Faithful Generations

Faithful Generations

Race and New Asian American Churches

RUSSELL JEUNG

FOREWORD BY ROBERT N. BELLAH

RUTGERS UNIVERSITY PRESS

NEW BRUNSWICK, NEW JERSEY, AND LONDON

LIBRARY OF CONGRESS CATALOGING-IN-PUBLICATION DATA

Jeung, Russell, 1962–
    Faithful generations : race and new Asian American churches / Russell Jeung.
    p. cm.
    Includes bibliographical references and index.
    ISBN 0–8135–3502–6 (hardcover : alk. paper) — ISBN 0–8135–3503–4 (pbk. : alk. paper)
    1. Asian Americans—Religion. 2. United States—Religion. I. Title.
    BL2525.J48 2005
    277.3'083'08995—dc22

                    2004003827

A British Cataloging-in-Publication record for this book is available from the British Library.

Manufactured in the United States of America

CONTENTS

FOREWORD

The changing configuration of American society, at once the most secular and the most religious of all the advanced industrial societies, is full of surprises. A society that has "absorbed" immigrants more successfully than most comparable nations also continues to view people in racial categories. Some doors are opened while others are closed. If assimilation means rapid appropriation of English, and concomitant loss of the immigrants' original language in two or three generations, together with the affirmation of dominant patterns of lifestyle and career in a society that values upward mobility above almost anything else, then no group has failed to be "assimilated." But if assimilation means full acceptance without stereotypical pigeonholing, then, for all immigrant groups, but particularly for those who appear racially different, the process is slow if it occurs at all. Asian Americans seem to exhibit what might be called marginalization of the similar. The very characterization of them as a "model minority" is demeaning, as it denies difference while at the same time affirming it.

In the face of these peculiar but persistent characteristics of the American pattern, ethnic and racial minorities in America have adopted a variety of strategies. One minority that may be closer to Asian Americans than many, surprising in that it is not a racial minority, is American Jews. Having apparently assimilated successfully to the American pattern of occupational success, Jews, only partially in response to lingering anti-Semitism, have persisted in affirming their cultural difference. In earlier days Jewish identity could be affirmed in secular as well as religious associations. Today Jews are faced with the reality that they will identify religiously or lose their separate identity altogether. Though the situation of Jewish Americans is different from the situation of Asian Americans, the ability to retain cultural identity through religion, even when successfully assimilating in terms of social class, may make these cases interestingly comparable.

One of the many interesting findings of Russell Jeung's study is that the congregations he describes are not primarily interested in holding on to ancestral culture. The ethnic congregations of an older generation, often the parents and grandparents of those Jeung has studied, were very much concerned with holding on to the past and, if possible, passing along the ancestral language to their children. But Asian American congregations have an ambiguous, if not downright ambivalent, relationship with their ancestral culture. Having largely lost the immigrant language and having learned little about the ancestral cultures in American schools, they, even their ministers, are far from at home in Chinese or Japanese milieus. On the one hand, they do want to assert pride in their heritage and to learn more about that part of their past; on the other hand, they experience a degree of alienation from the parental generation, particularly over childhood experiences viewed as involving too much parental pressure and not enough parental reassurance. The Asian American culture that is developing in these congregations is, then, only peripherally related to geographical Asia. Primarily, it grows out of the shared experience of being Asian American in a period when everyone, except perhaps the dominant majority, is supposed to have a culture and to be proud of it. But in a heavily commercialized society where making it is the national ideal, holding on to any distinct culture, majority or minority, is a problem.

As Jeung makes clear, the creation of racial solidarities has several sources. Shared experiences of racial exclusion lead to common material interests and a degree of political mobilization. But in a very privatized society where most people are engaged in improving their life chances, if they are fortunate enough not to be worrying about how to pay the rent, political mobilization is never easy, even when there are shared material interests. In this situation, the vitality of American religious life provides opportunities not present in most other spheres. Emile Durkheim laid the groundwork for all subsequent sociology of religion by pointing out the correlation between shared religious symbols and the creation of social solidarity. For Asian American Christians, whether conservative or liberal theologically, the new panethnic congregations have provided a fruitful context, culturally and socially, for working out new understandings and new forms of solidaristic relationships. So far the new congregations have attracted mainly Chinese and Japanese Americans, though Korean Americans are beginning to join as well. These congregations are very much a work in progress and there is much variety among them, helpfully described by Jeung. American religious life, though more persistent than many other cultural spheres, is hardly changeless or even very stable. What Jeung has told us is a story very much in progress of unfolding. It gives us a window into salient features of American religion, a window into which it will be worth looking again as time goes on.

Robert N. Bellah
December 2003

PREFACE

I have a question. A lot of you have said that part of the reason why Yao is so popular is because a lot of Chinese people are rooting for him (a type of nepotism or ethnic pride). However, how do those of you who are Chinese feel about other Asian groups sharing the same views about Yao? Of course, these other Asians do not share exactly the same feeling of pride as a true Chinese blooded person, but I can imagine the feeling is pretty close. I'm just curious because I am a non Chinese Asian person who thinks Yao is representing not just Chinese but Asia as a whole. Why is that? I mean yes, we are all Asians but we come from different cultures. Do you think people of Italian descent get excited over a German born player like Dirk? I don't think so.

> —Submission to "Why Is Yao So Popular?"
> discussion thread on YaoMingMania.com[1]

Does anyone know if Yao is Buddhist?
I'm 99% sure Yao is not a Buddhist. Why? For the reason I posted earlier, almost no Chinese born after the 80s is associated with any religion. They might be agnostics, deists, atheists, etc. but definitely not Buddhists, Christian, or Muslims. However, because China had been a religious nation before, some traditions of Yao's might look religious. For instance, he wears the red band on his wrist, which can be understood as some religious symbol.

> —Submissions to "The Functions and Exploitation of Religion"
> discussion thread on YaoMingMania.com[2]

Why do Asians from different cultures come together to root for Yao Ming, a seven-foot-five-inch Chinese center who was the first player picked in the National Basketball Association 2002 draft? As stated in this sports Web site posting, European Americans do not get as excited over a German-born player, but Asian Americans from various ethnic backgrounds have taken great pride in this Chinese-born player. In fact, the creator of the Web site is John Takahashi, a Japanese American who spends thirty-five hours a week after work writing detailed analyses of Yao Ming's every game. Besides gushing over Yao Ming, members share new Korean basketball prospects, debate the gung fu abilities of different actors, and review Asian American films. Yao Ming mania has swept over the Asian American community, but why does Yao represent not just Chinese but also other Asian Americans? This book examines this question and why Asian Americans have come together to generate a panethnic identity and to form solidarity along racial lines.

For an increasing number of Asian Americans, religion has become the means by which they have organized panethnically. Although it has received scant attention in research literature about Asian Americans, religion—both personal faith and institutional traditions—plays a central role in the lives of the 12.5 million Asians in the United States. It provides comfort and meaning, shapes our ethical and political beliefs, and influences our culture and arts.[3] Even on YaoMingMania, a basketball fans' Web site, the members discuss the role of religion in the community and wonder whether certain Asian symbols are religious. Having become a symbol of the Asian American community, Yao Ming represents the emergence of Asians in the United States and draws together this group. Symbols drawing from religion are especially powerful because they represent and draw life from the hopes, sacred aspirations, and faith of entire groups. *Faithful Generations* is also about how religion, especially the symbols it employs, can define a new group and create Pan-Asian subcultures.

Another epidemic also illustrates this emerging Asian American panethnicity. When the SARS epidemic hit, the University of California at Berkeley initially banned from its summer programs all students from China, Hong Kong, Taiwan, and Singapore. The ban did not apply to Canada, even though the country had more cases of deaths from SARS than Singapore at the time. In the heavily Asian populated area of San Gabriel Valley, anonymous e-mails warned readers to stay away from specific Asian American stores and concluded, "Friends, please take care of yourself and your family. Avoid going to ASIAN areas!!!" (Chong and Hall 2003). Due to these institutional and racist responses, Asian American activists have complained that hysteria over SARS has led to acts of racial profiling against anyone coughing while Asian (CWA). Asian Americans, regardless of their origin or health status, may be regarded as carriers of a foreign disease (Vongs 2003).[4] The epidemic has become racialized in that it has become associated with an entire continent and people. Those with Asian physical features, not just those from China, Hong Kong, or Taiwan, are suspect.

As a fourth-generation Chinese American, I strongly identify as an Asian American as well. I grew up in San Francisco and attended Lowell High School, where Chinese Americans would later sue to eliminate its ethnic quota system.

Even though I am Chinese American, I did not join the Chinese Club. Instead, I joined the Korean Club and the Japanese Club to be with my friends, and probably because I wanted to see what it felt like to be a minority. The real model minority students at our school were the whites. When our class wanted to have a band for our annual boat dance, the student government faced an impasse. Should we hire a band to play rock music or a band to play soul and funk music? Fortunately, we did not suppress the rights of the minority but simply hired two bands for two boats. As I recall, Asians mostly boarded the soul boat and whites mostly danced on the other. This racialization of musical tastes, where different groups adopted different musical and dance styles, did not affect me, because I cannot dance. But I recognized that even in the late 1970s, friendship networks, tastes in popular culture, and even dress—the guys all wore black Derby jackets with hooded sweatshirts—revealed the contours of a nascent Asian American panethnicity. My Chinese, Japanese, Korean, and Filipino American friends from student government have continued to engage in racial politics and community activism, indicating that Lowell High School did socialize us with an Asian American political consciousness.[5] My high school friends have since worked as an aide to President Bill Clinton and legal professor of race, a community organizer for Asian Community Mental Health Services, a radio personality for Filipino and Asian American media, and a professor doing research on Asian Americans and education.

These three cases of Asian American panethnicity show that being Asian American entails more than checking off an abstract census category. Asian Americans, as in the case of SARS hysteria, become lumped together by institutional policies and racism. Common racial experiences help establish a reactive solidarity, where we bond together in the face of marginalization and discrimination. As a result, my friends from high school have continued to engage in identity politics to address persistent racism and inequality. Our racial experiences are not all negative, however, and Asian Americans celebrate proud traditions, collective efforts toward community development, and strong personal bonds. Just as my Asian American high school friends and I played basketball together in the same neighborhood playgrounds, I continue to live in a neighborhood with a strong Asian American community. Along with my Mien and Cambodian neighbors, we have banded together for better housing, welfare reform, and youth services.[6] Beyond reactive solidarity and these common interests, Asian Americans create a group identity by connecting with new symbols, such as Yao Ming or Margaret Cho, a comedian. These symbols represent and tighten group boundaries as Asian Americans subjectively relate to them. Yao Ming is thus more than a basketball player; he is also a role model and source of racial pride for Asian Americans.[7]

In graduate school, I wanted to examine panethnic formations at the grassroots level. I investigated Southeast Asian gangs that formed in response to neighborhood violence and racialized power dynamics within the inner city (Jeung 2002). To coincide with my fondness for basketball, I also wanted to research Asian American sports leagues that attract large numbers of participants. Instead, I discovered that another institution close to my heart had begun a panethnic movement. Churches that were once Chinese and Japanese American congregations now faithfully claim to be Asian American and embrace a broader racial identity rather than an ethnic-specific one.

Faithful Generations is about Asian American panethnic churches, how they develop, and how they organize themselves. When I was younger, I attended a Chinese American Bible church that taught its members to interpret scriptures literally. After reading passages like Galatians 3:28, which states, "There is no longer Jew or Greek, there is no longer slave or free, there is no longer male and female, for all of you are one in Christ Jesus," I wondered why we met as a *Chinese* church. We did not sing in Chinese, fellowship in Chinese, or hear sermons in Chinese. In fact, non-Chinese wrote the songs we sang and the Sunday school materials that we used. So why go to a Chinese American church? Our pastor and others explained that the Chinese American church could better evangelize and reach out to other Chinese Americans. So we went to summer Bible camps to meet kids from other Chinese American churches, and we went Christmas caroling, after which we ended up in people's homes to have *jook* (rice porridge) for *siu yeh* (midnight snacks), and we memorized Bible verses as much as possible. My fundamentalist church preached separation from the world while developing its own hybridized Chinese American Christian practices.

In college, I participated in Asian American Christian Fellowship, a ministry of the Japanese Evangelical Missions Society (JEMS), as well as every other Asian American student organization. I was not surprised that these social worlds did not intersect very much. With Asian American Christians, I would go to Bible studies. With Asian American student activists, I would help teach ethnic studies, organize statewide conferences, and protest cuts to education and affirmative action. The concerns of the evangelical Christians and the activists, although both organized around Asian American identities, seemed to be mutually exclusive. For me, being Asian American and being Christian were parallel identities that were not explicitly integrated, although they did influence each other.

On a personal level, this research is part of my spiritual and academic journey to understand Asian American churches, my friends who belong to them, and myself. Along the way, I have developed my own convictions about the relationship between ethnicity, race, and faith, which I will discuss in the conclusion. Currently, I attend an evangelical, multiethnic congregation that engages in urban ministry, and my own involvements certainly influence how I interacted with the congregations. Although I have my views, I want to share the voices and the stories of Asian American ministers themselves. They shared with me remarkable stories of calling and healing, of redemption and faithfulness. Knowing the needs of their church members intimately, they pay attention to and understand how race and ethnicity affect the spiritual lives of individuals and the organization of congregations as a whole. Their sincere desire to help build new generations of the Asian American church are inspirational, and I hope that I capture their insights faithfully.

FAITHFUL GENERATIONS is based on my doctoral dissertation research at the University of California, Berkeley's Department of Sociology. My chair, Professor Robert Bellah, provided a model of what sociologists can write and what we as scholars should do. I am extremely grateful for his comments in the foreword. Professor Michael Omi and Professor Claude Fischer also made invaluable theoretical and methodological contributions.

I wish to thank my teachers and classmates at the University of California whose stimulating discussions kept me going: Andy Barlow, Jaeyoun Won, Linus Huang, Sheba George, and Carolyn Chen. Their comments and review of my work have made significant contributions, but I prize their friendship even more. With the help from the Dean's Dissertation Year fellowship, I finally graduated from Berkeley.

Colleagues from the Asian Pacific Americans and Religion Research Initiative (APARRI), the Pacific Asian North American Institute, and the American Baptist Seminary of the West's Asian American Center have mentored me on the study of Asian American religious life. Their company and guidance along the way have made research and writing much more enjoyable ventures: Anthony Alumkal, Rudy Busto, Peter Cha, Chris Chua, Karen Chai Kim, Jung Ha Kim, Sharon Kim, Debbie Lee, Tat-siong Benny Liew, Fumitaka Matsuoka, Pyong Gap Min, Youngmi Pak, Paul Spickard, Timothy Tseng, Fenggang Yang, and David Yoo. From the start, Jane Naomi Iwamura and David Kim have been especially instrumental in our field of study and in my own academic life. Other scholars of religion and race have been helpful as well, including Charles Marsh and Michael Emerson.

Through the generosity of the San Francisco State University Affirmative Action Award and the San Francisco State University Presidential Award, I have been given the time to complete this manuscript. I am grateful for the support of SFSU's College of Ethnic Studies and Dean Tomas Almaguer, the Cesar Chavez Institute and Professor Rafael Diaz, and the Department of Asian American Studies and Professor Marlon Hom. I am glad to find an academic home where both scholarship and teaching aim to effect change in our communities.

My own church families, Grace Community Fellowship Church in San Francisco and New Hope Covenant Church in Oakland, have shown me what God can do through families of believers. Each of the ministers I interviewed have impressed me with their commitment to their faith communities. Two of these communities, Grace Faith Church and Park Avenue United Methodist Church, graciously allowed me to join them and witness their ministries to Asian Americans. I owe much appreciation to these fellow believers.

David Myers and Kristi Long of Rutgers University Press demonstrated great patience as I worked on this book. Their comments and editorial skills made it that much better. Shauna Olson Hong offered her sharp eyes to edit sections, too.

I wish to honor my family and my parents, Albert and Bernice Jeung, for their love. I thank God for all these people in my life and for the opportunity to write this book. May I be as faithful as the generations before me and as helpful to the generations to come. I hope my new son, Matthew Kim Jeung, will inherit this rich legacy.

Finally, I dedicate this book to Joan Jeung, whose own editorial skills, sociological insights, and commitment to the church influence my writing and work. More important, her partnership and love have been more than I could ever hope for or imagine.

Faithful Generations

1

Introduction

Paul would say, "To the Jews I'll be a Jew and to the Greeks I'll be a Greek." So maybe, in order to share the gospel among Asians, you must first understand what does it mean to be Asian. Why is it that you can do outreach to Asian Americans while another Anglo congregation can't? What is it that attracts people to each other?

–Pastor Isaac, Chinese American minister of a Pan-Asian congregation

While China and Japan were at war, Chinese and Japanese in the United States found themselves to be enemies of one another as well. Christian churches enthusiastically organized members to support homeland nationalist movements. When his son joined the Imperial Japan Army to fight the Chinese, a Japanese American minister cheered proudly *"Banzai!"* in support of his son's decision.[1] One Chinese American Christian, in a two-page autobiography, made a point of Japanese wartime atrocities by recalling, "When the Japanese invaded Hong Kong, we had no food. The Japanese treated the Chinese badly; we were afraid that they would come into our home, and we never knew where our next meal would be coming from."[2] Buttons that declared "I am Chinese" were worn to distinguish Chinese Americans from Japanese Americans who were being rounded up for internment camps. As one of the primary social institutions in the community, religious congregations served to maintain ethnic ties and reinforce specific linguistic and cultural identities.

Two generations later, Chinese and Japanese American congregations are undergoing a significant transformation into panethnic congregations. Groups that were once at war now pray and worship together with common songs, liturgies, and religious understandings. Those who had distanced themselves from each other now unite under a single group identity and a new subculture. In fact, half of this study's churches in the San Francisco Bay Area now target Asian Americans instead of focusing on a single ethnic group. As church entrepreneurs, Christian leaders have chosen a newly constituted racial group as their spiritual market niche.[3] Overcoming ethnic conflict to establish group solidarity, Asian American churches have generated a new institutional identity as well.

Although touted as the "model minority," Chinese and Japanese American Christians have not assimilated fully like other white immigrant groups but have adopted a new panethnic identity. Churches of previous white immigrant groups to America have tended to evolve from ethnic institutions to nonethnic, denominational churches (Dolan 1985; Herberg 1955; Wind and Lewis 1994). As members acculturated so that they were culturally indistinguishable from other Americans, ethnic churches no longer had to meet needs for a particular group. Unable to sustain themselves by serving only one ethnic constituency, immigrant congregations either died out or moved to the suburbs without retaining ethnic specificity. The building that remained would house a new congregation meeting the needs of the local population (Ammerman 1998; Davis and Wilson 1966; Douglass 1927). Just as generations of individuals transitioned from being immigrants to ethnics to Americans, so did their ethnic institutions (Dolan 1985; Hansen 1937; Niebuhr 1929).

American-born generations of Chinese and Japanese Americans have now become acculturated, have moved away from ethnic neighborhoods, and out-marry in high percentages (Alba and Nee 1997; Fugita and O'Brien 1991; Gans 1999). We would thus expect these groups to assimilate into local congregations and for their congregations to close. For example, Mark Mullins (1987) argues that over time, Japanese ethnic churches will de-ethnicize as they adapt to generational differences. However, contrary to expectations, Chinese and Japanese American churches are not dying out or becoming open to all but are adapting by becoming Asian American.[4]

Given the traditional enmity between Chinese and Japanese and the historic American pattern of assimilation, a Pan-Asian church seems an unlikely new form of religious congregation.[5] Yet facing demographic and generational change, congregations have had to reorient themselves toward a new target population in order to survive and grow. Instead of assimilating into the American denominational landscape, these congregations have established themselves with a racialized identity now legitimated in multicultural America. By integrating their church theology and their understandings of panethnicity, Asian American ministers have strategically and faithfully constructed new ways of doing church and being the people of God. This study of fifty congregations in the San Francisco Bay Area tells the story of the generation, growth, and expressions of panethnic Asian American congregations.

Why Study Asian American Ethnic Churches

The development and role of churches in the Asian American community have received scant research attention despite their long history and the increasing numbers of Asian immigrants and churches to serve them (Min and Kim 2002; Yoo 1999). Their growth not only reveals the significance of religion in the lives of the individuals, but also challenges the stereotypes about Asian Americans and their beliefs. Furthermore, study of these Christian churches sheds light on the relationship between religion and race. Religion provides symbols, narratives, and discourses with which ministers construct racial identity. At the same time, race both limits and structures new ways for these churches to organize themselves.

Chinese and Japanese congregations have served as religious homes for their ethnic communities in the San Francisco Bay Area since 1852 and 1879 respectively.[6] Yet the stories of past and current faith communities need to be detailed to counter the invisibility of Asian Americans in American religious history. To demonstrate the agency of our forebears, we need to uncover the rich and complex ways that Asian Americans have made sense of their lives (Busto 2003; San Buenaventura 2002; Yoo 1999). In 1882, when the U.S. Congress passed the Chinese Exclusion Act, Christians had already established five Chinese missions and churches in San Francisco and Oakland. By 1924, when Congress restricted immigration to the United States from Japan with the National Origins Act, at least seven denominations had founded twelve Japanese congregations in the area. When Chinese began migrating to the United States again in large numbers in the 1970s, the number of new Chinese American congregations rose dramatically through church splits, church start-ups, and denominational new church developments. James Chuck's (1996) research reveals that the number of Chinese congregations in the San Francisco Bay Area grew from 15 in 1950 to 158 in mid–1996. One hundred of these new Chinese congregations (both Chinese- and English-speaking) have been established since 1980. In the meantime, the 18 Japanese American congregations in the area planted only 2 new congregations in the 1980s and 1990s, both of which became Asian American congregations.

This book focuses on Chinese and Japanese congregations because these groups have been in the United States longer and have more English-speaking congregations than other Asian subgroups. Consequently, these churches reveal better the issues of generational transition and the development of ethnic churches. However, many Korean American churches have begun establishing English-speaking ministries for second-generation Asian Americans, as well as planting multiethnic congregations.[7] I examine some of these congregations in my conclusion. Filipinos, Asian Indians, and Southeast Asians have established religious institutions in the United States in increasing numbers, but they are less likely to be Pan-Asian or Protestant Christian because of the religious and ethnic diversity within these groups. A recent survey found that the percentage of Asian Americans who identify as Christian nationwide fell from 63 percent to 43 percent from 1990 to 2000, while those professing other religions (Hindu, Buddhist, Muslim) rose from 15 percent to 28 percent because of new immigration (Kosmin, Mayer, and Keysar 2001).[8]

In 2000, an estimated twenty-four thousand worshiped weekly at 180 Chinese Christian churches and about two thousand congregated at 18 Japanese churches in the San Francisco Bay Area.[9] These numbers make religious institutions the largest voluntary association within these ethnic communities where people have regular, face-to-face interaction.[10] Although Asians are stereotypically oriented toward education and business, more Asians participate in churches than in parent-teacher associations or business/professional groups (Lien 2001). Overall, 25 percent of Asians participate in organized religious activity, as compared to 15 percent engaging in PTA and 13 percent in business/ professional groups.[11] Given this high level of social interaction, which promotes "thick ethnic ties," religious groups are the community's primary social institution in maintaining ethnic solidarity and promoting ethnic identity (Kurien 2002; Min and Kim 2002; Zhou, Bankston, and Kim 2002). Beyond their spiritual and religious functions, these churches offer social services, language and citizenship instruction, business contacts, and political education (Chen and Jeung 2000). Understanding the roles of the church within the ethnic community can thus serve church leaders, community activists, and policy makers (Cha 2001; J. H. Kim 2002).

If one could wear one's religion on a shirtsleeve, then two T-shirts would neatly summarize the stereotypes of Asian American popular religion. In 2002 the corporate retailer Abercrombie and Fitch marketed T-shirts with a laughing Buddha that read, "Buddha Bash—Get Your Buddha on the Floor." Besides mocking the faith tradition of Asian Americans, it portrayed Asians as the exotic, religious "other" who have strange beliefs (Strasburg 2002). Ironically, American Evangelical Protestantism has seen the greatest gains of all faiths within the Chinese and Japanese American communities. Although the numbers of these Protestant churches are not as staggering as that of the Korean American or Latino communities, they do challenge this "perpetual foreigner" stereotype of Asians (Tseng 2003).[12] Nationally, 819 Chinese American churches and over 200 Japanese American churches held Protestant Christian worship services in 2000. In contrast, only 120 to 150 Chinese Buddhist groups and 61 Japanese Buddhist churches provided religious services (Luo 2002; Yang, 2002; Yoo 2002).

More than six hundred students sported a different T-shirt when they walked around the University of California, Berkeley, campus during the spring semester of 2000. In bold lettering on fluorescent orange shirts, they proclaimed, "I agree with Paul." Paul Lai, a poster child for the Campus Crusade for Christ fellowship, had published his Christian beliefs in a full-page ad in the student-run *Daily California* newspaper to spark conversations about Christ. According to Lai, he was picked because he was Asian American and could bring together the other sixty-four Asian Christian groups at the university behind this effort (Johnson 2000). On college campuses, Asian Americans now dominate certain Christian fellowships, so much so that Rudy Busto (1999) raises the issue of another stereotype—these Asian American students are the "model" of the model minority. Not only are they smart, hardworking, and graduating from prestigious universities, but they are godly as well![13] Asian American students have become the icon for these campus groups who aggressively evangelize other students. Unfortunately, this stereotype of Asian American evangelicals as otherworldly, politically disinterested students masks the complexity and range of Asian American evangelical presence (Tseng 2002).

To challenge these stereotypes, this study aims to give voice to the Asian American Christian community and particularly to the narratives of ministers. Understanding how ministers construct meanings is important, because ministers are the primary narrators of the congregation's story as well as the performers and interpreters of the symbols, rituals, and activities of their churches (Hopewell 1987; Wuthnow 1992, 1994). Their sermons, teachings, and writings make up religious discourse that establishes not only the categories by which their congregations view the world but also the ways in which they might interact with the world. Week after week, congregational members hear and process messages about the sacred, their identity in the world, and their role in their given faith community. What ministers say—and do not say—about ethnicity and panethnicity in front of the congregation represents their articulation of ethnic and racial meanings. Furthermore, their leadership mobilizes congregations into the public sphere, and how churches do ministry also defines their racial position in the broader community.

As ministers create panethnic understandings, they operate within a context in which racialization by the state and other institutions heavily influence the self-understandings of Asian Americans. Yet some scholars of religion continue to analyze Asian American faith communities by employing an assimilationist paradigm. In the introduction to the anthology *Gatherings in Diaspora: Religious Communities and the New Immigration*, R. Stephen Warner stresses "the continuity of the immigrant religious experience between the nineteenth century and the present" (1998, 14). By likening the current ethnic experience to previous white ethnic immigrants, Warner privileges the assimilating capacity of the United States and argues that religious identities should outcompete and outlast other traditions and identities. He therefore asserts that racial dynamics, although currently operative, are not permanent factors affecting the life cycle of ethnic churches. Even though contributors to his anthology argued that race is a basic organizing principle in the United States (Kurien 1998), he believes "the irreducibility of 'race' applies primarily to the African American experience."

In contrast, Asian American scholars of religion highlight the primacy of race in the development of our faith communities (Iwamura 2003; Min and Kim 2002; Singh 2003). The fact that Chinese and Japanese Americans band together along panethnic lines—even despite acculturating—indicates that racial dynamics continue to play a significant role in their lives and in the lives of their institutions.[14] Groups no longer assimilate into a triple melting pot, as Will Herberg (1955) once argued in *Protestant-Catholic-Jew: An Essay in American Religious Sociology*, but into a multicultural America that establishes racial, ethnic, and gendered categories for groups to align with, resist, or rearticulate (Portes and Rumbaut 1996). Also, an increase in the salience of an American and religious identity does not necessarily signal a concurrent decrease in ethnic or racial identity, as assimilation theorists predict. Even though Chinese and Japanese Americans have primarily converted to Christianity, their new religious identities do not always conflict with their ethnic or racial identities (Cha 2001; Kibria 2002; Yang 1998). In fact, religious and racial identities may intersect and become integrated rather than competing. This new, self-defined group boundary is the critical focus of this study.

Basic Questions

Why and how have Chinese and Japanese American congregations reorganized around a new panethnic identity as Asian Americans? Or, as Pastor Isaac, quoted in the beginning of this chapter, asks, "What is it that attracts people to each other?" The establishment of these congregations around racial identity instead of national culture or language raises three issues for this study of ethnic and panethnic institutions. First, what factors led ministers to adopt a panethnic identity for their congregations rather than maintaining an ethnic one or following the path of white immigrant churches? In this case, demographic shifts, regional politics, and power dynamics within the churches structure the identity and development of new panethnic congregations. This group identity involves the conscious self-definition of the group, the boundaries that encompass who is in and who is out, and the members' subjective attachment to the group.

Second, how do leaders build fellowship and solidarity around a new group identity? Today, as in the past, congregations bring together groups of people who shared no prior association. Chinese and Japanese American Christians now have a group solidarity that includes a sense of identification with Asian Americans, obligations to other Asian Americans outside their own ethnic group, and regular social interactions with each other.[15] If previous generations of these ethnic groups distanced themselves from one another, then what types of interactions or cultural activities might now bond them?

Third, how do congregations give appropriate expression to group identities that are new? As these new groups emerge within congregational spaces, they may draw from a variety of cultural resources, traditions, and visions to develop their own unique narrative. However, making their worship, teachings, and ministries authentically and distinctly Asian American is a difficult and slow process, precisely because Asian American panethnicity is such a new phenomenon.

Ethnicity, Race, and Panethnicity: Concepts, Dimensions, and Theories

Ethnicity

In response to the persistence, rather than the assimilation, of ethnic groupings in the United States, sociologists have developed theories on the emergence, revitalization, and social construction of ethnicity. Ethnicity is a socially constructed group around a common ancestry, shared history and culture, and shared symbols of peoplehood (Cornell and Hartmann 1998). When groups immigrate to the United States, they often first form organizations based on regional ties of kinship, village, and primordial ties rather than around ethnic grouping (Barton 1975; Bodnar 1985; Gjerde 1985; Handlin 1951; Yans-McLaughlin 1977).[16] Indeed, Chinese and Japanese first formed religious organizations through family and village networks, and today new Asian immigrants continue to group religiously along dialect or region (Hayashi 1995; Yang 1998). However, over time these groups reorganize within the United States into larger-scale ethnic identities as a result of modernization, competition over resources, and discrimination (Barth 1969; Hannan 1979; Hechter 1975; Olzak 1992; Tilly 1986). For example, in 1882 six separate Chinese district associations organized to form the powerful Chinese Consolidated Benevolent Association, also known as the Six Companies, in order to respond to the social needs, political concerns, and official exclusion faced as ethnonational Chinese in the United States (Chan 1991; Lien 2001).

Groups holding common interests find that mobilization along ethnic and racial boundaries make them more competitive (Glazer and Moynihan 1975; Nagel 1986; Olzak 1992; Spickard 1996). Indeed, competition and context are the main variables that shape the formation of different types of group institutions. William Yancey, Eugene Ericksen, and Richard Juliani (1976) regard ethnicity as an emergent phenomenon produced by the structural conditions of modern society. Given their time of entrance into the labor market and their skills, immigrant groups find themselves concentrated occupationally and residentially. The authors explain that "each of these factors—lifestyle, class interests, work relationships and common residential areas—facilitated the development of group consciousness" (394). Within the earliest urban neighborhoods, ethnicity crystallized under conditions where local institutions and interpersonal networks developed and were maintained. Lon Kurashige (2002) explains the initial success of Los Angeles Nisei Week, an ongoing Japanese American festival that started in 1934, as due to a combination of these same racial, urban, and political factors. Segmented into an ethnic enclave because of racial discrimination, the second generation needed to stimulate their local economy and improve their public image with the broader community. The festival, which received widespread support, provided an opportunity for the second-generation Nisei to understand and rearticulate their own role and identity as Japanese and Americans.

As groups mobilize around material interests, they build solidarity. However, as groups acculturate and enter the middle class, lessened economic competition also causes ethnic interest groups to wane. Symbolic ethnicity theorists argue that European Americans no longer need group solidarity but just an ethnic identity. By the third generation, the ethnic identities of white immigrants tend to be more symbolic and optional so that involvement with an ethnic congregation, if any, is intermittent at best. Symbolic ethnicity is a new form of ethnic behavior and affiliation in which the old culture is only an ancestral memory and provides no useful function (Steinberg 1981). Because regular practice and participation in ethnic communities is not essential for the maintenance of symbolic ethnicity, identification with a group can be developed through allegiance to group symbols that are visible and clear in meaning. These symbols may include ethnic festivals, foods, and political representatives or sports figures. Mary Waters's study of white ethnics reveals that symbolic ethnicity embodies a great deal of choice, "something that is enjoyed and will not cause problems for people" (1990, 158). Attendance and participation at an ethnic congregation for third-generation Americans, then, is a choice to express one's identity without requiring significant cost (Alba 1990; Gans 1979; Steinberg 1981; Waters 1990).[17] Indeed, this free expression and choice of identity— under the banner of multiculturalism—may constitute "white privilege." Whites can claim ethnic identity similar to other groups while ignoring the economic and racialized advantages of their group position (McIntosh 1988).

In her book *Forever Foreigners or Honorary Whites?* Mia Tuan interviewed ninety-five middle-class, third-generation Chinese and Japanese Americans about their ethnic identities. Similar to studies of other white ethnic groups, Asian Americans reported a decline in ancestral language capabilities and a loss of cultural traditions. Tuan concludes that her respondents do maintain symbolic ethnicities: "Our respondents are more concerned with expressing an ethnic identity than with maintaining traditional cultural practices. Furthermore, they feel free to choose those aspects of Chinese or Japanese culture that fit into their lifestyle and discard what does not" (1998, 156). However, Tuan asserts that the ethnic identities possessed by Asian Americans differ from white ethnics' because of their "racialized ethnic experiences." While whites enjoy ethnicity as voluntary and optional, Asian Americans continue to face expectations from others to be culturally different because of their ethnic and racial markers. Marginalization as foreigners or as individuals who are not "real" Americans thus excludes Asian Americans from America's ethnic and racial center.

Race

The personal and collective costs that Chinese and Japanese Americans face as ethnic minorities indicate the significance of race. While ethnic groups usually organize around shared culture or ancestry, racial groups are socially defined on the basis of physical characteristics (Cornell and Hartmann 1998). Racial group formation is an ascriptive process conducted both at the level of the state and in the everyday lives of racial minorities (Omi and Winant 1994). On the state level, governmental bodies and public policies lump groups together, whether for census counts or distribution of funding, to create official racial categories. In the 1890 U.S. census, Chinese and Japanese were first conceived as separate races, both of whom were deemed inassimilable to American society (Gotanda 2001). For the 1980 census, however, the Census Bureau categorized these two groups under one of four umbrella races, "Asian and Pacific Islander."[18] By the 2000 census, the Asian and Pacific Islander race was divided in "Asian" and "Native Hawaiian and Other Pacific Islander." Although shifting and historically contingent, this group categorization and the implementation of racial policies establish the language and discourses by which racial groups get assigned stereotypes or positions in our racial hierarchy.

Furthermore, structural racial inequalities provide impetus for mobilization. Groups may organize around issues of political disenfranchisement or economic discrimination. For example, in California state hearings for redistricting after the 1990 and 2000 census, Asian American political organizations and community nonprofit agencies testified together as the Coalition of Asian Americans for Fair Reapportionment. To advocate for the creation of electoral districts favorable to Asian Americans, the coalition testified that Asian Americans are a "community of interest" despite the fact that Asian ethnic groups vary widely in class background, political orientation, and place of origin. One attorney for the Asian Law Caucus claimed in 1991, "I would argue at this stage of the game that you look at the category of Asian Pacific American, particularly in Southern California. We can show that we live fairly close to each other. And kind of shop in the same areas."[19] By noting the voluntary concentration of Asian Americans into certain neighborhoods and their daily interactions in local economies, he suggested that Asian Americans do have an emerging group solidarity.

Reactive solidarity to racism also draws Asian Americans together. Following the murder of Vincent Chin, a Chinese American killed because his attackers thought he was Japanese, Asian Americans formed political coalitions in Detroit, Denver, Toronto, Chicago, New York, and the West Coast to combat anti-Asian violence. Yen Le Espiritu asserts, "For Asian American groups in the United States, Asian American identity is not always an identity of choice. Largely on the basis of race, all Asian Americans have been lumped together and treated as if they were same. When manifested in anti-Asian violence, racial lumping necessarily leads to protective pan-Asian ethnicity" (1992, 259). This protective response and the joining together for greater power occur on the street level, too. In my study of Southeast Asian gangs, youth also form panethnic gangs, with names like Asian Street Crips and Oriental Boyz, to resist anti-Asian violence in their neighborhoods. Because non-Asian gangs often mistake Asian American youth as being part of an Asian gang, they attack them. Mien, Chinese, and Filipino youth thus join forces as a panethnic gang to avoid being harassed regularly (Jeung 2002).

On this personal level, Omi and Winant suggest that Asians in the United States face similar treatment and preconceived expectations of how they are to act and think. In her book *Becoming Asian American*, Nazli Kibria (2002) interviewed sixty-four second-generation Chinese Americans and Korean Americans about their ethnic and racial identities. In a chapter entitled "The Everyday Consequences of Being Asian," she identifies several common incidents that Asian Americans experience. Non-Asians expect Chinese and Koreans in the United States to speak Chinese or Korean languages fluently and to possess traditional values. Others expect these two groups to be the same, even though they have different histories and heritages. Kibria explains that in response, Asian Americans regularly engage in "racial identity play," an interactive negotiation process by which they confront and challenge the stereotypes and racial identities assigned to them. Some of these processes include asserting ethnic uniqueness, disidentifying with foreign appearances or demeanor, and taking advantage of "ethnic identity capital"—that is, the opportunities that accrue to them from others' perceptions. Race thus structurally shapes group identities and individuals' personal opportunities.

Panethnicity

Race and *panethnicity* are terms that are used fairly interchangeably in sociological literature. Panethnic groups, as defined by David Lopez and Yen Le Espiritu (1990), are politico-cultural collectivities made up of people of previously distinct tribal, ethnic, or national origins. Pan-tribal American Indian activist groups or Latino political organizations, made up of both Puerto Ricans and Mexican Americans, exemplify such collectivities (Cornell 1988; Padilla 1985; Ricourt and Danta 2003). In San Francisco today, community nonprofit organizations such as the Asian Law Caucus and the Asian Pacific Islander Health Forum serve multiple constituencies of ethnic groups and also advocate on behalf of the Asian/Pacific Islander population as a whole.

Racial formation theory focuses on structural, state designations, official categories, and the discursive representations of people grouped by physical traits. The U.S. government does not recognize Latinos or Hispanics, however, as a race of people (Ricourt and Danta 2003; Rodriguez 2000). Panethnicity is instead a newer concept coming out of the 1960s movements for Black Power, Brown Power, Red Power, and Yellow Power. Fighting for group rights, visibility, and racial pride, these movements succeeded in the government implementation of affirmative action programs that recognized four umbrella groups, including Hispanics (Espiritu 1992). Recently, even European Americans can be seen as coming together as a panethnic group to compete for jobs or housing resources (Alba 1990; Gans 1979; Roediger 1991).

Because panethnicity is a relatively recent phenomenon, as well as one that was initiated for ideological and political aims, scholars have debated whether people have begun to hold a panethnic consciousness as part of their individual identities. The major critique regarding panethnicity is that, as a political construct, it homogenizes the internal diversity of the groups and does not represent any "real" groupings (Espiritu and Ong 1994; Garcia 1997; Kibria 1996; Oboler 1995; Omatsu 1994). New, smaller entities within panethnic groupings might have interests and cultural practices that differ from the ethnic groups that are dominant. For example, Filipino Americans or South Asian Americans may feel inadequately represented within Asian American organizations (Kibria 1996; Mendoza Strobel 1996). The term *Asian American* may be an institutionalized group category, but is it a viable identity that affects conscious self-understanding and group identity?

Nazli Kibria (2002) found that some of her respondents stated that the identity *Asian American* was an artificial construct in contrast to the seemingly more "natural" and primordial ethnic identity of being Chinese or Korean. For instance, one Korean American noted that Chinese and Japanese communities "were unfazed" by the riots in south central Los Angeles in 1992 and did not identify with the issues facing the Korean American community. She claimed, "Why do we have to go around pretending that Asian Americans are the same?" (2002, 123). Additionally, others found that both ethnic and panethnic labels were irrelevant and stifling to their individuality and friendship networks.

Another question relates to the source of panethnic group solidarity. Researchers differ on whether Asian Americans might find unity in primordial culture, in a common narrative, or in common interest. Although these elements are not mutually exclusive, researchers usually focus on one of these factors more than the others. Given the different sources of solidarity, one might expect to find greater panethnic identity and solidarity among certain Asian groups.

First, some assert panethnic group consciousness may be based upon a primordial, common culture that ethnic groups share. Internal bonds of common peoplehood bind panethnic people together in groups. For example, leaders of Latino groups have sought to rally their constituencies around the mother tongue of Spanish (Fox 1996; Padilla 1985). Religion, such as Catholicism or Confucian ethics, may be another basis of panethnic solidarity.

Pyong Gap Min (2002) argues that Asian American panethnic identity and solidarity are more established among native-born Asians who share similar cultural and physical characteristics, such as Chinese, Korean, and Japanese. In a collection of fifteen essays of Asian American professionals, he finds that these Asian ethnic groups maintain more frequent panethnic contacts than

Filipinos or South Asians. He concludes that primordial ties of culture and religion, along with differences in physical characteristics and premigrant historical experiences, divide Asian Americans into two groups, East Asians and South Asians.[20]

Second, panethnic groups may not objectively share a language or religion, but they may share a symbolic narrative in that they come to believe in their common roots. While the specific groups may differ culturally or linguistically, they may all understand themselves to come from similar descent. A charter of origin, whether a story or language, represents the group's mythic origins. In his study comparing American Indian and Asian American panethnicity, Richard Trottier (1981) notes that American Indians have been more successful as a panethnic group because they have both a common political interest and a shared unique relationship to the land. Since most American Indian tribes lay claim to sacred, indigenous roots to this land, they may see themselves as a common people. Richard Alba (1990) hypothesizes that a common European immigrant narrative, that of coming to the United States from the old country and succeeding through hard work, may be a defining boundary for European Americans. By identifying with a common sense of origin, panethnicity is a grouping similar to ethnicity based on national ancestry (Alba 1990; Cornell 1988; Portes and Rumbaut 1996).

Nazli Kibria (2002) supports this notion of "pan-Asian ethno-genesis," or the development of an Asian American collectivity as an ethnic group. Her respondents report feeling neither authentically ethnic nor truly American. Instead, Chinese Americans and Korean Americans only maintain core ethnic values in the form of a "distilled ethnicity." These second-generation Asian Americans retain values such as hard work, loyalty to family, and education but view other ethnic traditions and values as optional. Sharing common values from distilled ethnicity, as well as common racialized ethnic experiences, these professionals now interact and intermarry more. Kibria claims that for these individuals, being Asian American is "another possible way, besides ethnonationality, 'to be ethnic,' to think about and define one's ethnicity" (2002, 196).

Third, panethnic solidarity might be based on common interests and affective ties (Calderon 1992; Nagel 1995; Okamoto 2003). When reviewing four panethnic groupings—Latinos, Asian Americans, Indo Americans, and Native Americans—Lopez and Espiritu conclude that neither common primordial culture, a common set of cultural symbols, nor a common racialized experience is sufficient for panethnic solidarity. They observe that structural conditions limit access to material resources for panethnic groups and that efforts to obtain resources form the basis for panethnic mobilization: "Clearly, structural factors, not cultural commonalties, better explain the emergence and success of panethnicity. This conclusion emerges from examining the incidents that have led to increased panethnic solidarity: all have drawn subgroups together on the basis of some common material concern, not on the basis of common cultural symbols" (1990, 218). Panethnic organizations build affective ties and develop panethnic consciousness where they did not exist prior to the organization.

Political scientist Pei-te Lien agrees that panethnic identity and solidarity are primarily political phenomena that emerge as Asian Americans organize for their rights and material needs. To illustrate, she cites the establishment of nine Pan-Asian national organizations since 1986 based in Washington, D.C., that address health, legal, and labor issues within the Asian American community. Other issues that have mobilized Pan-Asian organizing include combating anti-Asian violence, institutionalizing Asian American studies, and seeking greater political voice. She writes, "The construction of panethnic consciousness not only has to be forged from the political front and led by community organizations that are panethnic in orientation, but it also needs to be embedded within community's struggles for liberation and empowerment" (2001, 49).

2002 Multisite Asian American Political Survey

A recent study by Pei-te Lien, M. Margaret Conway, and Janelle Wong (2003) challenges these three theories on panethnic solidarity. Their groundbreaking, national survey of Asian Americans in 2002 revealed surprising trends about Asian American panethnic identity and solidarity.[21] Not only do six out of ten Asian Americans claim an Asian American identity; this identity cuts across class, place of birth, and generation.

Only 15 percent of the respondents chose to identify as an Asian American when asked about how they identify in general. Not surprisingly, the majority (64 percent) chose to identify as an ethnic American (that is, Chinese American) or by ethnic origin (that is, Chinese), with only 12 percent identifying as just "American." However, when those not identifying as Asian American were asked a follow-up question, "If they *ever* think of themselves as Asian American," about half responded affirmatively. This high percentage of Asian Americans (57 percent) who now possess an Asian American consciousness is much higher than a 1996 survey of Asian American high schoolers indicated.[22] Asian Americans hold both ethnic and panethnic identities simultaneously, and the employment of either identity depends on the situation or context.

Lien et al.'s results defy most expectations of the previously mentioned theories. Sociologists who base panethnic solidarity on primordial culture, such as Min, would predict that East Asians with similar Confucian worldviews would identify more strongly as Asian American. However, Filipinos (66 percent) and South Asians (60 percent), two non–East Asian groups, had higher percentages of respondents identifying panethnically. At the same time, "the perception of a common culture" among Asian Americans does correlate significantly with panethnic identity.

Theorists who view panethnicity as a new form of racialized ethnicity, such as Tuan and Kibria, would hypothesize that U.S.-born Asians would have a stronger Pan-Asian consciousness because of their racial experiences growing up here. In contrast, there is little difference between the U.S.-born and the Asian-born in the percentages reporting "Asian American identity." Interestingly, those who report experiencing racial discrimination, as well as women, actually are less likely to identify as Asian American.[23]

The last group of researchers who view panethnicity primarily based on common material interests, such as Espiritu and Lien, would believe that panethnic identification would be divided along lines of class and education. Nevertheless, Vietnamese Americans report just as much Pan-Asian identification as Chinese or Japanese Americans despite the former's lower economic status and more recent immigration. In fact, perception that Asian Americans share a common fate, or have similar interests, did not correlate to Pan-Asian identity. Participation in politics and Asian American causes, though, do make respondents more likely to identify with other Asian Americans.

To summarize, this recent survey finds that Asian Americans seem to have overcome obstacles of ethnic, class, and generational divisions to identify panethnically with each other. Although the category "Asian American" may be seen as artificial or stifling to some, a majority of Asian Americans have at one time or another self-consciously thought about themselves as Asian Americans. Factors that most influenced panethnic identity include integration into U.S. mainstream political parties; perception of a shared culture among Asians in America; citizenship status; involvement in Asian American political causes; older age; and employment.[24] Thus, panethnic solidarity involves a combination of cultural, political, and age factors.

A Theory of Symbolic Racial Identity and Solidarity

Given these elements of panethnic identity, how are they employed to develop solidarity and to mobilize Asian Americans? I argue that Asian Americans have group solidarity based on a symbolic, racial identity. Racial identity is symbolic in that it is not simply based on common traditional values, a primordial sense of homeland, or common material interests. Instead, panethnic entrepreneurs mobilize around symbolic group boundaries and strategically construct who belongs to the group. At times, community activists may organize Asian Americans around the idea that they are politically marginalized and possess a shared fate in the United States. At other times, they may argue that Asian Americans share an emergent common culture of shared upbringing. The group boundaries that are employed then determine the content of the identity and consciousness of the group members (Barth 1969).

According to previous theorists, symbolic *ethnic* identity is relatively meaningless, is subjectively invoked, and has little consequence on daily life. In contrast, I argue that symbolic *racial* identity is institutionally reinforced, self-defined, and regularly practiced. As a result, being Asian American is not an identity that is only intermittently evoked, but a significant one embedded in our social structures. Institutions of the state, as well as institutions of American Christianity, now recognize and promote the concept of Pan-Asian identity. Community leaders, including ministers, articulate Asian American group boundaries by using symbolic narratives of common, representative experiences (Barth 1969; Nagel 1994; Smith 1998; Taylor and Whittier 1992).[25] Ministers specifically use theologies and religious understandings to develop concepts about what constitutes race and to bring racial groups together.[26] Not only do they understand race in conceptual and symbolic terms; their religious practices organize how race is lived out in concrete ways. For example, Catholic festivals or small-group fellowships accentuate what characteristics are emphasized in their life together.[27] These symbols, then, establish a racialized sense of self and community that constitutes a meaningful identity, and not just a racial category that is ascribed from the outside.[28]

Because racial group boundaries are symbolic, they are not fixed but are subject to different articulations and interpretations. For Asian American evangelicals and mainline Protestant ministers, religion provides differing organizing logics for panethnic self-understanding.[29] The specific narratives or experiences of Asian Americans that these ministers choose as most representative are the ones that most resonate with their religious viewpoints. Also, because organizational fields have narrow sets of concepts, they limit the ways their members can think of racial groups.[30] Boundaries that determine "who is an Asian American" are permeable so that groups may employ different symbolic narratives. Evangelical Christians define Asian Americans around symbols of the common upbringing and the professional status of Asian Americans to build their churches.[31] In contrast, mainline Christians highlight the marginalized status and the cultural heritages of Asian Americans to mobilize around community concerns.[32] By consciously organizing themselves to address the perceived group needs, new Pan-Asian congregations collectively establish new symbolic racial identities.

The emergence and generation of new Asian American churches demonstrate how new symbolic racial identities are institutionalized and meaningful, fluid and subject to rearticulation. The symbolic boundaries of Pan-Asian churches are meant primarily to distinguish them from the ethnic churches from which they develop. Understanding the new Asian American identity, therefore, first requires an examination of Asian ethnic churches and their self-understanding of what it means to be ethnic.

2

Chinese and Japanese Churches in the United States

When I visited Chinese Grace Church (CGC), I was struck by the Chinese architectural motifs that conveyed the tranquility of a Chinese walled home and courtyard.[1] I stepped through a round moon gate into a small vestibule and paused at the goldfish pond. As I entered the main sanctuary, large Chinese characters inscribed in the wall greeted me with grace and blessing. Rectangle lanterns ending with curves hung from the ceiling.

I visited on Thanksgiving and joined the high school Sunday school class, where six kids cut out pictures from magazines to create collages. There was no prayer, no Bible teaching, no lesson—at the end, the students merely presented their works. As we cleaned up to go down to the worship service, the young teacher announced, "Time to practice our Chinese." A collective groan of resignation rose up from the kids, who all chafed at the thought of a long service that had two sermons—one in Cantonese and one in English.

The service was dry, formal, liturgical, and slow-moving. Hymns were sung ceremoniously and prayers were recited reverently. During the Chinese sermon, which lasted only about fifteen minutes, the teens in the back squirmed noisily as they whispered and passed notes to one another. They lasted through the hour-and-a-half service and then helped clear out chairs for the Thanksgiving potluck.

At this potluck, we lined up for traditional holiday fare: turkey and gravy, ham with pineapples, and sweet potatoes with brown sugar and marshmallow topping. In addition, we sampled Americanized Chinese dishes: sticky rice for stuffing, tea for the drinks, and almond Jell-O for dessert. We gathered in age groupings to eat, so I sat with the young adults. Occasionally, one back from college would be called over to be reintroduced to all the aunts of the church. When I asked Sam, my tablemate, why he was attending this church all the way from Contra Costa County, he replied, "I like it and my mom comes here, so. . . . "

Why do Chinese and Japanese Americans continue to attend ethnic churches? Like Sam, those living outside ethnic enclaves often make an effort to drive to these churches instead of going to ones in closer proximity. Although these second-, third-, fourth-, and perhaps fifth-generation Asian Americans are English-speaking and often acculturated, they participate in institutions such as Chinese Grace Church that have traditional twentieth-century American ways of doing church, albeit hybridized. Most Asian Americans continue to maintain ethnic affiliation when deciding upon their place of worship and fellowship. Amid fluctuating political and racial climates, Chinese and Japanese churches in the United States have established ethnic solidarity around transnational and cultural ties. Yet what ministers consider as *Japanese* nationalism or *Chinese* culture remains only represented in symbolic terms and not concrete, objective, or fixed traits. Definitions of what constitutes these ethnicities have themselves shifted over generations.

Like his grandfather before him, Sam maintains a Christian and an ethnic American identity. How to relate these identities is not always clear. In terms of nationality, should he make his allegiance to China or the United States? As a Christian, what Chinese and what American cultural traits should he value and which should he renounce? And as a minority, how does Sam interact with the American church that often reinforces the racial inequalities seen in broader society? Just as Asian American Christians wrestle with these identity issues on a personal level, Chinese and Japanese American churches have inevitably dealt with these issues of nationality, ethnicity, and race.

The establishment of congregational subcultures reflects these tensions and the diverse ways Asian Americans have negotiated their multiple group identities. The English-speaking churches led by the fifty Asian American ministers I interviewed divided into four main categories. Twenty of them remained ethnic specific, and their mission and ministries targeted only Chinese Americans or Japanese Americans. Another six identified their churches as both ethnic and Pan-Asian. In these cases, pastors used ethnic terminology to signify the cultural heritage or the ethnic legacies of their church and employed panethnic language to represent their members' newer social networks and political identity. Often, they comfortably interchanged the term *Asian American* with *Japanese American* or *Chinese American* to indicate the multiple identities of their congregants. Sixteen claimed a primarily Pan-Asian identity and eight desired to become more multiethnic.[2] To shed light on the diverse ways that Asian American churches have identified, this chapter explores the history of ethnic-specific Chinese and Japanese congregations and, specifically, how current ethnic-specific congregations respond to cultural changes.

Early Immigrant Churches and Iconoclastic Religious Nationalism

Orientalist discourses, the rise of the nation-state, exclusionary racism, and hostile reception from fellow countrymen paradoxically forged strong nationalist loyalties among the first Asian Christians in the United States.[3] Ideologically driven to build Christian civilizations, white missionaries first sought to inculcate "American ways" among the Chinese and Japanese immigrants. To mitigate anti-Asian sentiments arising from economic competition, the missionaries sought to demonstrate the civilizing nature of Christianity on the Asian laboring class. However, the Asian converts held strong nationalist tendencies, and subsequent legislation excluding them from American society drove home the fact their loyalties and hopes lay in their ancestral homelands. As a result, both Chinese and Japanese Americans developed their own religious institutions independent of American denominations. Their radical break from traditional institutional affiliations—both American and Asian—demonstrated the authenticity of their conversions and their loyalty to their homelands.

The missionaries who worked with early Asian immigrants in the United States held Orientalist notions that dichotomized the East from the West, asserted Western supremacy and progressivism, and established paternalistic relations between the two (Tseng 1994). Not only did Americans hope to Christianize the Chinese and Japanese; they also held the burden of civilizing them and their nations.[4] The initial immigrants, who came as students, provided hope that this vision could be realized. In 1847, Yung Wing, Wong Shing, and Wong Foon were the first Chinese to arrive in the United States for study. While the other two returned after a few years, Yung Wing graduated from Yale University in 1854 and went on to establish the Chinese Educational Mission in the United States. The 120 students brought by this mission during the 1870s became China's first generation of railroad builders, engineers, Western medical doctors, diplomats, naval militarists, and college presidents. They also established in 1878 the Chinese Christian Home Mission, an effort to transplant Christianity in their homeland.

The first Japanese Christians, mostly from the samurai class, also came to obtain their education.[5] Shimeta Niijima, one of these samurai, fled Japan in 1864 and pursued seminary training at Andover Theological Seminary. He eventually returned to Japan to establish Doshisha University and trained Japanese preachers to further spread the gospel. Historian Brian Hayashi suggests "Shimeta Niijima's extraordinary impact on Meiji Japan may have intensified the white missionaries' eagerness to teach English to the newly arriving Japanese students" (1995, 26). Missionaries used Yung and Niishima as models, encouraging converts to return to Asia and to build their own nations, where they truly belonged.

In 1852 the Presbyterian Board of Foreign Missions appointed Rev. Dr.

William Speer to develop mission work among the increasing numbers of Chinese arriving in California during the gold rush. Church historian Tim Tseng, in examining Speer's lectures to garner San Franciscans' support of the Chinatown mission, argues that Speer's discourse "established the language of paternalistic advocacy which would eventually dominate Protestant missionary rhetoric" (1994, 37). In both lobbying for the interests of the Chinese and seeking to remake them after the white man's image, he pushed for the evangelization of the Chinese domestically. He argued that the return of converts to China would spur the Christianization of that nation, a corresponding renewal of its institutions, and redemption of even its gender practices: "The Chinese who emigrate here will, on the opposite side of the earth, imitate our social institutions, will adopt our manners to some degree, and be elevated by examples of Christian virtue; and the female sex will obtain through them a respect, and be allowed intellectual and social privileges they have never before known" (Speer 1853, 21).

Tseng notes that Speer, his idealistic rhetoric notwithstanding, believed the Chinese to be "heathen idolaters," a "debased race," and "free hired servants." The Chinese immigrants were no longer coming for education, but as laborers from the peasant class. In order to uplift the Chinese and to establish a stronger and more docile workforce, Speer set up schools for Chinese that taught English, geography, arithmetic, science, and business education.[6] In a span of ten years, the Methodists established sixteen such schools throughout the Pacific Coast. Although many Chinese attended the classes, only 2 percent of the Chinese, or 6,500 individuals, eventually converted by 1910 (Moy 2002).[7]

Similarly, schools set up for the Japanese, such as the Methodist Gospel Society that was formed in 1877 in San Francisco, offered classes in the English language, American culture, and democratic politics. The United States passed the Chinese Exclusion Act in 1882, so the Japanese had strong incentive to disidentify with the Chinese and avoid being labeled as "inassimilable," as the Chinese had been. As a result, Japanese American missions gained many more converts through revival efforts in the 1890s than the Chinese ones. By the early 1900s, the Anglo Japanese Training School in San Francisco enrolled an average of three hundred students a year at its peak in its efforts to acculturate the Japanese (Suzuki 1991). Given their Orientalist discourse, the Western missionaries preached and taught accommodation to the values of the dominant European American social order that they felt were superior (Woo 1983; Yung 1995).

Although the missionaries advocated on behalf of Asian immigrants, the Chinese Exclusion Act of 1882 and anti-Japanese legislation that followed discouraged full social integration of Asians into the United States. Consequently, Chinese American Christians saw the relationship between their excluded status and their homeland's weak international status and mobilized for national reform. Jee Gam, a Chinese minister who converted seven years after arriving in

San Francisco in 1867, argued that the Chinese needed Christianity to save not only individuals but also the nation.[8] Likewise, Kan'ichi Miyama, who converted in 1877, encouraged his Japanese brothers to adapt themselves to American culture, remain temperate, and avoid gambling. Yet because of the racist anti-Japanese laws that were promoted in the early 1900s, he preached that Japanese Americans' fates were linked ultimately with Japan:[9] "Oh brothers! Let us consider it our honor that we are of the Japanese race. . . . Laziness and misdemeanors will not only bring distress on you but will also harm our unbroken national structure which has existed from time immemorial. Such acts will also bring dishonor upon our 30 million countrymen in Japan" (Hayashi 1995, 36).

Conversion to Christianity reinforced incipient nationalist loyalties by minimizing traditional obligations to clans, villages, and districts. Chinese Christians, perhaps resenting white denominational control, established their own autonomous and interdenominational Christian society, the Youxue Zhengdaohui. These associations drew Chinese from throughout China, in contrast to the other social organizations in Chinatown, the district and family associations (huiguan), which organized around more localized clan affiliations. In fact, the family associations persecuted converts, thus forcing Chinese Christians to look to each other for mutual support. At its peak in 1890, this society had thirty branches in twelve states and provided temporary lodging, arranged social and recreational activities, and helped those departing back to China. By doing so, this society fostered a Chinese and Christian identity as opposed to an American or clan identity.[10]

Similar religious and ethnic factors reconfigured Japanese American Christian identity and solidarity toward a reinvigorated nationalist stance. The arrival of Buddhist missionaries to California in 1898 posed major religious competition for the Japanese American missions. Beyond attracting many converts, the presence of Japanese Buddhists raised an identity question for Japanese converts: could they be both Japanese and Christian? To prove themselves as true Japanese, Japanese American Christians felt even more inclined to support nationalist efforts. Just as the Chinese Youxue Zhengdaohui extended beyond village parochialism, the Japanese churches in Los Angeles drew from different Japanese prefectures that reinforced a stronger ethnonational Japanese identity. Other Japanese American social institutions organized around ties based on regional prefectures (kenjinkai). They eventually sought financial independence from American mainline denominations, which had been decreasing monetary support anyway. As the ethnic churches relied more on the Japanese American community for support, they reflected the community's more nationalistic sentiments.

Homeland politics, the rise of the nation-state, and international conflicts in Asia provided opportunities for the Japanese and Chinese to express their national loyalty. During the Russo-Japanese War of 1904–1905, Japanese American Methodists prayed for Japanese victory that would bring peace and freedom to Asia. Rather than merely providing humanitarian financial assistance, they donated more to the military effort to win the war.

Chinese American Christians helped to mobilize and lead Sun-Yat Sen's Republican Revolution of 1911 in China. Already having broken from traditional Chinese religions, they challenged other feudal practices, Confucian thinking, and the monarchy that kept China underdeveloped.[11] Like the Japanese Americans, they did not merely seek peace but also sought a change in government that would reflect Christian values. The Chinese American Christian newspaper, the *Chung Sai Yat Po*, editorialized: "The Christian teaching brings the idea of a republican form of government such as we find in the United States. . . . Are we going to continue to have a monarchy? Monarchies will never bring prosperity and freedom" (Tseng 1999, 33). Excluded from American society and marginalized within Chinese society, these Chinese American Christians envisioned a new nation-state for China that would match their patriotic ideals.

The remarkable similarities between the early Chinese American and Japanese American churches—ethnonationalism combined with Christian missionary zeal—arise from their analogous treatment in the United States and crises in international relations. Orientalist discourse, which simultaneously denounced Chinese culture as superstitious and Japanese culture as beautifully refined, nonetheless painted Asian cultures as traditional and static. Westernization and Christianity, then, became primary means for national progress. Combining a desire for progress with their own patriotic fervor, Chinese and Japanese converts in the United States adopted this strategy for their respective nation's salvation. They adopted Christian cultural values, but they could not socially assimilate into the United States because of racial discrimination against Asians. Facing religious competition within their own ethnic communities and declining mainline denominational support, both Chinese and Japanese Americans developed autonomous ethnic institutions to support evangelization within the United States and in Asia. War and revolution focused their loyalties back to Asia and their visions toward the future when their countries could obtain peace, independence, and prosperity. In these ways, Christianity helped to establish new ethnic group boundaries away from village and clan and toward an imagined nation-state.

From Transnational to Bicultural: The Early Second Generations

Once established as financially independent and indigenously run ethnic institutions, second-generation Chinese and Japanese American congregations moved from transnationally bound relations to solidarity based on common culture. For the second generation, racial segregation and Japanese American internment during World War II prevented social assimilation. Instead, Asian ethnic enclaves became institutionally complete, with a host of ethnic businesses, organizations, and social groups that paralleled those in mainstream society. Although Chinese and Japanese Americans grew up with American education and mass media, most of them primarily interacted within their own ethnic communities. The resulting hybridized ethnic American subcultures combined certain selectively maintained Asian values, new American traits, and transformed ethnic ones.

Initially, Chinese American congregations maintained loyalty to both China and the United States while keeping a primordial sense of peoplehood. Diane Mark (1989), in recounting the story of Chinese Christians in Hawaii, describes how the First Chinese Church of Christ was designed with a pagoda-style bell tower, a Chinese-style portal, and other cultural motifs. The second generation of this church supported China relief efforts alongside other churches during the 1930s and 1940s through "chop suey dinners." The president of the women's fellowship, Mrs. Kai Fai Li, described her primordial sense of solidarity with those in China suffering from civil war and famine in 1930: "We must strive to aid our fellow country-women in that far-away continent, the home of our ancestors. Last Sunday when Rev. Davis reminded us of the famine in China, our hearts burned with sympathy" (Mark 1989, 60). During its seventieth-anniversary week celebrations in 1949 that included a nine-course Chinese banquet, Mark notes that "while American and Island-style elements were evident in the celebration, the events reflected an unabashed pride in the congregation's Chinese roots and culture. This incorporation of cultures into a unified whole was indicative of a unique 'local Chinese' identity that not only applied to the FCCC members but also reflected the broader Hawaii Chinese population during that period" (1989, 65).

Other Chinese churches in Hawaii sponsored plays, Moon Festival dinners, "Bowl of Rice" fashion shows, and Qing Ming, a gravesite ceremony in honor of family ancestors. These special occasions offered members the opportunities to reaffirm their ethnic identities, especially through ethnic symbols such as foods and traditional costumes. One photograph in Mark's book shows the cast of the play put on by Saint Elizabeth's Episcopal Church in 1952. The male actors dressed flashily in traditional Cantonese Opera costumes with scary masks and beards, flowing gowns, and ornate headpieces. The female actors, in Mandarin-collared silk dresses (qipao), held fans with cocked wrists at waist level. However, the host on the side of the photograph signals the cultural shift occurring for the second generation. Wearing a Western suit and a bow tie, he holds a lei and a microphone. The title of the drama characterizes this cultural transition even more: "So Long, Oolong."

This cultural transition reflected the change in the Chinese American church's demographics in the 1940s and 1950s. The Chinese missions had become family-centered congregations as the influx of Chinese male laborers declined. Female church leadership shifted church concerns from overseas nationalist politics toward providing better family opportunities in Chinatowns and transmitting ethnic culture (Tseng 2002). Yet church research on the Chinese American community, applying the assimilation paradigm that was dominant at the time, predicted declining ethnic practices. In a study commissioned by National Conference on the Chinese Christian Churches, authors Horace Cayton and Anne Lively (1955, 72) concluded the following:

> As the power of the family and benevolent associations declines, the Church will find a more congenial atmosphere in which to expand its influence. . . . For a time, the young Chinese may be satisfied with the Chinese church as it now exists, and become its leaders. Eventually, however, if the force of democracy continues to strengthen within our country, these members may break off entirely from a strictly Chinese congregation.

Their data backed up this conclusion. Of the sixty-two Chinese Protestant churches in the United States in 1950, the majority of the members were English-speaking young people. Only 31 out of the 298 Sunday school programs taught in Chinese and 114 out of the 152 church activities reported were conducted in English (Cayton and Lively 1955). Ministers reported that their sermons concentrated on the issues most affecting this population, such as parent-child relationships and race relations. Although many of the ministers also acted as principals of Chinese-language schools, the study acknowledged that the youth showed little interest. Denominations thus attempted to integrate ethnic churches by eliminating separate, provisional conferences. In 1952 the Methodist California Oriental Provisional Conference, made up of Chinese, Korean, and Filipino churches, disbanded and merged with geographic conferences.

As demographic change and the American acculturation process began to reorient Chinese Americans' needs from the church, the Communist takeover of China in 1949 fully redefined this church's mission. With their hopes for a democratic and Christian China dashed, Chinese American Christians were left without a political homeland and outlet for their missionary zeal. In addition, American Cold War anti-Communist policies discouraged Chinese American involvement with their homeland (Tseng 2002). Instead, Chinese American Christians developed a self-understanding that being Chinese was a cultural identity, not a political one. Since 1949, this reconstitution of ethnic boundaries in turn affected the focus, theologies, and ministries of the Chinese American church.

Japanese American congregations followed a similar selective acculturation process. They passed on Japanese customs and values to the second generation even while encouraging Americanization through the use of English and attempting moral reform efforts. After the passage of the 1924 Immigration

Exclusion Act aimed at Japanese, Japanese Americans pushed less strongly for full assimilation. At this time Japanese American Protestants formed their own denominational conferences that were financially independent from white denominations. Their churches attracted the Nisei more than Buddhist temples because of their sports and social programs (Spickard 1996).[12] In the early 1930s, Nisei youth in church learned traditional folk dances, songs, martial arts, and traditional athletics, such as sumo wrestling. They viewed the ethnic church as a "cultural bridge" to promote peace between the East and West. To that end, churches sponsored Japan nights at white churches with displays of Japanese dolls and cultural objects to explain things Japanese.

The churches rarely incorporated Japanese religious practices, except for the Japanese Shinto custom of holding *tsuitokai,* or wakes, to placate recently deceased spirits (Hayashi 1995). Yet they also failed to introduce American Christian normative values. Japanese American ministers rarely addressed temperance when that movement was strong in the United States.[13] Instead, they offered a transcendent, otherworldly message that provided space for the retention of ethnic solidarity and an ethic that reinforced Japanese *seishin* philosophy. This ethic denounced decadent Western materialism and in contrast promoted the virtues of filial piety, loyalty, and honesty.

The second-generation Japanese Americans responded more favorably to Christian work supporting their ancestral homelands, just as the Chinese did, than to calls for American Christian relief efforts. They donated clothes and financial aid to people suffering from famine, fire, and earthquakes in Japan in the 1930s, rallying around the cry, "For the sake of our Japanese brethren." By claiming brotherhood or sisterhood to the suffering in China or Japan, the second generation called upon a sense of primordial attachment and common bloodline.

Racism also fostered a reactive ethnic identity. In 1910 the Northern California Japanese Christian Church Federation was founded "to keep up the morale of the community due to incidents of racial prejudice and persecution in business, school, and work" (Yoo 2002, 131). At the 1939 Young People's Christian Conference, supported by Japanese American churches throughout California, Nisei delegates addressed how to develop a Christian response to the discrimination that they commonly suffered. The internment of 120,000 Japanese Americans during World War II clearly challenged the second generation's faith in the U.S. government, and the Japanese American Christian ministers helped resist the government's efforts to Americanize the internees. Instead, they upheld ethnic values of filial piety, family loyalty, and ethnic solidarity (Okihiro 1984; Yoo 2002).

The Wartime Relocation Authority in 1942 found that 22 percent of the Issei (first generation) and 35 percent of the Nisei affiliated as Christian at the camps, compared to the 68 percent and 49 percent identifying as Buddhists.

Unlike earlier ministers, who saw America as an example of modernization and civilization, Rev. Lester Suzuki held a more chastened perspective about the United States. He reflects on the government's wartime executive order: "Perhaps America is like St. Paul, she can will what is right but cannot do it, and the evil she does not want to do, is what she did, that is, calling for the wholesale evacuation of all people of Japanese descent on the West Coast" (Suzuki 1979, 332). Because of this shared experience of racism, which Suzuki terms "a time of exile for all of Japanese descent," he argues that "the Japanese ethnic people, through the churches, through the vernacular newspapers as well as newspapers like the *Pacific Citizen*, tend to have a common ethnic consciousness that will be in existence for a long time to come" (339).

For this second generation, the Christian Church provided institutional space where they could practice their faith as both Asians and Americans. The missions initially started with efforts to Americanize the immigrants, so their activities paralleled other American churches, with Sunday schools, temperance efforts, youth leagues, scout troops, and choirs.[14] Because the immigrants instead took control of the congregations, especially to further nationalist efforts, their children grew up in churches that valued the members' primordial roots. Within this ethnic institution, the second generation received not only language instruction but also cultural training to maintain their sense of cultural loyalty. Watershed historical moments, especially Japanese American wartime internment and the Communist takeover of China, suppressed transnational political ties. Although the native-born generations became both culturally and structurally assimilated into American society, they still retained an ethnic identity organized around ethnic institutions and cultural hybridity.

Resurgent Cultural Identities in the Civil Rights Era

Despite declining support from mainline denominations, churches persisted in serving Chinese and Japanese Americans through the 1970s. Even before the influx of new immigrants through the 1965 Immigration Act, Chinese and Japanese American ministers maintained that distinct cultural bonds continued to hold their congregations together. In response to the pessimistic outlook of the Cayton and Lively report, Chinese American churches formalized the National Conference of Chinese American Churches (CONFAB) in 1955 in order to promote a Christian perspective sensitive to Chinese Americans. During the same time, Japanese American churches also resisted expectations of assimilation and maintained family-centered ministries. Like other groups during the 1960s, Chinese and Japanese Americans began to assert resurgent ethnic pride. Even evangelicals, who did not attempt to establish specific Chinese or Japanese Christian outlooks, promoted ethnic-specific congregations that maintained family unity.

Youth ministries began to receive greater emphasis in Chinese churches in the 1950s and 1960s. The popular Chinese Christian Youth Conference, an annual camp held at Lake Tahoe, California, offered programs for the entire family. The metaphor of church as family can be seen in this youth group advisor's narrative about his church work. Byron Chan writes:

> One of the great joys of our lives, as a young married couple, was the calling and challenge to assume the responsibility of being advisors for the Senior High young people at the First Chinese Baptist Church in 1964. For the next seven years, these young people became our surrogate children. . . . Looking back, the saving grace for us has been the church as our extended family, where as families we are able to support and encourage each other. (Chuck 1996, 188–189)

While CONFAB was a mainline denominational effort to encourage Chinese American Christian faith perspectives and fellowship, the 1960s also saw the emergence of evangelical Chinese American churches and fellowships. In the early 1960s, Ambassadors for Christ established campus ministries for Chinese students and the Chinese Christian Mission promoted evangelism of diasporic Chinese outside of mainland China. Within churches in the San Francisco Bay Area, 59 percent of the members predominantly spoke English so that their bonds were ethnic rather than linguistic. Of the nineteen new Chinese churches planted in the region between 1950 and 1972, sixteen were theologically conservative and nine were independent (Bird 1968). By 1972, when the North American Congress of Chinese Evangelicals formed with more than three hundred Chinese evangelical leaders across the continent, the number of Chinese evangelical congregations far outnumbered those in mainline denominations.

Despite sociologists' predictions, cultural solidarity around kinship systems persisted among the Chinese.[15] Seeing American culture as fallen and chaotic, the fundamentalist churches sought to establish an environment to protect the unity of the Chinese family. Writing about Chinese American churches in the 1970s, Lawrence Palinkas found that "the one factor that brings them together is their attendance of Chinese Christian churches. . . . In such a church, members enjoy a substitute for the traditional kinship system and may both interact with and seek help from fellow Chinese immigrants" (1981, 616–617).

After the war, Japanese Americans returned to the West Coast and rebuilt their congregations in ways similar to Chinese Americans. As families reestablished themselves residentially and financially, they continued to support the ministries of their churches. Within the Methodist denomination, thirteen new sanctuaries and thirteen new educational buildings were built or dedicated in the late 1950s. Despite being invited to merge with the larger denominational conference in 1948, the Japanese Provisional Conference remained autonomous until 1964.

Mergers into mainstream denominations resulted in decreased autonomy and funding for Chinese and Japanese American congregations. Denominations failed to recruit new English-speaking ministers and planted very few churches in the 1960s. Lester Suzuki, a Methodist minister at the time, wrote of his fellow Japanese American pastors and their involvement with the larger denominations: "Although they voted for the mergers, they really didn't belong in spirit in the new Conferences. Their psychology and activities were still ethnically oriented. . . . The English-speaking ministers and lay people tried valiantly to work together with Japanese in Conference and district affairs, but in reality it was not a success" (1991, 133). Only four years after merging with the larger denomination, Japanese American Methodists called for denominational hearings about reconvening their members and "the need to undergird Asian American ministries with a theological base." The denomination's Board of Missions did not fund the caucus's efforts, but its Commission on Religion and Race did. This significant shift transformed the status of Asian Americans from a missions field to an advocacy group.

The Asian American Caucus of the United Methodist Church, along with similar caucuses in other denominations, saw themselves as both ethnic minorities and racial minorities. Formed in 1971, this particular caucus adopted a resolution that sought "to explore and to appreciate the values of our ethnic cultural and religious heritages that make the gospel relevant" and to gain "liberation from the elements of racism within the United Methodist Church and society" (Chang 1991, 141).

One cultural value that persisted among Japanese Americans was the concept of *iemoto*, or family household relationships. In their study of the Japanese American community in the late 1970s, Steven Fugita and David O'Brien argue that structured social relationships as "quasi kin" distinguished Japanese Americans from other ethnic groups.[16] Fugita and O'Brien (1991, 43) argue the following:

> The most important voluntary associations in Japanese American communities are the churches. . . . What is perhaps most striking about this situation is the high degree of continuity across generations and across rural and urban areas even though there are substantial differences in affiliation with Buddhist versus Christian churches. These findings are further evidence for the perpetuation of the basic principle of Japanese culture that the preservation of social relationships among group members is of fundamentally greater importance than the specific content of such relationships.

These authors found that Japanese Americans perceive themselves as belonging to a community distinguishable from Caucasians, especially in regard to how they operate culturally in church. Almost three-quarters of Japanese Americans believe that Japanese and Caucasians act differently in church, while only 45.6 percent of them believe that these groups behave differently in business situations. The most commonly named characteristics that they see differentiating themselves from other Americans are the Japanese Americans' work ethic (41.2 percent), greater social reservation (33.3 percent), and their different physical characteristics (25.1 percent).

As the civil rights and black power movements spawned other struggles for liberation, Chinese and Japanese American churches also continued to foster a resurgent ethnic identity among their members. The civil rights movement paved the way for the 1965 Immigration Act that reopened the United States to Asian immigrants. The tremendous growth of the Chinese immigrant community in the San Francisco Bay Area resulted in the planting of twenty-seven new churches in the 1970s and fifty-four in the 1980s. Only twelve were planted by mainline denominations; the rest were evangelical.

Three factors account for the greater proportion of evangelical congregations within the Asian American community. First, the growth of Asian American evangelical churches corresponds to national trends in church growth and decline. Beginning in 1965, mainline churches began reporting significant membership declines, while evangelical congregations increased at rates higher than the nation's population growth rate (Roof and McKinney 1987). Second, as stated earlier, declining mainline financial support of Chinese and Japanese American churches in the 1960s coincided with a policy of assimilating Asian American Christians. Chinese separatist evangelicals began at the same time to form independent parachurch organizations and made greater efforts than the mainline to convert Chinese in the United States. Simply put, evangelicals evangelize and recruit more than mainline Protestants do. Tseng (2003) suggests that the failure of China's nationalist movement led these evangelists to become less politically active, more pietistic, and more focused on the Chinese diasporic community in the United States. This separatist evangelicalism, along with the desire for autonomy from outside control, has fostered the founding of independent congregations without denominational linkages. Third, Fenggang Yang (1999) argues that the orthodox and conservative culture of evangelicals meshes well with the Confucian values of East Asians. His church ethnography demonstrated how Chinese Americans employed evangelical Christianity and the Bible to reinforce values of family, respect for elders, and education. Because of its emphasis on evangelism, the desire for autonomy, and the cultural fit between conservative Christianity and Confucianism, Chinese and Japanese Americans have tended to join evangelical churches.

Cultural Solidarity in Contemporary Ethnic-Specific Congregations

Of the fifty contemporary congregations in this study, twenty are ethnic-specific in that they identify with and serve one ethnic group. Although these congregations differ in theology, denomination, and age, they all organize themselves around an ethnic tie that is based on a shared culture. According to their ministers, ethnic culture is an intuitive, taken-for-granted way of behaving and viewing the world that is transmitted generationally through families. These shared cultural traits foster a sense of comfort and familiarity among the people when they gather (see Nguyen 2000). Ministers also recognize that the minority experience of Asians in the United States reinforces this ethnic solidarity. Feeling different from other Americans, marginalized from the immigrant community, and occasionally discriminated against by wider society, Chinese and Japanese Americans find a safe and comfortable environment to evangelize and build community within their congregations.

The Boundaries of Ethnic Solidarity

Although native-born Chinese and Japanese Americans are raised in the United States, their ministers assert that they continue to be bound by cultural traditions, practices, and values from Asia that serve as a basis for ethnic solidarity. As later generations acculturate even more into American behavioral and cultural patterns, ethnic solidarity may be retained through a few major and specific cultural traits, which serve as the symbolic boundaries defining the group. The churches reinforce these boundaries by providing the institutional space to congregate and by sponsoring cultural programs, festivals, and language instruction. Even the more fundamentalist congregations, who tend to devalue this-worldly culture, utilize these cultural differences as a rationale for their ethnic-specific evangelism activities. As a result, ethnic congregations build upon and cultivate a cultural bond that seems natural, comfortable, and familiar to its members.

Ethnic culture, according to the ministers, consists of a set of values and ways of relating that have been socialized through home life. Even though the people cannot always articulate these traits or practices, someone like Sam, in this chapter's introductory vignette, knows it when he sees it. One minister says these cultural traits distinguish American-born Chinese (ABCs) from overseas-born Chinese (OBCs) and whites:

> When I go to a white church, and I'm using myself as an example, I'm not sure who I'm talking to. I know them well enough but I don't know them well enough where I can quickly identify with them culturally. The gap between me and the white is much less than the OBC and the white because we do share some cultural similarities. But when I run into a Chinese, and I assume his parents are Chinese, then I think I know the

kind of household family life he comes out of. I can talk to them. I can make some assumptions as to some of his likes and don't likes. It's that kind of thing that we sense with one another.

A European American minister, who is also a scholar of Japanese history, recognizes that these selectively maintained cultural patterns distinguish them from other American congregations: "The Japanese American church has something in it that's Japanese but you can't predict what it is. The places where you stumble across some Japanese pattern, you can't tell where it's going to be. Because each individual kind of picks and chooses in terms of their ethnic stuff."

While each individual retains different aspects of Japanese culture, group patterns do emerge that distinguish Japanese Americans from others. Cultural differences, for example, separate individual Asian ethnic groups. One minister recognizes that these distinctions justify the need for different ethnic congregations: "There're differences between Chinese, Japanese, and Korean. Chinese have a long tradition and are more conservative. They built a great wall around them. The Japanese, they are an island culture and absorb things from the outside. The Koreans, the church has become their social base."

This commonsense discourse of family-transmitted cultural traits as the basis for ethnic solidarity assumes an Orientalist dichotomy between East and West. The East is represented as the exact opposite of the West, with the East being more traditional, static, and inferior. Being culturally Chinese or Japanese stands at one end of the continuum; being white American stands at the opposite end, and in between is the ABC. OBCs and Japanese Issei would be the most Eastern in culture and they would pass down certain traits to the next generations. For example, one minister described this dichotomous thinking between American individualism and Asian group-orientation:

> The American culture values the individual over and above the community. They see the community and society as the way to help the individual succeed and prosper. The Asian community, if you talk about Confucius days, a lot of it is feudal. The individual is there to serve the larger whole. You have a very different approach in terms of worldview and the value of the individual. That usually comes out clashing intergenerationally. Many Asian Americans have a very weak self-image. The Caucasian world is really touchy-feely—give them positive regard and question authority. [But for Asians,] I've seen a lot of people emotionally starved. The need for positive, unconditional regard is not satisfied.

Because Asian parents may retain "feudal" thinking and do not provide emotional support or unconditional acceptance, Asian Americans often have inferior, weakened self-images compared to Caucasians.

Although each successive generation would be "less Asian," they would continue to receive specific traits that might distinguish them as Chinese or Japanese Americans. Ministers also believe that Asian traditional culture is itself static and that new "Chinese" or "Japanese" cultural ways are not authentic. One Japanese American notes the following about the ethnicity, the role of families, and changes in later generations:

> We don't stress ethnicity but it's kind of understood. I think generally Asians value the family and families are strong because of a national trait of Chinese and Japanese. There's some change now in the third and fourth generation. They are not quite as "Japanese-y" as their parents and grandparents. A lot of Japanese and Chinese seem to get along really well. They just think of themselves as Asian American.

These ethnic traits of being "Japanese-y" or "Chinese" are the taken-for-granted ways of behaving that create a subjective sense of peoplehood. In contrast to interethnic situations, interacting within one's ethnic community offers a sense of familiarity and comfort that makes attending an Asian religious institution easier than attending a non-Asian one. This minister discusses how some Chinese Americans can function effectively in dominant society and live in the suburbs but prefer to travel back to Chinatown for church:

> I think for this church most of our Chinese American youth and young adults, just by fact that they are still at church, are more comfortable in the Asian community. Certainly, most of them live out in the suburbs so have very much functioned in a more Caucasian, more American culture but for whatever reason, they feel more comfortable, feel more connected, tied, loyal.

Although the cultural style of an ethnic congregation is familiar to a member of that group, it is usually an unconscious way of acting and thinking that manifests itself "naturally." When asked how one's Christian beliefs affect one's ethnicity, one pastor responds: "I'm not sure. I would think that it happens naturally. You are a Christian. You are Chinese. It'll just come out. . . . What's it mean to be Chinese? I don't know. I've never not been so it's kinda . . . [trails off]." She assumed that one's ethnic background is a core part of oneself that would become integrated with one's religious values. Similarly, a Japanese American pastor believes his members' ethnic cultural orientation was tacitly assumed. He simply noted, "We don't stress ethnicity but it's kind of understood, I guess."

The comfort that co-ethnics share may be understood as a subjective sense of peoplehood that is derived from common backgrounds. Shared physical similarities demarcate Chinese and Japanese Americans from other Americans.

Other observable markers, such as accent, dress, and interests differentiate native-born from overseas-born Asians. Among co-ethnics of similar background, groups enter a comfort zone.

Distinguished from others by cultural traits that establish a primordial comfort, Chinese and Japanese Americans develop stronger ethnic identities when they voluntarily opt for such identities. Although some may choose to identify as ethnic Americans for political instrumentality or for economic advantage, those who affiliated with churches did so primarily for symbolic, cultural reasons. Repeatedly, ministers shared how parents wanted their children to attend an ethnic congregation in order to be around other Chinese or Japanese youth. The parents were concerned not only about raising their children with specific values, but also about their children knowing "who they were." The value of ethnic heritage and identity brought people together even when congregating was not convenient. This minister explains that this valued common identity also establishes a sense of comfort:

> They went to a Caucasian church because they are second, third generation Chinese here and they don't really speak Chinese at all. Now that they have kids, they like them to go back to a Chinese church. I say, "Why? You've merged into the culture." Somehow, their sense of identity is still very important to them. Even though a person is born here and definitely the whole person is American, except the color. Everything they learn, they're all American. But somehow, that sense of identity, of knowing that they are Chinese and they want to learn more about Chinese, learn the language, a little cultural background. So somehow the parents still want them to come back to Chinese church.

Although Sam could have attended a white suburban church, the conscious choice to attend his parents' congregation represents a claimed, resurgent identity. His ethnic identity is stronger when, given an opportunity to participate in either co-ethnic or mixed-race contexts, he freely associates with his own ethnic group.[17]

Ethnic boundaries established through these congregations thus coalesce around cultural traits that symbolize difference and offer subjective kinship. Such solidarity certainly differs from the religious nationalism of early immigrants or the reactive solidarity that developed in the mid-twentieth century around a shared racial fate. While many of these cultural understandings were implicitly understood, certain traits came to represent paradigmatic Chinese or Japanese values.

The Content of Chinese and Japanese American Cultures

Which Chinese or Japanese American cultural traits are selected to demarcate group members from mainstream society and maintain strong ethnic bonds?

The ministers highlight specific values shaping group behavior and interactions. These are Confucian virtues that include family harmony, obligation to the group, and a strong work ethic geared toward education and career.[18] Significantly, the values considered "Chinese American" or "Japanese American" by both broader society and ethnic communities may change given the sociohistorical context (Chan 1991; Okihiro 1994). The very cultural traits considered and promoted as quintessentially Chinese or Japanese today—family unity, education, hard work—also are legitimated by the American capitalistic system and its ideology of meritocracy and individualism. Thus, the traditional values that are selectively maintained, passed on, and highlighted tend to be those that are also adaptive and prized in this society. Other traditional customs, such as being buried with ancestors, become obsolete and are no longer practiced.

Many of the Chinese American ministers comment on how their congregations operate as an extended family in unity. They argue that just as Confucian ethic promotes filial piety (xiao) and harmony, Christianity supports honoring the parents and church unity.[19] These traditions reinforce one another to create strong bonds in a church. A minister observes what connects people in her church:

> I see it being a real strong family orientation. In fact, family is probably why the congregation stays together. So when you come in to the body, you're treated as one of the family. The older people become uncles and aunties. This kind of thing goes on. That's probably what it means to be Chinese. You have family orientation, you have people that look like you, you have people that have been brought up like you, probably the same values and parental experiences growing up.

Likewise, another minister encourages this family orientation:

> Ninety, 80 percent of our people commute. So my parish is all the way from Fairfield all the way down to San Jose. This is something different. They see a meaningful ministry here. They want to be a part of serving the community. They want to come back here to meet their friends, everybody comes back as a family gathering, which I believe is quite positive.

Japanese American ministers did not address family ties directly, but rather discuss the obligation and responsibility their members felt toward the overall community. This distinguishing cultural feature of the Japanese refers to the notion that the members are quasi-kin toward one another and the group.[20] One minister describes her members' loyalty to the group:

> They're very typically Japanese American. Their attitudes about why they have church and why they come to church is more based upon loyalty and obligation rather than a sense of worshipping and praising God. And

they come here faithfully and some have been here decades and decades. But none of their children come back to church. And they don't know what happened to their children.

As this pastor observes, the later generations of Japanese Americans seem to have less loyalty to the congregation. A minister of another congregation explains that this loss of loyalty hurts the older members because they feel responsible for the continuation of the group:

> I think there is this sense that the next generation coming along and our lives are some kind of investment in them. The strength of that is Japanese. I would say that people think that. Where that shows up in the church is that they feel an obligation to make sure this church exists for the next generation. They feel too much obligation for that. It really bothers them [when their kids leave]. They feel like somehow it was their responsibility to make sure the good things were available for the next generation, including the church.

The other strong cultural value that ministers identify is a driven work ethic. This ethic, combined with increased educational and employment opportunities, has made many of the churches more middle class in composition and financially self-sufficient. Almost all the ministers acknowledge this ethic and an upwardly mobile orientation among their members. One Japanese American minister notes: "[Education] is a cultural thing, not a church thing. We don't preach it but culturally there is this premium on education. You would find the kids here pretty much high scale as far as grades and going to colleges." And a Chinese American pastor complains:

> One of the powerful aspects of Chinese or Asian culture is a very strong work ethic. Asians tend to flourish just about wherever they go in this world. And I think it's because they work very, very hard. That's one reason. However, that cultural issue, which is esteemed in Asian culture, many times backfires. So you find a lot of the men going in at six in the morning and coming home at eleven at night and occasionally asking, "Are you my son?"

Confucian filial piety encourages a sense of responsibility and work ethic to provide for one's family. This traditional ethic, when coupled with immigrants' drive to survive and the capitalist system's ideology of meritocracy, becomes easily passed on as one of the defining characteristics of being Chinese and Japanese. Most Asian Americans take pride in their model minority status because it congratulates them for their own efforts and accomplishments.[21] Because of this ethnic pride and because the model minority thesis reinforces American ideology of equal opportunity, Asian Americans and others buy into the stereotype as hard workers. Asian culture thus gets distilled to encompassing hierarchical family relations, duty and obligation, and drivenness.[22] Just as the Protestant ethic becomes transformed as the capitalist system becomes an iron cage, Confucian virtues of *xiao* and *iemoto* have been reconstructed to fit into contemporary American society.

Ethnic Culture in the Church

Ethnic-specific congregations reflect the values and orientations that members bring to the congregation. Besides offering Sunday schools and prayer meetings, ethnic churches are usually distinguished by their attempts to transmit cultural values, language, and pride in heritage. Every ethnic-specific congregation in this study offers some language instruction for American-born children, and many sponsor cultural festivals and events.[23] As one minister explains, these types of programs are ubiquitous: "We have a Saturday morning Chinese language program that every Chinese church seems to have in that form or other. There's an element of holding onto your culture, especially for later generation kids to learn Chinese and to be around other Chinese kids."

With the exception of fundamentalist churches, which teach that all culture is fallen and in need of replacement by biblical values, most of the churches recognize and value their ethnic heritage. One minister of a suburban congregation explains that becoming Christian is not necessarily a step toward American assimilation:

> For instance, the Chinese schools we have here, the parents send the kids here because they want their kids to learn more Chinese. It's good for them and we promote this. The church's function is to provide this opportunity for the children to learn their own culture so that they can appreciate their culture and so they can still communicate with their parents. And also to be aware that they are unique.

Another minister again asserts that these practices are natural expressions of group identity: "I think the biggest thing [about being a Chinese church] that comes out is that we celebrate Chinese New Year or Mid-Autumn Festival. That tradition comes over and we don't see that as something pagan or foreign that we shouldn't do. It's just part of our culture." Holding pride in and practicing certain symbolic aspects of one's ethnicity are accepted in multicultural society even though other ethnic patterns, such as becoming too clannish or overachieving, are perceived as threats to mainstream society.

Many ministers note that members may come as much for the cultural and social activities of the church as the spiritual ones. Parents might send their children to church language schools but not attend worship services. Others visit churches only on special occasions. One pastor merely cites attendance numbers to illustrate the popularity of these ethnic programs rather than traditional, American events: "Last year, we did Halloween, Thanksgiving, Christmas and we were having like 40, 50 kids. When we did Mochizuki, we had 120 kids. So what does that tell me? Should we try to do this ethnic stuff or should we do this plain wrapper Christian stuff? We did 40, 50, 60 when we did Christian stuff and we had a bigger number with ethnic stuff, so . . . ."

Besides the cultural and social activities sponsored by the churches, cultural orientations affect the style of worship as well. Pastors observe that the hierarchical, authoritarian nature of the Chinese or Japanese family appear in how they relate to God and the pastor. One observes the difference between the fellowship time and the worship service:

> The main way that I see the worship being affected is that to me, it's more traditional and formal than what I'm used to. I see an element of culture in that because Chinese culture is more hierarchical and traditional in that sense. There's such a sense of being quiet and reverent before God. So that it's really hard to loosen up during worship.
>
> The fellowship time is just so loud. But the worship time is the time to be together. Worship is a time of reverence before God is the impression I have. I know that's certainly been so at other congregations. I think the seriousness of the liturgy is what hits me. The sermon is oftentimes more intellectual, not as personal, and I find that to be . . . sort of a distance. It adds to the distancing of worship. God's out there.

As described in this chapter's opening vignette, singing and prayers at Chinese and Japanese American ethnic congregations tend to be reverential and subdued. Again, the traditional formality of relationships and passive reception of instruction from authorities influence how they respond in worship. This minister complains about her members:

> When I first got here, when I was candidating for the church, I really thought I was at a JACL meeting. It was like they were running a program and I was just the keynote. They acted like the liturgist was the MC and it was an entertainment thing. People would sit in the pews, like they were being entertained. It was just a funny feeling. They were not including God in their worship. They were just doing their thing, going through the motions. I just felt really odd about that.

Chinese and Japanese Americans bring distinct cultural orientations that affect how they approach group efforts and church gatherings. For example, members can expect that everyone, including the children, will participate in group activities. As explained before, this motivation to participate comes from a sense of familial responsibility and obligation. One Chinese American minister complains,

The issue of obligation, shame and duty has been the fuel that has run this church for the past sixteen years. And it works for the second generation because they drink that in with their mother's milk. So they tend to filter their spirituality through duty and obligation.

And I think one of the felt needs of the Taiwanese youth is like, "Man, we've been serving and we don't have a life. We don't have any life other than this little, stinkin' church." They sacrifice all these things thinking that that's their Christian duty. But really, they've been given over to a family system.

In fact, this sense of duty and obligation derives from Buddhist and Confucian ethics as well. By mobilizing upon these Asian values, Christian churches employ a cultural resource to build solidarity. A minister explains the function of their annual bazaar and how they have attempted to make it a Christian event:

Our big bazaar involves everyone. Your worth is how much you sacrifice for the group. It's a fundraiser and trying to provide an atmosphere where people will just come and sit and have a second bowl of noodles. That's an emblem of the bazaar for us. When people are evaluating the bazaar, how many people stayed and how many people left. If someone's working really hard and a friend comes, they are encouraged to take a break.

I think it represents *matsuri* (festival). I think it's straight out of Buddhist scriptures. When you look at the village festivals in Japan, it sure looks a lot like it. The emphasis is on how hard the work is, how strenuous it is. It's the one time of the year where everyone will do it. It's a bonding, it's a little bit of competition with the other bazaars. It is a cultural expression. It's a survival thing. Your worth has to do with whether your values are extended to the next generation. That's a religious experience for Japanese people. That survival. That's not part of Western culture.

The festival itself represents the people's willingness to sacrifice for the group as a whole. As Christian churches sponsor these events, they assert that the events also represent one's commitment to God and his people. Ethnic culture plays a significant role in the type of activities, the worship style, and the members' approach to activities within the church. Whether ministers choose to reject, transform, or build upon cultural traits, ethnic culture heavily influences the solidarity of the groups.

Reinforcing Cultural Differences: Racism and Reactive Solidarity
Ministers also recognize the role that race has played and continues to play in maintaining group boundaries between Asians and other racial groups. While mainline liberal ministers mobilize around racism and social justice issues

more, fundamentalist and evangelical ministers acknowledge racism as well. Ministers observe that race has two effects on the members. It factors in the higher comfort level Asians experience when together, and it limits the opportunities that Asian American ministers have to serve.

Ministers share stories about the marginalization that Chinese and Japanese Americans face because they are not accepted as either authentically Asian or authentically American. Among immigrant communities or back in China or Japan, American-born Asians are culturally different and considered "bananas" in that they are yellow on the outside but white on the inside. Within Caucasian settings, some Asians of any generation are still considered foreign. One minister explains his own experience:

> Particularly for some Chinese who are born here but have Chinese parents, there is a tension of trying to figure out "How Chinese am I?" and "How American should I be?" You're not Chinese. Whenever you're with Chinese, you feel it's too awkward. And I don't want to sound racist here, but sometimes when you're with non-Chinese, it still feels uncomfortable as well. I'm still different from them. So I don't feel comfortable going to a non-Chinese church.

Another theologically conservative pastor cites racial prejudice and ostracism of foreigners as an expected experience of Asians in the United States:

> I have no problems with Caucasians. They are still my very best friends now. But definitely there is racial prejudice there. No doubt about it. If you are Chinese, then they treat you differently. What can you say? You're in other people's country. Even though you are born here, it makes no difference. You are Chinese, you look like that. So we have to accept that.

Despite the long history of Asians in California, this pastor feels that he and his members are "in other people's country." Ostracized from mainstream society and culturally estranged from the larger Chinese immigrant community, Chinese Americans are especially alienated. The church provides a safe place where Chinese and Japanese Americans can feel comfortable. Sadly, these experiences as racial minorities in the United States simply reinforce the boundaries established by the cultural differences that Chinese and Japanese American ministers observe.

Within the broader Christian church, racial policies also shaped the creation of ethnic-specific ministries. Limited opportunities to do missions work in Asia through Western-based missions agencies encouraged the formation of ethnic-specific missions agencies run for and by Asian Americans. The Chinese Bible Evangel, started in 1951, began only because the founder, Sen Wong, could not go back to China to serve as a missionary. He recounts the following:

I felt God was calling me to be a missionary to my own Chinese people. In fact, I approached the field director of the China Inland Mission. I approached him because I told him I was interested in ministering to my own Chinese people. I asked him, "Would your mission take me, a Chinese, to my own people?"

His answer was, "No, it's against our policy." He stated that they felt that having Chinese going back to their own native people at that time was not in their own program. Maybe they had trouble with it, I don't know, but nevertheless it was against their policy. And that was what precipitated our starting the Chinese Bible Evangel.

Another minister who planted a church in San Francisco complains:

I have had some very bad experiences with missions associations. When I finished my master's degree here, I wanted to go with OMF and go back to Hong Kong. They told me, "You came from Hong Kong, we cannot send you back to Hong Kong." I said, "Why not? I grew up there! And I'm familiar with the place."

I wanted some missionary group to send me back in. Most of the missionary groups have this stupid policy. They won't send you back to where you come from. Because they don't want the local people to think, "You're using American dollars and now you tell us what to do." They've got their point. But why send me to Thailand or Indonesia, somewhere I don't even know the language, the culture. But in Hong Kong, I had connections. I'd be more effective.

Similarly, the Japanese Evangelical Missions Society (JEMS) began in 1951 because Japanese Americans wanted to serve as missionaries to Japan but could not do so. As a result, they created their own sending agency that also focused on mission work aimed at Japanese Americans and now Asian Americans. Paul Nagano, one of the founders, remembers:

There are a lot of Japanese Americans who applied to the major denominations to be sent as missionaries to Japan. But the argument that most of the mission boards used was that, "You are a Japanese American. Your standard of living is so different, your culture is so different, you cannot adjust to these war-torn countries. And we cannot accept you as a candidate." They didn't want Japanese Americans to identify with Japan. They said, "We must assimilate them into our society."

From our perspective, Japanese Americans said they are the people that we love. That's a country of our ancestry, the country of origin. And we have this obligation to share this good news that transformed our lives. That is what got JEMS started.

Although some Asian Americans have pastored non-Asian congregations, the ministers face obstacles in getting hired and promoted in these churches. They recognize that most churches remain racially segregated as members choose where they wish to worship and whom they want for their pastor. In a *San Jose Mercury* article, "Leadership of Big, English-Speaking Churches Seems Out of Reach, Many Asian American Ministers Say," Rev. James Sun described the "stained glass ceiling" blocking English-speaking Asian pastors: "They're stuck. They are frustrated in the Chinese church because they don't share the same values system. And the Caucasians won't invite them to be their pastor" (Khanh 2002). The few exceptions are Asian American ministers of Roman Catholic parishes and mainline denominations that assign ministers to churches.[24]

Because ministers believe that major denominations and mainstream congregations would treat Asian Americans differently or simply neglect them, they feel a special responsibility to serve and evangelize their ethnic groups. One justifies the need for ethnic-specific churches by arguing that group members have the responsibility to reach out to families of their members:

> God has given us a concern. If we don't reach the Japanese people, we feel that nobody else may. So we feel the responsibility. As you notice, this is a family church and a lot of people have grown up in the church. Their parents were members of the Japanese-speaking congregation and they stayed in this church. So there's families that have three or four generations in the church.
>
> This particular church here started in 1929 and except for the few years when it was shut down, it's been here ministering to the Japanese community. We used to think as people get integrated or part of the whole society that there'd be less and less need for the church, but it seems like there's still a need and we need to be here. Without Christ, they're lost. If we don't reach out to them, they may not be reached.

Evangelism of Chinese and Japanese Americans by Chinese and Japanese American Christians illustrates the dual function that traditional culture and racial dynamics play in maintaining group solidarity. First, ethnic culture perpetuates among members a responsibility for group boundary maintenance. Chinese and Japanese Americans hold a special responsibility to their families and future generations. They establish church-based language instruction or sports programs to help maintain the family and pass on values and traditions to succeeding generations. Second, this desire to maintain cultural boundaries and the neglect of the broader church reinforce the ethnic church's role to evangelize co-ethnics. By providing cultural activities, Asian non-Christians, who otherwise might not be attracted to the Christian faith, are drawn to the church and may join as a result.

Conclusion

The intertwining of ethnicity and religion throughout Asian American history has resulted in some unique formations. Religious nationalism, in which Chinese and Japanese Christians hoped evangelism of their ancestral homelands would bring national salvation and modernization, developed as international students came to learn from the United States. They spawned movements—both religious and political—that contributed to Japan's war efforts and to the building of the Chinese nation. Bicultural congregations emerged as the second generation grew up acculturated by American ideology but isolated because of American racism. Although these churches sought to be cultural bridges that combined the best of two worlds, they also suffered from the worst of both worlds. The U.S. government excluded Asian immigration, interned Japanese Americans, and spied on Chinese Americans suspected as Communists. Japan's militarism and China's communism blocked Asian American Christian engagement with these countries. Retreating to work primarily within their American ethnic enclaves, Chinese and Japanese American churches became culturally oriented in their family-centered ministries. The civil rights movement of the 1960s encouraged resurgent ethnic identity despite mainstream denominations' attempts to integrate Chinese and Japanese Americans. Responding to the racial upheaval of the day, these groups formed national caucuses and conferences along ethnic lines. Today, these congregations continue to promote selective and adaptive cultural patterns to their members.

Ministers employ ethnic culture as a resource to draw people to the church. Cultural activities such as festivals and language instruction appeal to broad sectors of the ethnic community. They also use ethnic cultural traits to mobilize people around church activities. By appealing to members' sense of responsibility to the group, ministers can even rely on guilt and shame to encourage church participation. Ethnic culture also shapes how worship and Sunday school are conducted. The worship style of Chinese and Japanese American churches reflects the respect and reverence the people hold for higher authorities.

This book, however, contends that this cultural solidarity is waning as Asian Americans acculturate more. With the establishment of more panethnic Asian American congregations, new cultural and symbolic resources must be employed to build and maintain group solidarity.

3

The Emergence and Institutionalization
of Asian American Churches

Like the ethnic congregations described in the previous chapter, the Chinese Independent Church wanted to keep its families together in the church. The head pastor did not like to preach twice in two languages and was already overworked. To serve the youth who were put off by Chinese sermons and singing, they sought to hire an associate pastor. Then, as now, the demand for English-speaking Chinese American seminarians was high but the supply few. So they hired Pastor Rob, even though he was Japanese American, hoping that youth would appreciate the church family and that the English congregation would grow. However, Pastor Rob felt called by God to implement a broader vision than just ministering to Chinese American youth. He hoped to plant Pan-Asian congregations that would multiply in number, stating, "I think the way this church is going to survive is to broaden the base. I notice a lot of our young people, they're going to Peninsula Bible Church, which has a great multicultural ministry. And we lost a bunch of them to Grace Faith Church. They live on this side [of the bay] and they still go over there. Youth attracts youth, right?"

In the same city, Gibson Methodist Church, a Japanese American congregation nearing its centennial anniversary, also desperately needed another pastor. The congregation was elderly and most of their own children had left the church. Unless they did something drastic, such as becoming a Pan-Asian church, the church would close because of its dwindling numbers. So the members warmly welcomed Pastor Dan and his wife, Jan, hoping that the young Chinese American couple would bring other new families to the church. Pastor Dan dreamed of evangelizing non-Christian Asian Americans and making them disciples: "I grew up in L.A., went to UCLA and Berkeley, and so I've a much more intuitive sense of Asian Americans—meaning those who are Asian by background but grew up here in America, who identify with mainstream culture yet also view themselves as very Asian and American, who have a network of friends beyond their specific ethnicities. When I'm preaching, there are certain empty chairs where I have in mind the target, the unchurched Asian Americans, and I want to be preaching to them."

How did God grant such similar visions to Pastor Rob and Pastor Dan? In fact, so many pastors have caught this vision that the number of self-identifying Pan-Asian congregations has risen dramatically. In the San Francisco Bay Area, the number of Pan-Asian congregations has increased from one in 1989 to five in 1993. By 1998 an estimated two hundred churches in the area had congregations with a majority of Chinese or Japanese American members. Twenty-two of these specifically identified as Pan-Asian.[1] Eight were new panethnic startup congregations, and fourteen were originally Chinese specific or Japanese specific but now have a broader mission focus. The concept of Pan-Asian congregations is a radical break from the model of church found in ethnic-specific churches and from other American ethnic churches.[2] Ministers have mobilized around newly constituted racial groupings as the United States has attempted to become "the world's first truly multiracial democracy," as President Bill Clinton proclaimed in 1997. And rather than preserving ethnic ties or building transnational connections, these churches have established a new solidarity at the intersection of race and religion. What factors have led ministers to heed the call for building Asian American churches?

Factors external and internal to the churches account for the growth and institutionalization of Pan-Asian churches. Since the 1980s, the San Francisco Bay Area's racial climate has been particularly conducive to Asian American panethnic formation. Identity politics and multiculturalism heavily structure the racial discourses employed by the ministers and their members. Religious institutions that train, professionalize, and ordain ministers, also known as their organizational fields, adopt these discourses and promote new racial formations. Because pastors have little time or resources to innovate, they rely heavily on their organizational field for inspiration and models for church work. Both Pastor Rob and Pastor Dan worked as ministers with Asian American Christian Fellowship and drew from their campus work experiences.

Although trends in broader society and in religious institutions may encourage Pan-Asian formation, they tell only half of these pastors' stories. Dynamics internal to the ethnic communities also determine whether churches innovate or remain ethnically organized. First, demographic shifts within the Asian American community and their churches influence the opportunities that Pastor Dan and Pastor Rob had to fulfill their visions. The Japanese American church has a shrinking ethnic base from which to draw, while the Chinese American church has welcomed huge flows of Chinese immigrants. Second, these changes have altered the cultural viewpoints about church that members hold. New generations of leaders conflict with their elders about how to build their churches. Third, power dynamics within both these ethnic churches affect the possibilities for church renewal and growth. Pastor Dan and Pastor Rob have to operate within the same broader racial context but face different ethnic circumstances.

Despite these differences, internal dynamics and the broader racial context have encouraged the remarkable movement toward Pan-Asian churches that was unforeseen a generation ago. The growing numbers of Asian American churches indicate that panethnicity has become institutionalized. As a category, it has become an identity legitimated by institutions of the state and the church. As a new basis for solidarity, it has become an emergent means for church organization.[3] Through ideas and examples that get circulated within their organizational field, ministers perceive this model to provide opportunities for growth, for change, and for revival.

The Racialization of the Bay Area

Pastor Dan and Pastor Rob themselves developed Pan-Asian racial identities as they attended public universities in California in the 1970s. While they attended high school, more and more people appeared with faces that looked like them. With the lifting of immigration restrictions in 1965, the numbers of Asian Americans soared from 1.5 million in 1970 to 7.9 million in 1990. Having grown by 44.6 percent in the Bay Area in the past decade, Asians now make up 31 percent of San Francisco County, 20 percent of Alameda County, and 21 percent of Santa Clara County, according to the 2000 U.S. Census.[4] As the presence of Asian Americans impacted the public education system, the regional economy, and local politics, these institutions have responded with policies that have defined residents' ethnic and racial identities.

Today, when these pastors' children attend school, they become socialized into a system that recognizes students' ethnic backgrounds and advocates multiculturalism to a limited degree (see Moore 1998). Until the passage of California State Proposition 227 in 1998, bilingual education programs had provided instruction in pupils' first language, such as Cantonese or Vietnamese. Almost every school district in the area has adopted a policy regarding multicultural education and developing ethnic pride. As an example, Santa Clara Unified School District, with minority students making up 57 percent of the population, approved "Community Values and Beliefs" that include a "respect for diversity" among its seven core values.[5]

Institutions of higher education in the area recognize ethnic and racial groupings as well. At the University of California at Berkeley, where the undergraduate student body in 2001 was 41 percent Asian and 68 percent nonwhite, students must take an "American Cultures" course in which three of five racial groups are covered in a comparative manner.[6] Students not only learn about different racial groups but also divide into these groups socially. The school's Student Activities and Services Office lists seventy-one different types of Asian student organizations, ranging from Cal Asian Lesbian Bisexual Gay Alliance Yo-united to Pilipino Association of Scientists, Architects, and Engineers.[7] A report on the students' experiences of racial diversity at the university summarizes the school's impact on students' identities:

> When these students came to Berkeley, they report feeling a bit strange or awkward about being in an environment with so many Asians. Given that the label Asian American is not a category with which these students readily identify, several talked about having to *learn what it means to be Asian American*. . . . Regardless of their previous attitude toward their racial-cultural identity, Berkeley forced [Asian American students] to come to terms with their own racial identity in very new ways. (Duster 1991, 23, 25)[8]

While schools may not inculcate specific ethnic cultural traditions and values, they do categorize students into racial groupings and treat them differentially. This racialization, in which race becomes a significant factor in social relations, exemplifies how institutions such as the school system legitimate certain groupings.

Upon entering the labor force in the Bay Area, Asian Americans are located within a global economy where transnational Pacific Rim ties are valued. In Cupertino, a suburb on the San Francisco peninsula, the chamber of commerce targeted a membership drive toward Asian American businesses, which make up 22 percent of the businesses in the city ("Cupertino" 1998). The *San Jose Mercury News* includes the *Asia Report*, a weekly look at people and trends around the Pacific Rim. Other local media accounts report the presence of new ethnic malls, ethnic markets, and booming immigrant entrepreneurship (Casteneda 1998; Collier 1996; Tran 1998). As industries and businesses increasingly view Asians and Asian Americans as a viable market, a side result is a growing group consciousness among Asians of their common market identity. Asian Americans then network together to capitalize on this identity and to access corporations (Ho 2002).

In ways similar to the market, the state and political activities structure how Asians view themselves and organize. To gain power, groups need to mobilize money and voters. The increased number of Asian Americans elected to office in the 1990s, especially in the Bay Area, signals an ethnic voting bloc pursuing their own material interests.[9] Whereas Oakland had only one elected Asian American official in 1990, voters had elected three Asian American city council members, one county supervisor, and one state assembly member in

2002. In San Francisco, Asian American politicians attempted to mobilize ethnic constituencies through organizations such as the Chinese American Democratic Club and by appealing to local issues such as freeway reconstruction and
the sale of live animals (Epstein and McLeod 1997; Martin 1998). In fact, newspaper reporters proclaimed that a recent election "marked the emergence of a
potent new political force in San Francisco—a growing bloc of Chinese American voters and property and business owners from the Richmond and Sunset
districts who think City Hall consistently ignores them" (Epstein 1997). Furthermore, with the recent increased attention on immigrant issues, large voter
registration drives aimed at Asian Americans have been successful (see Chao
1998; Lubman 1998; Nakao 1996).

On the other hand, Asian American support of Asian American politicians
may not represent political mobilization as an ethnic interest group but simply
symbolic identification with candidates of the same background (Lai 2003). In
an editorial column in the weekly newspaper *Asian Week*, Filipino American
Emil Guilermo questions whether Asian Americans should support the campaign of Matt Fong as the Californian Republican Party candidate to the U.S.
Senate. He wonders, "Should Asian Americans—who tend to be Democrats—
support Fong? The ethnic bond is sacred. It's a reason why many Asian Americans have expressed strong outward support for Fong. He's sort of like us"
(Guilermo 1998). In the June 1998 primary election, Fong garnered 35 percent
of the Chinese American *Democrat* vote in San Francisco. Fong does not necessarily represent the interests of the Asian American constituency as a whole,
but his election supplied feelings of pride over his success.[10]

The San Francisco Bay Area, in sum, acknowledges the ethnic and racial
presence of Asian Americans even though they may be an invisible minority
throughout the rest of the country or caught between black and white (Chang
2001; Lien 2001; Okihiro 1994; Wu 2002). Through the educational system, business affairs, local politics, and the media, the Bay Area embraces a form of multiculturalism that accentuates and superficially celebrates ethnic and racial
differences while still promoting a common culture based on market forces
(Bellah 1998; Glazer 1997). Within this multiethnic, multiracial context in which
almost everyone is a minority and seeks a group identity, ministers of Chinese and
Japanese American congregations have the opportunity to build their churches.[11]

The secular climate in the San Francisco Bay Area is paradoxically suited
for establishing Pan-Asian congregations as well. The San Francisco metropolitan area has the lowest percentage of Christian identifiers of any area in the
country, at just 70 percent (Kosmin and Lachman 1993).[12] One minister in this
study noted the following:

> San Francisco is not a Bible Belt area. It's actually one of the most anti-
> Christian areas in the nation. The Chinese churches are fairly weak in

this area. You've got the flight of family people, white people from San Francisco. Even the Chinese people, you have the slow movement from Chinatown to the Sunset and Richmond and then they're moving into the East Bay for affordable housing or they're moving south to the Silicon Valley for work. So you have many factors against the stability of the church because the church relies upon family, longevity of its leadership, good numbers attract numbers.

The area's reputation for openness and tolerance supports an ecumenical acceptance of different types of religious innovation and group formation, including panethnic congregations. Mainline liberal denominations, in accommodating more to the ideological atmosphere of the region, also embrace the idea of diversity and therefore can accept the existence of ethnic and Pan-Asian congregations (Balmer 1996; Roof and McKinney 1987; Warner 1988; Wuthnow 1988). Evangelical congregations, on the other hand, find themselves more in opposition to the morally relativistic milieu of the Bay Area and maintain more tightly knit communities (Ammerman 1987; Hunter 1983; Kelley 1972; Roof 1993). Homogeneous ethnic and panethnic congregations can provide a more tightly bounded, sacred canopy by which members can practice their own beliefs (Berger 1967).

Institutional Legitimation of Asian American Panethnicity

Pastor Dan and Pastor Rob may have been racialized in the Bay Area so that they socialize along panethnic lines, but where did they receive the idea that a Pan-Asian church might be successful? They learned from teachers and gained information from peers whose expertise and authority they respect. In particular, their professional network, called their organizational field, strongly influences them as it supplies church models, publications, and trainings about the best practices (Scott 1998).[13] However, evangelical ministers and mainline, liberal ministers generally divide theologically and organizationally into two camps.[14] As a result, they receive divergent ideas about Asian Americans and develop different models for developing their churches.

The Mainline Organizational Field

Mainline church leaders look to their denominations, seminaries, and nonprofit organizations as sources of panethnic understanding. Mainline denominations recognized and established panethnic Asian American professional caucuses and youth camps as early as 1971. Seeing the need for Asian American leadership development, representation on boards, and resources for Asian American ministries, these caucuses advocated official recognition within their respective denominations.[15] For example, in 2001 the Presbyterian Church USA

(PCUSA) denomination sponsored its annual Asian American meeting. Rev. Syngman Rhee, a Korean who is the first Asian American moderator of the general assembly, encouraged the 250 delegates to get more involved with the leadership of the PCUSA (see Filiatreau 2001).

When a group in the South Bay wanted to develop a Pan-Asian congregation, they contacted the associate executive of the regional presbytery who had also come from their home church. The denominational caucus's work to increase awareness of minority needs, and the presence of Asian American leaders within the presbytery hierarchy, opened up opportunities to establish this church. A minister recounts why his denomination recognized the need for minorities to have their own congregations. It understood that white congregations might not be easily integrated with Asian Americans or other minorities.

> If you look at Santa Clara, there's easily half a dozen [Presbyterian churches]. Some of those churches might [be] 10 percent ethnic. I would say that's true for all denominations. You can probably pick [out] those churches that are genuinely multicultural. They would be the exception to the rule. So the Presbytery said, "Fine, go with our blessings. We'll even help with some funding and help secure leadership."

Official denominational recognition of the racial minority status of Asian Americans has made the idea of forming Pan-Asian congregations possible.

Mainline seminaries promote Pan-Asian identity and solidarity by educating seminarians about the particular theological perspective and concerns of this group. For example, the mainline Graduate Theological Union (GTU) has trained several Asian American ministers in the Bay Area. As early as 1972 the GTU provided institutional space for the Asian Center for Theologies and Strategies to develop new theologies based on Asian worldviews and experiences.[16] Today, the Pacific School of Religion, one of the seminaries in the GTU, hosts the Institute for Leadership Development and Study of Pacific Asian North American Religion. In its first two years of existence, it raised $3.25 million in endowment funds and program grants. It annually sponsors the Asian Pacific Americans and Religion Research Initiative conference, which brings together scholars, theologians, and ministers of Asian American religions. This institute and other schools of the GTU sponsor courses on "Asian American Religions," "Asian and Asian American Bible Hermeneutics," and "Asian American Church History." Through these conferences, classes, and other workshops sponsored by the seminaries, future pastors and ministers learn theology from an Asian American perspective.

Theologians and biblical scholars from these seminaries have written about Asian American Christianity to "bridge biblical studies and Asian American studies," according to Tat-siong Liew (2002). Recently, titles by mainline publishing houses include *Out of Silence: Emerging Themes in Asian American*

Churches (Matsuoka 1995), *Journeys at the Margin: Toward an Autobiographical Theology in American-Asian Perspective* (Phan and Lee 1999), and *The Bible in Asian America* (Liew 2002).

The community nonprofit world also furnishes models to the church. Mainline liberal congregations, who tend to be involved in community issues of race and social justice, work closely with these nonprofit organizations. Within the San Francisco Bay Area, the Asian American nonprofit sector is especially well established with longstanding organizations such as the Asian Law Caucus, Asian Neighborhood Design, and Asian Health Services. Because these agencies address the same kinds of concerns and work with the same constituencies as their congregations, mainline ministers conceive of their congregations as peers to these organizations.

Institutional structures within denominations, educational curriculum that recognizes Asian American panethnicity, and nonprofit organizational models shape how ministers think about congregational identity. As they respond and comply with institutional and professional expectations, they help make their own congregations similar in form and structure.[17] They establish Pan-Asian congregations with understandings from these institutional bases that circulate a broad definition of the group Asian Americans.

The Evangelical Organizational Field

Evangelical ministers work together and learn from each other in an organizational field separate from the mainline and thus have a very different understanding of Asian Americans. Just as mainline ministers receive formal training from certain seminaries, evangelicals learn about church growth methodology within their educational institutions. But instead of looking to denominations and the public nonprofit sector for insights on serving Asian Americans, evangelical ministers look more to leading evangelical publications and their professional networks to target and minister to this group.[18]

Since the 1980s, institutional campus ministries have recognized the growing presence of Asian Americans on campuses and have sought to evangelize students along these groupings. InterVarsity Christian Fellowship (IVCF) and the Japanese Evangelical Missionary Society (JEMS) have established Asian American Christian Fellowships (AACFs) throughout California and on elite university campuses in the United States. Once graduated, students seek similar fellowship and church settings because they find their ethnic home churches to be less oriented to their social needs and worship styles. Just as public universities racialize students, campus ministries also now emphasize racial identities by encouraging targeted evangelism and racial reconciliation.[19]

Like mainline seminaries, evangelical seminaries also promote and legitimate panethnicity by offering courses tailored toward this grouping. The largest seminary in North America, the evangelical Fuller Seminary in Pasadena,

California, offers the courses "Building Multicultural Teams" and "Communicating Cross-Culturally." Instructors use the text *The Wolf Shall Dwell with the Lamb* (Law 1993). These courses, texts, and Asian American instructors constitute official, professional recognition that Asian Americans are a valid "people group" to target. However, evangelicals usually do not attempt to develop theologies based on a localized, particular group experience in the manner that mainline theologians might. Instead, classes on Asian Americans at evangelical seminaries emphasize evangelism and ministry to this group rather than distinctive Asian American theologies.

Most important, evangelical pastors have professional and ministerial networks that introduce Pan-Asian models of congregational development. Online, the L^2 Foundation has established a Web site and resource network for Asian American Christians. This foundation's purpose is to "develop the leadership and legacy of Asian Americans by providing support and resources. L^2 serves ministry and professional leaders, empowering them to fulfill God's calling." This Web site took over the Chinese American Christians Listserv (CAC), which hosted discussion boards on a variety of ministry topics. In the San Francisco Bay Area, official networks have included the Bay Area Asian American Youth Fellowship, the Promise Keepers, and the Asian American Bay Area Fellowship.

For example, the Asian American Bay Area Fellowship is made up of about fifty Chinese, Filipino, Japanese, and Korean American evangelical pastors who meet irregularly. Since 1991, they have addressed similar issues as those posted on CAC, including the role of ethnic culture in the church and Asian American racial reconciliation between individual ethnic groups. These professional networks are the "interorganizational contexts" within which the discourse of panethnicity and race become circulated, appropriated, and infused with meaning. Whether Pan-Asian congregations or multiethnic congregations become the premier model for Chinese and Japanese American churches remains debated between ministers within these networks. These forums, along with seminary training and books on church growth, create the menu of options from which ministers can choose in building their congregations.

With limited options of strategies and rules about church growth circulating within the evangelical field, ministers often follow the leaders. Within the local Bay Area Asian American church networks, ministers perceive Pan-Asian congregations as being successful in attracting members and building the church as a body. For example, this pastor feels called to establish a ministry similar to other Pan-Asian ones: "Most of the successful churches, either in Southern California or here, they're mostly Pan-Asian. They have been very successful, not only in terms of numbers but also spiritual growth. So I thought that this church, that's why God placed me here." Pan-Asian churches emerge as new congregations copy other successful panethnic ones. In particular, pastors often referred to Evergreen Baptist Church and Newsong Church in southern California as large and growing Asian American congregations.[20]

Even if the innovations do not prove to be effective in increasing church growth, they are still adopted to demonstrate that the ministers are trying to effect some kind of reform and to meet the demands of potential members. Panethnicity, as a new model for organizing a congregation, enables ministers to start afresh and rethink every aspect of church. As a sectarian movement, its novelty encourages a reenvisioning of what church could be. This minister explains how people seek change and want to build something new:

> I think a lot of ministries have a tremendous desire to do something great and different. There's a lot of churches that I know that have great aspirations when they finally start up their English ministry. And it's funny because when they start it from their perspective, they always think that they're doing something radical like, "Wow! Let's do an English ministry!" And from their perspective, I'm beginning to see, yeah, that it is.

Another aspect of the perceived success of Pan-Asian churches is that they are new and cutting edge. These churches attract members who want to avoid the cultural baggage of ethnic churches. A minister explains that his new congregation was tailored for those who had left the church: "The original purpose was to be ministry designed for those who had given up on traditional churches, what we call the 'Silent Exodus' where a lot of Asian Americans are leaving their ethnic churches, seeking more of a contemporary worship environment." Asian American evangelical congregations, therefore, become established to mimic successful church growth models and to reform outdated elements of the ethnic church. With the large numbers of unchurched Asian Americans and the increasing percentage of Asian American young adults who are leaving the church, ministers look for fresh innovations in church form and in worship style that might attract these disaffected groups.

Demographic Trends toward Pan-Asian Solidarity

Not only do institutions external to their congregations racialize ministers, but demographic changes among church members also encourage a movement toward Asian American panethnicity. To be viable, a church must attract new members to volunteer for church activities, to provide a revenue base, and to serve the community. In Pastor Dan's church, the church session recognized that their elderly church would eventually die off unless they recruited new young families. However, the number of Japanese American families in that city was limited, so they widened their target to families and friends of their members. In Pastor Rob's church, the head pastor could not handle the workload of a growing bilingual Chinese American population. To meet the needs of the young families, they hired an English-speaking minister to nurture the youth fellowship. These two examples reflect two different impetuses for Pan-Asian congregations.

In terms of sheer numbers, ministers observe that Chinese American churches have a growing ethnic pool of people and resources to attract, but Japanese American churches have a much more limited one.[21] In San Francisco alone, the Chinese American population has seen a dramatic increase, 85 percent from 1980 to 2000. The Japanese American community, on the other hand, dropped 5 percent in San Francisco and now ranks only sixth among California Asian ethnic groups in population. Demographers predict that the Chinese American population in California will continue to grow by 38 percent while the Japanese American population will increase only by 7 percent into the next decade.

Population trends indicate that the growth in the Chinese American population has largely resulted from immigration. More of the Chinese American population is now foreign born, but the Japanese American population is predominantly American born.[22] Because the majority of Chinese Americans have arrived more recently, they are much more likely to seek out church services in their native tongues. Furthermore, immigrants prefer congregating with co-ethnics who share cultural similarities and value transnational connections. Chinese-speaking congregations have thus sprung up even in suburbs, where they make up a small minority.

Another problem facing Japanese American churches is that the Japanese American community is an aging population with smaller household sizes. Within California 34.6 percent of the population is under twenty-five years of age, but only 26.7 percent of the Japanese American population is this young. While the mean number of children per household in California is 0.72, Japanese Americans only average 0.42 children per household. Their churches reflect these changes so that congregations like Gibson Methodist Church increasingly cater to the needs of seniors. Without a critical mass of young families or young adults, churches cannot provide children's programs or singles fellowship that would attract this profile. In fact, younger members are more likely to leave the church to meet these needs. In contrast, Chinese American households roughly match the general population's profile. Congregations like the Chinese Independent Church, then, can maintain growth simply as their couples have children and fill Sunday schools.

Ministers also note that Japanese Americans no longer reside in ethnic concentrations and have moved out of urban centers. San Francisco Japantown is no longer an institutionally complete, residential neighborhood for Japanese Americans but more of a commercial neighborhood with a mix of Asian businesses. Since Japanese families are now in their fourth or fifth generation in the United States, they are less likely to return to their ethnic enclave for church.[23]

A Japanese American minister observes that Japanese American urban flight has caused his church's ethnic composition to begin shifting:

> Our congregation is 85–90 percent Japanese American, but the direction is Asian American. Two couples in our church who are members have married Caucasians. The majority by far have been with Chinese Americans. Most of them live outside the City. That's another difference between the Japanese American community and the Chinese American community. A greater percentage of the third generation have left the City, haven't had the same kind of family unit, family support and reason to stay in the City as the Chinese Americans have. In the case of Japanese Americans, it's the case that the third generation and younger all become professional people. Because of the professions, they've moved out. They don't have the same ties.

One demographic shift that has created opportunities for Japanese American churches is a trend toward Pan-Asian friendships and interethnic marriages.[24] Asian American youth overwhelmingly prefer having friends of the same ethnicity, but they are also more likely to choose a friend of the same race over a friend of a different race (Kao and Joyner 2001).[25] These friendships increase the possibilities of Pan-Asian marriages. For example, the percent of Japanese Americans marrying other Asians increased from 11.9 percent of all outmarriages in 1980 to 20.3 percent in 1990. The number of Chinese Americans marrying other Asian groups grew from 22.2 percent in 1980 to 32.7 percent in 1990 (Qian et al. 2001).[26] A transition from an ethnic congregation to a panethnic one is easier than becoming multiethnic. By building around a racial solidarity, Pan-Asian churches can draw on social networks developed in college and work. They also may build upon common cultural traits, such as Confucian virtues, and address similar causes, such as racial empowerment.

Demographic shifts within the Japanese American church have raised serious issues about its viability and even its necessity. Gibson Methodist Church, at a critical juncture in its history, chose to become Pan-Asian and to call Pastor Dan to its pulpit to attract new families. Chinese Independent Church, on the other hand, called Pastor Rob to minister to the youth in English but did not see the need to change the mission of its church. Tensions between English-speaking congregations and Chinese-speaking congregations have created another impulse for organizing Pan-Asian churches.

Generational Conflicts

While the Japanese American church faces a shrinking target population in the Bay Area, the Chinese American church faces a different challenge: welcoming more and more immigrants into their congregations. New immigrants now control most Chinese American churches, and their congregational practices exacerbate a tension already present between the first generation and the later generations. Indeed, maintaining the unity of a church with two separate congregations, one English and one Chinese, is the major source of strain for ministers.[27] Members not only speak different languages but also hold different generational perspectives about church.

According to ministers interviewed, the generation gap in the Chinese American church is primarily a difference in cultural viewpoints. Because he brought a more Americanized cultural style, Pastor Rob was at odds with the Chinese congregation. His church was similar to ethnic-specific churches, described in the last chapter, that seek to transmit ethnic culture, maintain formality and hierarchy, and employ a sense of group loyalty to mobilize members. In contrast, Pastor Rob had a different cultural approach to organizing church and drawing in new members. He felt his American-born members preferred his style, but it threatened the church leaders, and he eventually found another position. ABCs who feel that the immigrant church does not meet their needs are tempted to split churches and plant new Pan-Asian ones.

The group-oriented, Confucian ethic that Chinese and Japanese American parents wish to preserve and transmit at times contrasts with the individualistic and egalitarian values rewarded in the United States. While the younger generations appreciate "distilled" ethnic values such as family, hard work, and education, they react against the severe guilt and shame employed by their elders to raise them.[28] For example, Chinese and Japanese American parents often negatively compare their children with those who receive straight A's, win music competitions, or have other notable achievements. They expect their children to respond by trying harder and to save the "face," or the group reputation, of their families. These social controls maintain hierarchical relations and group harmony as children seek to gain status for their family and avoid standing out in negative ways. In contrast, the American school system and media socialize youth to desire egalitarian relationships, honesty, and individualism. The concerns for keeping quiet, controlling emotions, and avoiding embarrassment lessen as Asian Americans acculturate in colleges and workplaces. One pastor contrasts the older Japanese Americans' orientation toward saving face with the younger generation's desire for more authenticity: "I think shame in this culture is a really big thing, especially among the Japanese. I know in the Japanese culture that's really huge. If you lose face, it's just terrible. The younger Asians, whether they're Japanese or Chinese, it doesn't seem as important."

Pastor Rob had problems with his church leadership, first of all, because of his decision-making style. Values of group-orientation and face-saving affect Asian work relations because elder members and immigrants are more likely to seek harmony and avoid conflict. Pastor Rob preferred to directly address issues, even by raising differences of opinion. This approach jarred the elders and the first generation, who valued democratic debate less. In another church, a fourth-generation Japanese American complained that a few leaders within the church privately controlled funds and disbursed them. They acted without consulting the wider church, yet the minister could not reform church finances for fear of embarrassing these elders. Another Japanese American minister sums up this generational conflict that disrupts church administration:

> I see the third generation, the Sansei operating more as white Americans than I do. They're much more willing to be articulate, less consensus building. The Japanese approach is you do all your consensus building before you have your meeting. That's not the case for the Chinese American members and the third-generation people. They're more willing to express their opinions and differences in a public setting. My difficulty is how to get the more Japanese style and the younger style together. Since I'm more comfortable with the Japanese style, the difficulty has been with allowing and encouraging the younger generations to be as they are.

A direct style in preaching also bothers the older generation, especially when issues that were previously private become exposed. American-born pastors complained that some churches preferred to be ethnic social organizations over spiritual ones that address difficult issues about people's lifestyles:

> There's a second agenda to say that we also want to maintain Chinese culture. We want the church to reflect the Chinese culture so that it maintains it for the young people, it maintains it for those Chinese that have grown up here that have lost touch with their culture. And so there's an effort to say even though you've grown up in the U.S., you've been born in the U.S. and you really don't have very much to do with the Chinese culture, in the church we want to encourage you to remember that.

Indeed, another pastor believes that Asian American Baby Boomers and younger generations consider the immigrant church as hypocritical. They are overly concerned with preserving ethnic culture, maintaining status distinctions, and gaining face. On the other hand, he thinks the younger generation wants to go to church for authentic, "spiritual reasons":

> I think the Asian Americans really desire authenticity. And so I just spoke recently for [a] young adult retreat on the issues of holiness and godliness lifestyles. And it was a real threatening topic. I was extremely vulnerable because the topic called for it, you can't preach on holiness and godliness and just hide your life, you know!
>
> But I shared some things to a degree that just would never have gone

down or would have meant my termination or something [laughing] in this [Chinese] church setting. It's just ... well ... because there's families, it's a different story.

By referring that "there's families" in the church, this minister meant that immigrant parents would not want sex, drugs, abuse, or other sensitive issues to be discussed in church. Instead, he felt that they would prefer to maintain illusions of being happy Chinese Christian families with strong bonds.

To make church more authentic, less formal, and less status oriented, ministers like this one and Pastor Rob attempt to introduce a different worship style. They expect people "to come as they are" without dressing up to impress others. They want people to be free to express themselves individually without regard for the group. For example, this pastor explains his congregation's shift to a contemporary worship style that is more joyous and upbeat than reverent:

We do a lot of singing because again, we really feel like we want somebody to come to church and have a real positive experience that we're worshipping together. Maybe a little bit more experiential. We want to say that when we've come to church, we've actually met with God. He's there in our presence and we feel His joy worshipping Him. We're really focused on that.

However, this style of worship caters to younger generations and not the older ones, who may prefer more reverential music, traditional hymns, and orderly liturgy. Yet another generational conflict arises over the choice of music instruments. For example, one elderly church member in a Japanese American congregation confided to me that none of the younger members could play the organ. As a result, she "had to continue to play" as if the church could not do without a decent organist. While she raised this topic as a complaint, she was also proud that she had served the church in this way for the past fifty years. Needless to say, altering the music of the church and not using the organ would cause great consternation to these members.

Immigrant and elderly generations of Asian Americans desire to preserve ethnic unity and to transmit cultural values that include ordered relationships and group harmony. Ethnic-specific churches reflect this orientation in the formality of their programs, decision making, and worship styles. In contrast, younger Asian Americans may desire ethnic identities, but they have been socialized to value individualism and authenticity. Individualism, in which one seeks to have a voice and to assert one's independence, goes against an Asian group orientation traditionally understood as submission to the needs of the group. Authenticity, which includes admitting failure or avoiding false appearances, conflicts with the need to save face for the entire family. Asian American ministers like Pastor Rob understand the cultural orientation of the American born but face difficulties in meeting their needs while also pleasing the elders who pay them. How these conflicts get resolved depends on who wields power and how it is used.[29]

Power and Conflict

Chinese American Churches Becoming Pan-Asian

At Chinese Independent Church, the Chinese-speaking congregation held more power than the English ministry and, as a result, Pastor Rob was unable to implement his vision. With the power of numbers and money, they and most other Chinese-speaking congregations control the church's staffing, finances, and programs. In the Chinese American Christians e-mail discussion group, ministers have voiced such grievances about working within bilingual, bicultural churches. This minister, noting that the great majority of ABC pastors have few opportunities outside of the Chinese American church, offered suggestions about how to adjust to the cultural differences between ABCs and OBCs. Given the ABC pastors' limited power and the realities of Chinese American churches, he encouraged them to serve in humility and to defer to the older generations:

> Let me assume for the sake of discussion that most churches with an opening for your people graduating from seminary will be a church of about 150–200 people. It has an OBC pastor and is looking for someone to work in the English department. Maybe the board does everything in Chinese. There are few if any adults [in the English ministry]. The English ministry will be primarily youth ministry. I think this describes about 80–90 percent of the available positions out there. So, how would you prepare them? They have to be prepared to do cross-cultural ministry.

Ethnic church politics confronting English-speaking ministers include relating to immigrant church leadership, being considered a "youth ministry," and having to "do cross-cultural ministry."

Insisting on unity and harmony, both biblical and Chinese values, leadership of the older generation generally seeks to avoid conflict while at the same time resisting change. One minister complains that by controlling church functions through the use of language, the Chinese-speaking congregation effectively disenfranchised the English-speaking congregation, and, as a result, individuals abandoned the church. Not even one of the strongest ethnic sentiments, one's connection to the community through ethnic food, could keep these Chinese Americans coming:

> There's a luncheon. But it's hardly a joint lunch because it's catered Chinese food and the whole thing has this sense of flavor and environment of being really Taiwanese. They make announcements without translating, they make Taiwanese jokes without translating. And whenever

there's special occasions like a birthday, it's in Chinese and it's not translated. And so basically they're expecting the English [speaking members]
to kind of fit in and, "Oh yeah, this is wonderful time of community!"

Adding to the conservatism of the immigrant leadership is their need
to spend resources to please the majority rather than serving the English-
speaking minority of the church that usually does not give as much offering. For
example, Pastor Rob noted that the Chinese congregation had already sunk
costs in the church's architecture and hymnals. They would be unlikely to waste
more money:

> Look at the sanctuary. What do you see in the front of the sanctuary?
> People will come in and see [points to Chinese characters]. Even the col-
> ors they use are more Chinese-type colors. But there's a rule of thumb. If
> you're going to develop an Asian American ministry, or a multicultural
> ministry, that's the last thing you want up there. You don't want the lan-
> guage up there to indicate any particular loyalty. But since we share a
> sanctuary with a Cantonese congregation, we can't say you can't have
> Chinese up there.

Besides lacking resources, Asian American pastors and their English-speaking
adult members chafe against their status as the less important "youth ministry."
Cameron left his Korean immigrant church even though he had served as a dea-
con in the English-speaking congregation that had thought of itself as a separate,
autonomous entity. The Korean leadership consistently undermined Cameron
and his fellow deacons by dictating their agenda and budget:

> For some reason, a lot of English ministries seem to have generational
> conflicts between the first and second generations. The English min-
> istries would have differences in budget, ministry activities, and the
> main thing would be the purpose of the English ministry. A lot of times,
> the Korean and English pastor would have conflicts and leave. From what
> I've seen, the Korean congregation thinks the English ministries are an
> older version of youth ministries, not a ministry that can stand on its
> own. I guess English ministries want the freedom to minister and wor-
> ship the way they felt was right.

Similarly, Nic, a twenty-four-year-old Chinese American engineer from the
East Coast and a leader of a Pan-Asian church, recounts the story of his previous ethnic-specific congregation's hiring process as an example of the younger
generation's disenfranchisement. The second generation wanted to hire a new
English-speaking pastor who was very inspiring and filled with conviction to do
evangelism. However, the Chinese-speaking deacons had previously hired an
English-speaking pastor with similar missionary tendencies, and he left within

a year. In this case, the deacons went against the wishes of the second generation because they wanted someone who would be less likely to leave or encourage their children to become missionaries. Like many other 1.5 and second-generation Asian Americans, Nic expresses his frustration and resentment about their elders' seemingly arbitrary use of power: "And they were, like, 'We don't want that to happen again. We want someone to be here to help build the ministry.' So they shot down this hiring, which caused a number of defections from the English congregation. We couldn't even choose our own pastor, so. . . . "

Furthermore, requiring younger generation Asian Americans to "do cross-cultural ministry" and to go against their own Americanized ways and religious beliefs is a bitter pill to swallow for Asian American ministers and English-speaking members. One cross-cultural difference is how leaders are selected and authority is granted. Often, the older generations claim authority and expect filial piety based on traditional Confucian grounds and biblical references. Simply because they are the older, younger members are to defer to them and respect them. Additionally, in Confucian contexts, those with higher educational degrees and professional status are honored and awarded church leadership positions. However, younger members who grew up in the United States hold different views of authority and leadership. Instead of following authorities because they are older or have higher socioeconomic status, Asian Americans prefer capable and efficient leaders. One leader contrasts the older immigrant generation with Asian American culture regarding leadership selection:

> Taiwanese or Chinese, they have a much higher deference for age. I think they tend to be more hierarchical in their thinking. [Examples are] issues of authority, issues of degrees, and formal signs and symbols of leadership, and cultural designators of who's a leader and what-not. In Asian American culture, there's less of a deference for people's vast experiences in the company or what-not. And more, you know, "Is it working now? Can you deliver the goods now?" And almost regardless of if you have a Ph.D. or whatever, well, "Can you deliver the goods? Are you relevant to me now?"

Due to their lack of autonomy, resources, and status, Chinese American ministers seeking to introduce major changes to worship or ministry focus must resort to establishing new churches.[30] Chinese American ministers have started seven of the eight new panethnic congregations. One justifies his rationale to create a new Pan-Asian church by claiming that it would not face the competing agendas that a bilingual, bicultural church might have. Instead, it would be more effective in accomplishing the spiritual mission of the gospel:

> The obvious issue is that in a bicultural church, there develops an infusion of particular agendas. One agenda [is] the preservation of the mother

culture. There's that agenda but [there's] also the Christian agenda of evangelism, church growth, edification, outreach, prayer and worship. And
those two agendas don't necessarily hold. If the church leaders think that
having the young people exposed to the language in the mother tongue
is a priority, trying to choose that will cost them outreach opportunities.

Japanese American Churches Becoming Pan-Asian

Japanese American congregations have become panethnic through a more grad-
ual process than Chinese American ones, but not without contestation, either.
As in the Chinese American churches, the older Nisei generations control power
and claim that traditional respect for the elderly legitimates their authority.
The Japanese American churches that shifted to a Pan-Asian identity did acknowledge the need to broaden their church target. Those that consciously and strategically decided to change had faced closure and had very old members who were
willing to give up power.

Although older Japanese Americans would like to maintain their congregations as an ethnic institution, they have had to come to terms with the demographic changes facing the community. A minister, whose congregation had
dropped to twenty-five at worship service, observes that the shift to panethnicity and concurrent reforms of church worship and programs had emotionally
affected the older members. He explains that he was brought in as pastor to
change the church's focus toward Asian Americans, and, soon after, the older
members resigned from their committee work:

> Sometimes I hear rumblings that we're neglecting those who were
> founders of the church or those who were the backbone of the church.
> But at the same time, the older folks realize that within their own fami-
> lies—like their own children—they're not marrying just Japanese. So
> they're coming face to face with personal change and the church had
> been the last bastion for them of what they were as Japanese people. And
> now that's changing too. So I think they're not feeling as secure. That's
> part of the reason, too, they withdraw from leadership. They always say
> it's the young people's turn. But I think some of it has to do with the fact
> that it's changed so rapidly.

Another Japanese American congregation, whose attendance had shrunk to
about fifty on an average Sunday, also shifted focus. From their historic and cultural context, the older Nisei did not understand how an Asian American community could be established:

> The difficult thing was with the older generation. I remember speaking
> with the seniors in our group, the Nisei, and they're asking questions
> like, "Boy, how does the events of World War II, how does that affect the
> Chinese who are coming in?" It is in the back of their minds, especially

older Japanese Americans, . . . if Chinese come in, can we blend together
and be this body?

With few members and resources to hire more staff, Japanese American
congregations have had to recruit pastors strategically. Hires had to be able to
serve a more Pan-Asian audience and yet be sensitive to the vested interests of
the different Japanese American generations. One Caucasian pastor recognizes
that he was hired as a transitional person to help the congregation shift to
panethnicity:

> At the end of the last minister's ministry, there was a shift, barely per-
> ceptible. Mainly, the new people coming in were no longer Japanese or
> Japanese American. And it's my sense that the church became aware
> that they were changing.
>
> And yet they needed to maintain some continuity with the Japanese
> heritage and the Japanese language. As so I, as a Japanese speaking Cau-
> casian, could help the situation because I'm an outsider. So I'm not going
> to participate in the second generation–third generation dynamics of
> parent-child dynamics. I'm an outsider and can cause trouble and take
> the heat.

He points out that as the recognized authority—despite being an outsider—he
could make needed reforms and be a neutral sounding board:

> Transition to Asian American has been difficult. One reason I'm here is
> that difficulty can be put upon me . . . they don't have to face it them-
> selves and recognize that Japanese Americans look down on . . . Ameri-
> cans and think Chinese Americans are noisy, boisterous, and pushy.
> They have articulated that to me, the Nisei especially. The third genera-
> tion doesn't operate that way at all.

An understanding of the power dynamics within Chinese and Japanese
American congregations helps to explain why some congregations innovate and
others do not. Relegated as junior partners in ministry, Chinese American pastors seeking church growth and more opportunities have had to split from the
Chinese-speaking mother church. Japanese American congregations, facing
closure and demographic changes, shifted only when older Nisei members
relinquished power and gave new leaders authority to make reforms.

Conclusion

In summary, despite the numerous constraints toward organizational change,
both Chinese and Japanese American congregations now identify as Asian
American. Institutions of the state and of the church recognize Asian Americans
as a legitimate grouping. Because of the widespread use of this racial category,

Asian Americans have been able to organize around it to gain power, resources, and a new group identity. Demographic shifts require a change for the institutional survival of Japanese American congregations. With a smaller market niche, these congregations have gradually shifted focus and target. Immigration and generational differences have prompted Chinese American ministers to start new Pan-Asian congregations. Lacking opportunity, resources, and freedom of ministry, they have seceded to begin new congregations.

Needing to restructure their churches because of these internal dynamics, ministers select from their limited options to adopt specific changes. They lack time to be creative and they lack resources to try radical changes, so they look to their professional networks. In their organizational fields, they have found models for new Pan-Asian churches. Furthermore, ministers observe that their members have already been adopting Asian American identities and developing Pan-Asian social networks, so the notion of panethnic congregations seems feasible.[31]

Due to these institutional pressures for efficiency and legitimacy, ethnic congregations are very similar and tend to adopt similar innovations. The great number of churches that now claim to be Asian American indicates that panethnicity has become an institutionalized model of organizing a congregation. Within ethnic church circles, ministers perceive panethnicity to provide opportunities for growth, opportunities for change, and opportunities to be cutting edge. Even if becoming Pan-Asian does not make a church more effective in terms of outreach and church growth, ministers and their members *believe* that it can be helpful. As a result, panethnicity obtains the status of a mythlike rule. It becomes a taken-for-granted category for ministers to use and mobilize around.

Congregations become alike as they copy successful churches and as the church organizational field establishes jargon, methods of ministry, and professional tracks for ministers. Ministers employ the term *Asian American* and embrace its accompanying models for congregational form because it serves as a cultural resource for change. Because evangelicals and mainline ministers hold different theological orientations and operate in different religious worlds, they generate different understandings of Asian American panethnicity.

4

Evangelical Constructions of Asian American Panethnicity

There is a subculture, an Asian American subculture that is different from Chinese culture and that is different from mainstream culture. Although I want to be the same as everyone else, I still feel a little bit different. I'm not as Americanized as my non-Asian friends. If you don't have that many Asian Americans around, then it feels sort of weird. We get together as [Asian American] English speaking pastors, and there's a big identity struggle with us right now. What is the Asian American culture? What is the specific identity and draw to say that you should come to an Asian American church because we provide this and this. I'm not sure there is a specifically Asian American experience.

—Pastor Carl, evangelical minister of a Pan-Asian church

Pastor Carl's church is named the "Chinese Baptist Church" and houses a Cantonese and an English congregation. Despite this name, Pastor Carl states, "Right now, we feel like our strongest target [of the English congregation] would be professionals, primarily Asian but not exclusively." As he met with other Asian American ministers, he learned that similar evangelical churches were no longer planting ethnic-specific churches, but Pan-Asian ones. Although the concept of a Pan-Asian identity was vague to him, he recognized that even for himself, he felt comfortable neither in predominantly white settings nor in solely Chinese-speaking contexts. He concludes: "We still want to have an Asian identity but recognize that it's not met in Chinese terms. It has to be something new, something different."

The term *Asian American* stands for a large umbrella group that has primarily been used as a political category. Asian Americans range in ethnic ancestry, class background, cultural traits, and racial experiences. New immigrants to the United States from Asia do not understand themselves as Asian Americans, although they do identify with their ethnic-specific or national backgrounds. In fact, many Asian Americans themselves complain that this racialized concept is inauthentic and does not refer to any group with real solidarity. How could Pastor Carl possibly define the group Asian Americans? And without a specific Pan-Asian culture, what might draw Asian Americans together? To understand how he develops his own understanding of his congregation, this chapter examines how evangelicals as a whole construct their Asian American identities.

In the past two decades, American evangelicals have developed a "subcultural identity" that distinguishes this group from past evangelicals and mainline Christian denominations. Most scholars agree that evangelicalism has three tenets: (1) the literal interpretation of scripture; (2) a born-again experience; and (3) the commitment to converting others (Ammerman 1987; Emerson and Smith 2000; Hunter 1983; Miller 1997; Shibley 1996; Smith 1998; Warner 1988). These tenets have their own inner logics that translate into a peculiar form of American religiosity that is engaged with this world, therapeutic, and market oriented. Significantly, these logics frame how evangelicals respond to race relations and how Asian American evangelicals think of themselves.

Pastor Carl later came up with some "general principles" about who Asian Americans are: "Off the top of my head, these are the people we're going to draw and how we're going to minister to them:

- The idea of the focus on education or the idea of accomplishment.
- The idea of having parents that were not as affirming or affectionate.
- Dealing with Asian friends as well as Caucasian friends.
- Many Asian American Christians have a very bitter, past experience with the Chinese church.
- We have had to deal with two cultures and that comes into play as well."

He and other evangelicals agree that Asian Americans are a group of people with particular felt needs and spiritual issues. Churches "draw" and "minister to" Asian Americans by concentrating on meeting these needs. His evangelical perspective especially addresses Asian American concerns that stem from their families and ethnic backgrounds. Explaining why and how evangelical ministers define the Asian American experience in this way requires an examination of the organizing logics of their beliefs.

The Inspired Word of God and Its Relevance to a Multicultural Society

Evangelicals believe that the Bible is God's inerrant, inspired Word and the standard and final authority on all matters, including race relations and ethnic identity.[1] Ministers, in their interviews, continuously appealed to the Bible and biblical principles as the authorization and justification for their church activities, their understandings of ethnicity and race, and their view of congregational life. One minister explained his strategy for building his church, "When

I first came here, it was first to establish a real foundation of basing your life on the Bible."[2] Sermons always involve some Bible exposition so that members receive God's Word about a topic instead of blindly accepting the "world's perspective" on issues (Alumkal 2002).

In understanding the church's relationship to the ethnic heritage of Asians, evangelicals employ the Bible as the arbiter of what is good or valuable to retain from ethnic culture and what should be rejected as sinful or idolatrous. This fundamentalist minister denounces all human culture, including Chinese ethnic culture and American popular culture, as fallen in comparison with biblical standards. Valuing one's ethnic background is only helpful in understanding what one needs to redeem:

> What we need to understand is that our culture's teaching of what is good and what is the right way to do things are not true. I take it from Romans 12:2. It says don't be conformed but be transformed. The contrasts are heaven and earth, which should say to us, "This culture and thinking, and ways of a people, needs to be scrutinized and transformed." If we understand that the instruction of Scripture is to transform our culture, then the value of having a Chinese culture is that we know what culture we're trying [to be transformed from].

More moderate evangelicals may not take such a hard stance against the world or ethnic culture, but they agree that the Bible should provide transcendent answers to questions of truth and faith.

However, the interpretation of the Bible around certain issues is not always clear-cut. As a result, evangelical pastors, to keep relevant with the times, engage in creative interpretive work that allows flexible engagement with the world (Smith 1998). Evangelicals now place less emphasis on the literal interpretations of the Bible and show more concern for relevant interpretations of the scripture. One minister in this study characterizes contemporary evangelicalism's adjustment to changing values in society:

> To me, Christianity has to be relevant. Once it becomes irrelevant, then there's no reason for us to be here. So the key is to be relevant, to have a Christianity that really fits into this world. Of course, relevance is hard. You have to figure out what culture you're in, what community you're going to invest in. We have to make sure our Christianity is real.

To be relevant and real, ministers' sermons often address people "where they're at," as one pastor puts it. They take the concerns and issues that people face, such as parenting, work stress, emotions, and seek biblical principles or promises that might address them. Besides helping individuals with their immediate concerns or their "felt needs," the pastors also try to further people's relationships with God, which is their more important, spiritual need. One pastor explains how he tries to take what is relevant to the members and help them to see how they need God as well:

> [Asian American Christians'] felt needs connect with the unchurched in terms of emotional stress or transition and change. But what is the gospel, the good news in any given situation? Felt needs are always a window into real needs. So when I'm preaching and try to address a given situation, I try to figure out what is good news to these people. All those felt needs [are a] window into the real need, which is receiving Christ.

Evangelical pastors thus attempt to balance between dealing with people's concrete circumstances and their personal relationships with God.

Given their emphasis on the Bible, evangelicals need a theology of diversity and a biblical rationale if they want to target panethnic groups. If they take what the Bible says about ethnic distinctions literally, then the church should not be divided along ethnic or racial lines. One pastor questions the paradoxical existence of ethnic churches by quoting the Bible passage in Galatians 3:28. Primarily concerned with doing what's biblical, he wonders if Asian ethnocentrism and ethnic-specific churches are appropriate:

> Actually, if you look at Scripture, having an ethnic ministry is almost against what it teaches. We're taught "there is no Greek or Jew, there is no male or female but we are all one." Part of Asian ministries is the fact that we deal with certain prejudices and certain bias that come over and they don't go away in one generation or two or three generations. In my sense of things, they're not biblical. But how do you work within the confines of these churches and give them a broader sense of whom Christ is?

Two arguments that Asian American evangelicals make in response to this challenge is that God has created a diversity of peoples and that God affirms these differences. At one extreme, a fundamentalist minister explains that racial divisions are God ordained and that racial reconciliation will not occur until heaven: "God has set the separations. God was the one who set the races. We didn't. And therefore, we are happiest when we are within our own culture, within our own ethnic group. So we're one in Christ. That is positionally. But until we get to heaven, there's still going to be these distinctions." However, most evangelicals hold to the ideal of the multiethnic Christian body and support the idea of multiethnic unity. They believe that we are all brothers and sisters in the family of God, but that we also retain our distinctive ethnic and racial differences, even in heaven. They appeal to a passage in Revelations 21—"The nations will walk by its light and the kings of earth will bring their splendor into it"—and provide a picture of diversity in heaven:

Our physicalities are not an obstacle to spiritual maturity but precisely the raw material with which God works. And if that is true about our bodies, then doesn't that also embrace our communities and our families and our identity? And if you look at the end picture in heaven, the ethnicities are represented. There is continuity in heaven. I think we find our cultural identity still retained and recognizable.

If God had created ethnic diversity and if ethnic distinctions continue into heaven, then humans should also value these differences. Another pastor exclaims:

I've been going through Genesis in my series. I've been trying to stress that we belong to just one human race, but there are many colors. What I also try to stress is what gives the human race value or dignity is that we've been created after the image of God. There shouldn't be any prejudice, racism. We try to stress the one human race concept, that all human races are created after the image of God, that all have value and dignity.

A campus minister continues this line of thinking about our common human dignity and our valued differences:

I propose that on this rich, beautiful day [when Christ returns, as described in Revelations], our differences are not something that will ultimately divide us. Nor will our differences be something that God will mute. It is in our full expressions of our backgrounds that God is glorified—through each person, each tongue, each nation.

Ethnic and Pan-Asian churches provide the institutional spaces where individuals can develop their identities and the groups can develop the "full expressions" of their culture with which they can glorify God. This pastor asserts that identity development, including an ethnic/racial identity, is a critical part of one's spiritual journey. The Pan-Asian church can help foster group and individual identity by providing a spiritual context to explore this process:

At a personal level, I've certainly found I still have a whole lot of growing to do in my own awareness of my ethnic/racial identity and its role in shaping my thoughts, feelings, values, and choices. Yet I know my ethnic/racial identity is a huge part of my conscious and—probably even more so—my subconscious identity. That's why I think it has to be a big part of the spiritual journey I'm on and the spiritual journey I can help others be on. But since by my own admission it's a part of my identity I have only begun to explore, understand, and offer to God, I need a place that affirms and supports me in such efforts.

So with their theology of diversity, ministers have a biblical basis to address what they see as a very relevant and important need among their members, the affirmation of one's identity. Questioned about the needs of Asian Americans, one pastor answers that

> as ethnics, we like an affirmation of who we are. We want to be a blend, not necessarily fully white. We cannot have a healthy identity because every time we look in the mirror, we're not white. So the basis is that we need to affirm one another. We don't want to have to choose between the Asian part of us in order to be fully American.

Beyond concerns for identity, the ideology of multiculturalism in the San Francisco Bay Area raises three other concerns that evangelical ministers must address. They have to respond to racism, determine their relationships to other groups, and concern themselves with the representation of Asian Americans. Again, their conservative theology guides how evangelicals think about these issues.

Most evangelical ministers recognize that Asian Americans have faced racism and discrimination in the past and that this legacy continues today:

> There's a historical side to this about how we have been made "Asian Americans" in contemporary society. All of the historical, legalized oppression of Asians in the past, that sort of thing. Those things are there in our history and they're manifest now. It's been passed down through generations, where some white kid learns to sing "Ching-Chong-Chinaman."

Others noted that the glass ceiling in corporations keeps Asian Americans from being promoted. However, most evangelical ministers do not view racism as a sin that Christians need to address on a systemic level. Instead, they tend to view sin in terms of its consequences for the individual, not for the group. One explains that man's sinfulness in general causes alienation within oneself and that only God can restore one to wholeness:

> These are sin issues. When you talk about self-image, identity issues, that's an alienation issue from oneself. From an orthodox Christian perspective, these are all the result of original sin. Christ is the basis for hope and reconciliation. We have to be reconciled to God to reestablish relationships with ourselves and to find an identity that transforms our upbringing.

In this quotation, the minister defines "hope and reconciliation" as individual transformation and restored relationships to God and others. Hope and reconciliation does not imply social justice for minorities or redistributive economics. Salvation from the consequences of racism, then, relates primarily to how an individual can have a healthy identity and be nonprejudiced in one's personal relationships.[3]

To avoid appearing prejudiced, the ministers make a point about not being exclusive or racist in relations with others. They say that that their churches would welcome anyone and often they mentioned the non-Asians who attended their congregations. Pastor Carl explains, "Right now, we feel like our strongest target would be professionals, primarily Asians but not exclusively." Another asserts the following:

> For some people, having a non-ethnic focus is fine. But for some people, having some kind of ethnic thing [is also fine]—not exclusively—but to realize, "Oh, here are some Asian kids. They all have somewhat similar values." Not speaking from a racist standpoint, it's just knowing that people sometimes tend to feel more comfortable and it's okay to have a setting like that.

As evangelical ministers operate within a diverse environment, they are also aware of the identity politics in the Bay Area and its concern for positive images, role models, and authentic representations of Asian Americans. For churches to claim to be truly Pan-Asian, they diversify their staff to have representation from different ethnic groups. Also, ministers try to make sure that those with visible roles in the church, such as the worship teams, are Pan-Asian. This minister observes that positive images of Asian Americans in leadership are necessary to help their members feel better about their faith: "If you're not given a good model about Christianity when you're young, if you grew up the whole time just thinking that Christianity means being Chinese and everything your parents represent, you'll say Christianity is boring. I think if we have Asian Americans that are committed to God and they are happy and joyful, that's the best model." This concern for role models to develop a positive racial identity leads another panethnic church of Korean and Chinese Americans to work with Southeast Asians: "We do outreach to Asian kids in Oakland—Hmong, Mien, Chinese. We want to be role models to them, so we provide intensive academic and spiritual instruction. There are fewer Asian churches reaching out to Asians than white churches reaching to whites. Plus there's a lot of Korean Bible studies and we didn't want to be redundant."

In summary, evangelicals, with their acceptance of the Bible as the external authority for truth and direction, have sought to make scriptures relate to all spheres of life. In their quest for relevancy and practical application of the Bible, Asian American ministers have had to address modern, cultural issues such as race relations and ethnic identity. The different interpretations of these topics by pastors illustrate how the doctrines and boundaries of evangelicalism itself change with the culture (Hunter 1987). These changes are not necessarily accommodation or capitulation to the secular world, but examples of dynamic, religious identity negotiation and construction (Smith 1998).

The flexibility with which evangelicals now engage the world also enables them to creatively construct and validate racial identities as well. These ministers see group identity issues as relating to one's personal self-esteem, but they do not emphasize the racism or structural inequalities that result in the marginalization of Asian Americans. As a result, they preach in order to develop healthy individual self-worth but not to facilitate group empowerment. This individualistic emphasis of their theology leads to a focus on personal health, which we turn to next.

Jesus as Personal Savior and the Asian American Self

Born-again evangelicals accept Jesus as one's personal Savior and Lord. This process involves repentance of one's sins and spiritual rebirth through the atonement of Jesus Christ. Today, however, churches emphasize more the personal benefits of Christianity and less the repentance of sins, the concept of hell, or one's guilt before God. This minister discusses his church's plans to start a new congregation and its major aims: "What the new church plant is trying to have is a real narrow focus in terms of what our mission is. And that's basically to start off with bringing people into a celebrative encounter with God. And then to help them grow in their personal lives. Those are two things we're focusing on." These two objectives, a celebrative encounter with God and personal growth, are contemporary evangelicalism's positive new spin on personal salvation. By providing worship experiences that are uplifting and intimate, as well as programs to aid an individual's own spiritual formation, congregations have contextualized the Gospel to the postmodern American setting.[4] Jesus still saves, but not only from the future punishment of sins. He also saves people from career and work stress, family and personal dysfunctions, addictions, and relationship problems. Jesus saves the individual who is in need of emotional and spiritual wholeness. In addition, God is present in the here and now. God's immediacy might be accessed through rousing worship experiences that help individuals get in touch with love and grace. God is not just transcendent and otherworldly but immanent and inner-worldly.

Whereas Christianity was once a source for the recognition of individual dignity and human agency, it now becomes a path toward personal autonomy and individual fulfillment. Biblical individualism has always asserted individual dignity and equality of all before God (Berger 1967; Bellah et al. 1985). Protestantism's break with Catholicism further democratized the faith and made salvation a personal choice for individuals (Weber 1958). Americans, who have long held a "mythic individualism" that venerated moral courage, independence, and self-reliance, now have a cultural tradition of utilitarian and expressive individualism (Bellah et al. 1985). We are utilitarian individualists in economic and occupational spheres such that we attempt to maximize our own self-interests. We are expressive individualists in private spheres such that we need to express ourselves to become self-realized.

The 1960s counterculture embraced the individual even further so that self-understanding, self-improvement, and self-fulfillment became the primary ends of life. American evangelicals, in spite of their tradition of self-renunciation and asceticism, have also adopted this value system (Hunter 1987). Wade Clark Roof found that fundamentalists and evangelicals were similar to others in their agreement with the statements "I feel the need to find more excitement and sensation in my life" and "New insights learned about the self are said to have a strong influence." He concludes, "It is clear that the values of self-improvement and self-fulfillment have deeply influenced the conservative Christian community" (Roof 1993, 108).

Evangelical congregations and ministries have responded to Americans' need for expressive individualism by promoting positive new religious experiences and becoming therapeutic.[5] Worship services, marked with long periods of joyful singing, establish a proper mood and frame of reference to mediate one's encounter with God. These moods switch from being upbeat and inspirational to melodic and reverent. Services may conclude with time for "prayer ministry," during which individuals receive prayer from others for personal healing. Often, Christians seek "inner healing" from Jesus, who restored lepers and the lame in the past and now heals contemporary Americans from emotional scars and childhood abuses.

Evangelicals, because they focus more on the individual as the site of the church's moral project than mainline churches, have become preoccupied with the self. That is not to say that evangelicals have become selfish narcissists with no regard to others around them or the community. Instead, given their theological orientation upon the individual within the contemporary American context, they tend to see members as individuals with privatized emotional and moral needs.

Asian American evangelicals, such as Pastor Carl, view Asian Americans in this way, as a people with common family dynamics and psychological issues. In his description of Asian Americans, he identifies negative family or ethnic experiences that require healing, such as "having parents who are not as affirming or affectionate" or having a "very bitter, past experience with the [ethnic] church." Pan-Asian churches are necessary in order to help individuals resolve these specific therapeutic concerns. With a similar perspective, InterVarsity Christian Fellowship, a national campus ministry, has published three books about Asian Americans: *Invitation to Lead: Guidance for Emerging Asian American Leaders* (Tokunaga 2003), *Following Jesus without Dishonoring Your Parents* (Yep et al. 1998), and *Losing Face and Finding Grace* (Lin 1995). Each discusses handling pressures from Asian parental expectations, dealing with shame and perfectionism, and establishing one's identity.

Despite the range and diversity in Asian American family experience, from low-income refugees in inner cities to fifth-generation professionals growing up in affluent suburbs (Lowe 1991, 1996), Asian American ministers highlight certain family histories as being characteristically definitive. They note that since Asian American parents raise their children with high expectations, their offspring often must deal with issues of self-worth and perfectionism. One explains that "typical" Asians share a family pressure to succeed with little emotional support:

> You look at the typical childhood experience for many of us growing up. I share this at different camps, retreats and it strikes an instant nerve. What was it like when you were a kid? You come home, you got a test and you got a score of 98 percent. Your parents shower you with positive affirmation that you did so well? Hardly ever. If anything, they might yell at you for missing the 2 percent!

Asian Americans gain parental affirmation if they work hard and achieve in school and work. These family pressures to succeed then shape how they grow up and interact with the broader society:

> The third generation of Japanese Americans have utterly the identical experience of growing up as the Chinese Americans. They're peers! They went to the same schools, they were friends, they had the same difficulties, the same problems in relating to wider society as Chinese Americans. From my outside perspective, they look and behave the same way and they're marrying each other. Their experiences in school and society were the same—they faced the same obstacles and problems while their parents still are very much Japanese and Chinese with cultural differences.

Family dynamics affect not only one's self-worth and one's self-image among peers, but also, evangelicals believe, how one approaches God. According to the authors of *Following Jesus without Dishonoring Your Parents*, Asian Americans fear a judgmental God in the same way they fear their parents, who tend to criticize. Younger generations are unaccustomed to receiving gifts of grace because they are taught to earn acceptance. Given their personality temperaments and need for emotional healing, Pan-Asian congregations seek to create worship services that mediate a direct, intimate experience with God. This pastor contrasts the reverent, fearful attitude that the older generation maintains: "We want to be more experiential. The Chinese would say we have to be more solemn and reverential in order to worship and experience and appreciate God, which is fine. But as I said, for those of us in the English congregation, we want something more energetic and that was a big thing."

Another church issue arising from Asian Americans' perfectionism is an orientation toward legalistic works and active church participation to prove their worth. Active members often burn out from teaching the Sunday school classes, organizing activities, and participating on committees within ethnic churches. In reaction, ministers of Pan-Asian churches consciously promote personal spiritual formation, quiet times of Bible study, and an active prayer life to nurture their members' relationships with God. This minister explains that his members' wounded experiences with the ethnic church and their motivations based on perfectionism have led his Pan-Asian church to emphasize grace: "I've seen signs of burn-out all around because of that motivation. I try to model a balanced life, try to model that our primary motivation is God's grace. All ministry is an overflow of God's grace. If the overflow is not there, you're not gonna get it by serving on three or four more committees or just serving more." In working with Asian Americans, this minister recognizes that he cannot rely on ethnic group loyalty to encourage service to the church. Instead, he preaches that ministry and service flow out of God's goodness to the individual.

Seeing Asian Americans as a group with specific identity, psychological, and emotional issues, ministers believe that these distinctions make Asian Americans a viable grouping to serve. Although they teach and stress spiritual development and one's relationship with God, they find that common upbringing and a psychological profile bond Asian Americans together:[6]

> [God is calling us to] building an Asian American church where people of Asian American descent feel comfortable coming. We don't exclude non–Asian Americans, but there are definitely needs, concerns, family issues, relational issues that a lot of Asian Americans face that people from other ethnic cultures or races don't. We want a ministry designed for those Asian Americans.

In this quotation, the minister points out that Asian Americans have "relational issues" rooted in family dynamics that later affect individuals' marriages and interpersonal communication at work. Similarly, Pastor Carl noted that Asian Americans have social issues, such as "dealing with the struggle of Asian friends as well as Caucasian friends" and work problems that relate to "the idea of accomplishment."

Sharing the Faith: Targeting Asian American Professionals

The third defining characteristic of evangelicals is their commitment to converting nonbelievers. As one minister explains, "We think evangelism should be a theme that permeates the entire ministry of the church." Seeing that personal salvation only comes through acceptance of Jesus Christ as one's personal savior and lord, evangelicals view the church's primary mission as evangelizing non-Christians. They consider non-Christians as the "lost" who need to find an eternal home or the "unchurched" who do not have the benefit of having a church experience of faith. With their exclusive approach toward salvation,

Asian American evangelicals must be committed to evangelism or else their friends and families are destined for hell.[7] An individual's foremost concern should be the restoration of his relationship with God that has been broken by sin. A minister preaches that once that relationship has been reconciled, then a person's second concern is to share the Gospel with others:

> Salvation is accepting God's friendship. We can't do that because our sins get in the way. Jesus died to restore this relationship. So if you believe in Christ, then you accept your relationship with God.
>
> Our mission statement has been basically that we seek to bring people to know Christ and seek to help them mature to the point where they are also sharing their faith. When you know what you believe, then you are able to share.

However, just as the meanings of "Jesus as Personal Savior" and the "Bible as God's Inerrant Word" have shifted for evangelicals, they now approach evangelism in new, sophisticated forms. Besides their biblical reasons for affirming diversity, evangelicals argue that targeting racial groups is simply a more effective way to win converts. They often refer to what is known as the "homogeneous principle," that the fastest growing churches are those that recruit others of similar background.[8] Ministers in this study assume that Asian Americans are homogeneous and that Asian Americans can evangelize other Asian Americans better than others: "One of the best illustrations of the importance of Asian American churches is in terms of missions; the whole strategy is that people respond better to people who they can relate to, who look like them, and who experience things similar to them. In missions, it's obvious that's the best strategy."

Given that God's creation is diverse and that people can be evangelized better by others like themselves, ministers justify the segmentation of congregations to meet the different needs of groups. Rejecting assimilation or a multiethnic congregation as the end goal, they argue that a spectrum of ethnic and panethnic churches is necessary to meet the market demands of religious consumers. Since Asian American individuals range from being bilingual/bicultural to being assimilated, their churches should also tailor themselves to subgroupings:

> You could see Asian Americans coming to the campus and filtering into the different ministries and the different groups based on their issues of identity. And there were some Asians that were anti-Asian and they wouldn't want to touch another Asian with a ten-foot pole for fear of being seen as clannish. There were other Asians who were like, yellow power Asians who were saying, "We gotta be with our people." And then

there are others who were really struggling with, "Okay, I'm American but anywhere I go people see me first as Chinese American." Or, "the majority of my networks is pretty Asian American although I have other non-Asian friends." So I think there's this whole spectrum. And so you would think that because there's this spectrum, not one church fits for all, not one ministry fits for all.

All of the evangelical ministers referred to "church growth" leaders and principles that are renowned within the broader American evangelical subculture. While they do not attempt to model their congregations exactly according to textbook prescriptions, they do employ three general principles of church growth that affect the formation of the Asian American subculture. First, ministers build churches upon the personal networks of existing members. Second, the church should remove barriers that keep people from attending church today. Third, they market programs based upon what they believe are the needs and desires of their audiences. Together, these methodologies reinforce communities of race and lifestyle affinities. Leading innovators in the evangelical field that are emulated include Bill Hybels of Willow Creek Community Church in Illinois,[9] Rick Warren of Saddleback Community Church in Southern California,[10] and Donald McGavran and C. Peter Wagner of Fuller Theological Seminary.[11] Each of these individuals has built or studied large megachurches, has written books to recount their successes, and has held seminars to provide others with their principles.

Perhaps the most influential principle about being a seeker-sensitive church is that the growth strategy is one of "friendship evangelism." Instead of relying on large-scale events, such as a Billy Graham crusade or a revival meeting, churches seek to grow one by one as members invite their friends to church small groups and activities.[12] This way, over time, church members can introduce Christianity to their non-Christian friends in a nonthreatening, nondogmatic manner. In his book *Becoming a Contagious Christian*, Bill Hybels develops a formula so that Christians might have a "maximum impact (MI)" for evangelism: "HP + CP + CC = MI." Christians need high potency (HP), meaning that they should be authentic, compassionate, and sacrificial for others. They need to be in close proximity (CP) with others and they need to clearly communicate (CC) the Gospel message so that they can have maximum impact (MI). Hybels recommends the following:

> If we're going to impact our world for Christ, the most effective approach will be through friendships with those who need to be reached. We'll have to get close to them so they can see that we genuinely care about them individually and that we have their best interests in mind. Over time, that will earn their trust and respect. (1994, 97)

When looking at the friends and personal networks of their church members, ministers saw that they were primarily Asian Americans. The Pan-Asian congregation, then, developed out of a focus of building churches around the personal networks and friendship circles of existing members. Chinese and Japanese Americans born after the civil rights movements of the 1960s no longer remained confined to friendships with co-ethnics or participation in ethnic institutions. Instead, as explained in chapter 3, growing up in California racialized Chinese and Japanese Americans so that they now have increased contact and more relationships with other Asian Americans. One pastor explains:

> We draw more through relationships, relationships that we build. That is what we're focusing on right now. Not trying to minister to all these strangers, but to say, "Who are our natural contacts?" You may find that for Asian Americans, still a lot of our natural contacts still may be Asian. With those personal contacts, we draw them in.

Pastors surmise that if church growth comes from members inviting other friends, then those friends will also most likely be Asian Americans:

> A lot of times, Asian Americans tend to hang around with Asian Americans. I worked at Xerox for ten years and on my team we had Japanese, a guy who was Irish, had a black, Filipino, just the whole thing. And I found while I liked them all and we all worked together, I found for some reason I talked a little more to the guy who was Filipino and the guy who was Japanese.
>
> That's why I think, initially [in the new church plant], we'll be much more Asian just because this is the place for our members to start from. I'm expecting they'll be more of an Asian influx more than anything else. Just because of networks. We're not going to deliberately eliminate anybody, but just acknowledging the way that the Asian community operates, we tend to see more Asians.

By assuming that churches grow fastest when they are homogeneous, that friends of church members most likely share the same needs and desires as the members, and that these needs tend to be individualistic in nature, Asian American evangelicals build a certain type of community. It is not only racially Pan-Asian, but also similar in class and generational composition.

Congregations move toward panethnicity precisely because it makes them more seeker-sensitive to people belonging to Asian Americans' personal networks. "Seekers" are individuals who are looking to join a church or at least interested in learning about spiritual matters. To attract a new generation to come to church, churches have reoriented their own practices and rituals. One pastor of a church plant states, "Audiences and needs have changed. In Christianity, it's important to meet their spiritual needs. If the church isn't sensitive to those needs, it could drive people away and people won't come. Our basic overarching philosophy is that we want to reach people for Christ. So some of our ministries have changed pretty radically here." Being Pan-Asian and seeker-sensitive enables them to reach out to a broader target group than just their ethnic constituency. It also frees them from ethnic patterns that the younger generation dislikes. Korean American churches, who find the Korean American community already heavily Christian and attending a church, may become Asian American so that they may have a larger pool from which to draw:

> We deliberately made the shift [from being Korean-specific] because we're a church for the unchurched. We don't want to be a holy club for saints only. We're sitting on a campus that's so Asian and I wanted to open the doors of the church to all Asians. Becoming Pan-Asian changed us significantly. It's not a shift to panethnicity that changed us. What drove the change was becoming more seeker-sensitive.
>
> We knew that in college life, a lot associate according to race rather than ethnicity. It's also a generational thing, too. A 1.5-generation Korean American has more in common with a 1.5 Chinese American than he does with a third-generation Korean American. The values, flavor, color of culture seem similar to those children of Asian immigrants.

The second church growth principle is that to become "seeker-sensitive" or "seeker friendly," congregations are to remove cultural or institutional barriers that keep people from attending church. Another evangelical "textbook," Lee Strobel and Bill Hybels's *Inside the Mind of Unchurched Harry and Mary* (1993), provides "fifteen key insights into why people steer clear of God and the church." Suggestions include changing the language, dress, name, and even the sacred symbols and rituals of the church. To avoid religious language that the unchurched might not understand, ministers use new translations of the Bible and tend not to sing hymns from the past. To encourage people to "come as they are" and feel comfortable, the pastoral staff and members wear casual clothing and provide name tags so that no one is anonymous or left out. One minister explains their conscious efforts to be welcoming:

> We do a lot of things on Sunday to make people feel comfortable. We don't welcome people and ask them to stand up and introduce them-selves. We don't pass an offering plate. Our sermons are topical and there's a lot of practical application in the Sunday messages. The music is geared to meet many people's needs. Mostly contemporary. It's a wor-ship team with two keyboards, one or two acoustic guitars. We're inves-tigating going multimedia this year.

Ministers of Asian American evangelical congregations consciously attempt to avoid negative cultural connotations of traditionalism and authoritarianism. Targeting people in their forties and below, they recognize that Asian Americans are like other Americans who might associate the church with inauthenticity, hypocrisy, or rigid formalism. In addition, young Asian Americans may be averse to ethnic traditionalism and formalism that they see in their ethnic churches, so ministers go out of their way to be seen as contemporary and non-hierarchical.[13]

In designing their programs and activities, evangelical ministers of Pan-Asian congregations attempt to keep in mind the taste and sensibilities of their target group. They recognize that their target group has options in whether they want to go to church and what kinds of church they attend. While the ministers are not pleased with this market approach toward church, they do acquiesce to it: "And the career people, the young career people really shop around and float around. They go to SCBC church, they to LGC, or they can go somewhere else. They tend to move around. If they go to LGC, then they definitely like the Asian American model. People choose and that's fine." This model of the religious market views Asian Americans as individual spiritual consumers whose tastes and preferences dictate church programs.

Third, churches that grow thus have programs tailored to meet the needs of their members and their prospective members. Rick Warren (1995) writes that evangelical churches must be purpose driven and must have a defined target audience. Arguing that "targeting for evangelism is biblical," he recommends that the target audience is determined by two principles: "You'll best reach those you relate to" and, "as a leader, you'll attract who you are, not who you want." Asian American pastors, therefore, would best attract and reach other Asian Americans.

Warren states that a target group like Asians should be defined culturally, and, as a result, many of the ministers look at Asian Americans in these particular ways. A culture refers "a lifestyle and mindset" and "to a people's values, interests, hurts and fears" (1995, 165). Understanding the culture of a congregation's target group is critical in ministering to them, dealing with their "felt needs" and "hang-ups," and then communicating effectively to them. Warren argues that in response to a target group's culture, the church should neither isolate itself nor imitate the culture but infiltrate it. He explains that Jesus "spoke the people's language, observed their customs, sang their songs, and used their current events to capture attention when He taught" (237). In particular, the church's worship program, music, and preaching should be oriented toward the target group.

The objective for ministers, then, is to identify the felt needs of their target group and then to develop a church with programs and a worship service that serves them. Another minister argues that by finding a group's "cultural code,"

Asian American congregations can grow numerically and spiritually. He observes,

> It doesn't surprise me that the churches that have been more successful in reaching the larger share of Asian Americans are Japanese American churches. Because ethnically, they're much closer, more intuitively and without even trying, and so they've inherited waves of Chinese Americans who have left Chinese churches. And so obviously if you want to do Asian American ministry or reach a larger segment of these people, you have to try to pay attention to what's going on there. And what they do implicitly without thinking, perhaps could be done explicitly with greater effect.

In looking at their target group, ministers have examined the lifestyle and mindset of Asian Americans and have seen a group of young, urban professionals.[14] They believe that Asians' work ethic and stress on education have led Asian Americans to share common class backgrounds and class interests. Congregations are remarkably similar in their professional status, their upwardly mobile families, and spare-time activities. Lifestyle affinities thus characterize these Asian American networks.[15]

The Asian American professional lifestyle and networks begin at a young age. To start, Asian American high school and college students have enormous parental pressure to do well and succeed: "When I went to Berkeley, these Asian American students were like Junior Republicans! I got a sense that they were there because their parents sent them there, because they wanted to go to the best schools, and they were gonna get their MBAs and they were going to get their engineering degrees and make six figures right off the bat." Another finds that this stress on professional and career success is a common Asian American trait:

> There is a shared experience in terms of being second *generation*, immigrant drive to success, focus on education. Again I also understand that's also some of the Asian American ethos. What draws the Chinese American or Japanese American together oftentimes is the fact that they come out of this environment which has stressed education, which has stressed success, family and that kind of ties them together in a way that I'm not sure is in Caucasian churches.

Upon graduation, the ethnic ethic for success combines with normative professional expectations for career advancements. The ministers see Asian American professionals as having to deal with work and financial stress, time management, and family relations strained by two-income careers. For example, I asked one pastor what issues his members faced: "Work is [an issue]. Basically in Silicon Valley, most people are working seventy-hour weeks. They work on weekends, some work on Sundays. They work like crazy. We have a lot of families who have a lot of little kids and I can't imagine how they can take care of their family. A lot of times, both of them work."

To deal with the individualistic concerns of professionals, one congregation plans to establish a ministry center using applied biblical principles for non-Christians:

> In terms of church planting, what I see is, a ministry center. I think worship services will draw the Christians, not too many non-Christians. But if we have a place where we can start up another group, could be a class or seminar or things like that from a Christian perspective—another parenting thing, financial management, could be marital counseling, whatever—people will say, "Hey, yeah, there's something good that's going on over there. Let me see what it is." And then if they like it, that's great because we're Christians and because we're doing what we're doing based on the Bible.

The felt needs that this pastor mentioned—parenting, finances, and marital counseling—are not exclusive to Asian Americans, yet those are the primary interests and fears that Asian Americans as a group share and that ministers have identified as needs of Asian Americans.

Using evangelical church growth methods, Asian American ministers have been strategic in identifying the cultural code of those in the networks of their church members, other Asian Americans. They have been conscious in understanding the lifestyle and mindset of their target group and have found them to be young professionals with career, family, and social needs that are particular to those in the same class background. Their churches respond to their target group by adjusting to the needs and tastes of these Asian American professionals.

Conclusion: The Evangelical Definition of Asian American Panethnicity

This chapter has argued that the main tenets of American contemporary evangelicalism are the organizing logics for Pan-Asian congregations. Given the organizing logic of evangelicalism and the discourse of church growth, Asian American evangelical ministers generate a particular understanding of who Asian Americans are. Because evangelicals stress personal relationships with God, they see Asian Americans as an aggregate of individuals concerned about their self-esteem and family dynamics. Due to the evangelical emphasis on friendship evangelism and targeted outreach, they view Asian Americans as a network of people who share common educational and professional concerns. Thus, the symbolic boundaries they draw around this target group are similarities in psychological makeup and lifestyle affinities. Although they may see themselves as a marginalized group, they do not see themselves as an exploited class or a particularly oppressed minority. Asian Americans are thus a group of people connected by ties of friendship, not by political or economic concerns, as other theorists have argued (Espiritu 1992; Vo 1996). One pastor sums up the Asian American experience based on psychological concerns:

> There are whole cultural nuances for Asian American men that are different than men in general in the United States. Stuff like self-esteem, how to be a godly husband in an Asian cultural setting where there are more family issues that Asian men have to face. Issues of work—a lot of Asian men feel like they're in a glass ceiling and how do you deal with those kinds of issues—how do you deal with perfectionism, being a workaholic, those kinds of things. Obviously there's a lot of common ground.

Using the organizing logics of evangelicals, these ministers understand Asian Americans to have a shared generational experience. Three characteristics of this experience include a similar family socialization; a general psychological orientation; and common personal networks. Because these issues draw Asian Americans together and mark them as a distinct group, new Pan-Asian churches address these concerns and organize activities around these networks. The symbolic racial identity of Asian Americans, however, does not have to be defined by these characteristics. Mainline ministers employ different themes and narratives as symbolic to Asian American group identity.

5

Mainline Christian Constructions of Asian American Panethnicity

The church does a disservice to our core belief when we don't accept people as they are. [Unfortunately, we instead] first try to find out who they are and then try to put them in some category. For my experience and for many Asians when they come in contact with wider society, when [others] can't tell what your ethnicity is, they try to find out. But they're not always good about coming out and asking what your ethnic background is.

It's more like, "Where are you from?"

And you say, "I'm from San Francisco."

"No, no, where are you really from?!?" they ask.

–Pastor Rod, a Chinese American mainline pastor
of a Pan-Asian congregation

Pastor Rod was called to a church planted by a mainline denomination that was specifically aimed for Asian Americans. Located in suburbs outside of San Jose, the initial founders of the congregation had grown up in a San Francisco Chinatown church and moved out to pursue their careers in Silicon Valley. However, they never found other churches to be very comfortable, so they started a fellowship group. Eventually, they wanted to establish their own church. Pastor Rod explains their motivations: "It was designed as an intentional, Pan-Asian American ministry. It was an understanding that second and third generation or English-speaking Asians have more in common than they do different . . . the Asian American experience has very similar qualities when you look at their history of being in America."

In contrast to evangelical ministers who describe the family patterns and social networks of Asian Americans as their defining characteristics, mainline Christian ministers like Pastor Rod acknowledge the historical, racialized experiences of this group as the primary bond of Pan-Asian solidarity. In the opening example, he describes the Asian American experience of being categorized and treated as a foreigner or newcomer to this country. The mainline ministers interpret this everyday assignation as a symbol of the marginalization of Asian Americans. Even though this group has been here for generations, they remain perpetual outsiders to American society who still face discrimination. At the other extreme, even if Asian Americans are conceived by wider society as the model minority who have successfully integrated, the ministers would argue that such labeling is also an act of categorization that imposes mainstream values upon this group.[1] Instead, they insist that the church must accept Asian Americans as they fully are. Pastor Rod continues to explain what being "accepted fully" entails: "We want to be in a position where we feel that who we are is valued and lifted up. That our experience, our history, our culture, our art, our festivals, our foods are celebrated and are experienced as valuable things."

The recognition of both the historical disenfranchisement of Asian American communities and their Asian cultural/religious traditions differentiates mainline Christians from evangelicals in identity, community, and focus. To become more authentically Christian, evangelicals seek to transform Asian cultural patterns, but mainline Christians reconstruct their identity with Asian traditions and cultural resources. Evangelical Pan-Asian congregations make a conscious break from past ethnic congregations to create a new community, but mainline Christians remain rooted in tradition, geography, and congregational history to reconnect with community. Although evangelicals and mainline Asian Americans are comparable in their professional status, evangelicals accept upward mobility as the norm for Asian Americans, while mainline Christians accentuate a common, racial legacy of discrimination and injustice. As a result, they tend to work on issues of service and justice instead of primarily proselytizing. With a dissimilar orientation from evangelicals, mainline ministers generate a different understanding of Asian Americans.

Mainline Christianity is a loose religious family of churches with a similar theological orientation, denominational affiliation, and historical tradition. Dean Kelley (1972) characterized the mainline as the main body of the ecumenical movement.[2] Wade Clark Roof and William McKinney (1987) grouped mainline religious families as either liberal or moderate Protestants on the basis of their theological heritage and access to power in society.[3] Christian Smith (1998) surveyed American individuals and found that they clearly self-identified as Fundamentalist, Evangelical, Mainline, or Liberal. Individuals who strongly identified as mainline or liberal Protestants felt that they belonged to an old, established denomination that is quiet and respectable.[4] Similarly, I grouped ministers as belonging to the mainline through their self-identification, their denomination (United Methodist, Presbyterian USA, Episcopal, American Baptist) and their theological orientation. I include contemporary Catholics to the mainline because of their "enlivened sense of social responsibility" (Marty 1971).

The Organizational Logics of Mainline Liberals

Just as evangelicals have organizational logics that frame their understanding of race and panethnicity, mainline liberals have general theological orientations that govern their congregational values and practices. American mainline Protestantism has fewer clear-cut boundaries to distinguish itself than evangelicalism has. In fact, its very definition as "mainline" is that its members resemble and make up the mainstream of American society. According to Wade Clark Roof and William McKinney, "So wedded were the liberal, mainline churches to the dominant culture that their beliefs, values, and behavior were virtually indistinguishable from the culture" (1987, 22). Despite the broad range of churches in this grouping, mainline or liberal Protestantism does convey specific meanings for the ministers in this study. The three main traits of "lay liberalism" that structure racial understandings are its belief in tolerance, its historic ties to community, and its prophetic morality.[5] In their belief in tolerance, mainline Christians reject the orthodox teaching that Christianity is the only true religion. This relativism allows Asian American ministers to more easily accept and embrace Asian traditions and religious beliefs as part of their faith experience and congregational practice. To hold an Asian American Christian identity, then, involves reclamation of one's roots and heritage. In their historic ties to the community, mainline Asian Americans have connection both to an established denomination and a geographic parish. This recognition of the past and of old ethnic enclaves (San Francisco Chinatown, San Jose Japantown) privileges the group's historic experiences in the United States as a major boundary marker. In their religious role as being a prophetic voice to the community, mainline churches address concerns of peace and social justice. When examining the Asian American situation through these lenses, ministers identify issues of racial discrimination and community development as major arenas of struggle. This chapter covers the organizational logics of mainline Christianity and how they establish symbolic boundaries for Asian Americans around their race, reinvented ethnicity, and minority status.

Lay Liberalism and Asian Cultural Traditions

The tolerance of mainline and liberal churches toward other religions and traditions opens up space for the exploration of Asian traditions by Asian American congregations. One pastor wonders, "Specifically, how do we acknowledge and lift up the fact that God created us Asian? It's not meant to replace biblical values. It just means that culture becomes a dynamic that we're cognizant of. We didn't want to say 'Christ Against Culture,' but 'Christ with Culture,' to borrow Niebuhr's way of looking at it." Like the evangelicals, mainline ministers attempt to contextualize the Gospel to the Asian American experience. However, recognizing that American Christianity has Eurocentric cultural orientations and practices, they seek to correct the notion that "Christianity is a white religion." By combining Christ with Asian American culture, they hope to establish a distinctive Asian American Christian theology and practice. So they desire to be relevant to Asian American's current professional lifestyle and also to incorporate their heritage.

Mainline ministers in this study did not unite around common creeds or doctrinal beliefs, but they did share a rejection of orthodoxy and embraced a tolerant view of other religions and traditions.[6] They maintain that faith in Jesus Christ was central to their beliefs and that this faith distinguished them from the secular world and other religions; yet, other faith traditions also hold truth. One minister explains how Christianity is true for him but other religions are not necessarily invalid:

> To me, it's the Christian gospel that motivated me, as far as I'm concerned, to have a concern for community. Now it may be true that another kind of approach is found in Buddhism. And if the end product is compassion and unity and community, or if the values of equality and justice come out of a Japanese or Chinese culture, to me that's fine. I really feel we need to try to identify the richness of God's revelation in all kinds of approaches to reality, or different religions.

Mainline churches are thus more "lenient" than evangelicals about the belief that Christ is the exclusive pathway to salvation (Kelley 1972). Instead, Dean Hoge, Benton Johnson, and Donald Luidens describe the theological perspective that they call "lay liberalism": "its defining feature is a rejection of the orthodox teaching that Christianity is the only true religion. Lay liberals have a high regard for Jesus, but they do not affirm that He is God's only son and that salvation is available only through Him" (1994, 112–13). Furthermore, liberals interpret the Bible less literally and are open to more allegorical understandings (Balmer and Winner 2002). Instead of assent to a doctrinal statement of truth, this perspective espouses that the heart of religion is its ethical standards. These standards comprise a general moral code of faith and good works.[7]

The tolerance and relativism of mainline Christians shape how they view evangelism and conversion. In Hoge, Johnson, and Luidens's study of five hundred American Baby Boomers, 61 percent disagreed with the statement that "only followers of Jesus Christ can be saved." In addition, because 55 percent of those sampled believed that "all the different religions are equally good ways of helping a person find ultimate truth," they had less need to evangelize others than evangelicals.[8] This Asian American minister sums up his views on evangelism by contrasting his theology with those of conservatives:

> The Lutheran, Presbyterian, Methodists, what you call the mainline denominations, we are more liberal in our thinking. The theology is a little

different, especially on evangelism and outreach. The Episcopal Church avoids trying to impose our conviction on others. Social needs become more a priority than the spiritual or theological or faith element. Salvation, soteriology in a more liberal church is that salvation comes on both sides—your spirituality as well as your social needs. We try to respond to both, versus the conservative churches. They feel salvation comes first. You need to be saved first. They can ignore even the social needs!

Their postmodern, relativistic view of truth stems from a critique of Western, missionary forms of Christianity. Along with other Asian and Asian American theologians, these ministers see Western Christianity as a colonizing mode of thought; it universalizes particular Western ideals as it delegitimates the Asian as the other (Loo 1974; Matsuoka 1995; Ng 1996; Sugirtharajah 1999). Indeed, they argue that this colonization of thought accompanied the economic and political oppression of Asians both in Asia and in the United States. One minister argues that neither mainline pastors nor their members can accept white Christianity as dogmatic truth anymore:

> The problem with that is a lot of Christian tradition is bad stuff. It's twentieth century stuff and it's Western, European stuff and has passed. The trick is, the people who can give us information about the spiritual stuff are the people who are struggling with it themselves. So it's not like they can come here and I'll read the Book to them or I'll teach them the lessons.

The denunciation of Asian traditional practices as heathen and pagan by missionaries to Asia and to Asian immigrants in the earlier part of this century created conflicts for converts in non-Christian homes (Tseng 1994; Woo 1983). For Asians even today, conversion to this version of Christianity may entail a rejection of family practices and sometimes their own family members. This minister describes the onerous decision Asian Americans may have to make between Christianity and their family or heritage:

> I did campus ministry at U.C. Berkeley for a year and a half and it was really painful that I would hear, mostly in a Korean context, that your parents are going to hell because they still do this and do that. What that can do to a person, especially an Asian person with the kind of family pressures and ties that we carry!
>
> This faith community tells you that your parents are going to hell because they aren't Christian or they're participating in this particular ritual. But, on the other hand, you are pulled because this is family. More often than not, in college circumstances, folks are choosing the Christian church and then going back home and pushing the family away.

As well as creating conflict within the family, the pitting of Christianity against one's own Asian heritage causes internal dissonance. As the convert seeks to be transformed, the self-denial that Christ calls for may lead to excessive guilt and self-doubt:

> Some of us come out of a missionary experience that said all those things [Asian culture, festivals, beliefs] are bad. And I don't necessarily see them as bad, they're just different. To call Chinese culture and Chinese ancestral worship heathen and to make it pagan and categorize it evil and other, versus Christianity and all that experience as good, can create self-hatred and tension.

Mainline ministers say this conflict between Christ and culture is unnecessary. Instead, Asian culture may resound with the morality of lay liberalism, which is a universal ethical code summed up in the Golden Rule.

If Western forms of Christianity are culturally biased and if other religions contain truth, then Asian perspectives and ideas could provide correctives and insights to the Christian faith. Mainline ministers look to Asian traditions as cultural resources that are rich in wisdom:

> I think what we consider Christian identity is not very clear because it's sort of a Euro-Western perspective of what it is to be Christian. So when [an Asian American] person goes back to his roots, you realize that within your culture and background there are a lot of realities from God—revelation that is from God and that can accentuate what we believe is the heart of Christianity.
>
> There's so many things within the Japanese, Chinese, Asian culture that can be affirmed within Christianity if a person studies it in depth. The Euro-Western approach is to say those things are maybe pagan or heathen or primordial or primitive. . . . Not so! There are ancient cultures which have been around longer than what we have in the West, and there is a lot of richness. If we find the contribution we can make toward reality or Christianity that comes out of culture, that'd be great.

Likewise, another minister challenges interpretations of the Bible that denigrated Asian spiritual practices and looked to explore Asian religious traditions as possibly helpful:

> I think we wanted to create a space that said, "Can we explore that?" Can we bring in somebody who can tell us about Confucius, Buddha? An authentic Christian faith says we're not scared to talk about that, that there's no problem.

An examination of one's Asian identity and heritage, then, provides Asian

American Christians with a fresh understanding of the faith that may build up the church universal.

Embracing Asian traditions not only corrects Western biases in Christianity but also helps Asian American Christians integrate their faith with their culture and heritage. By acknowledging both their religious and ethnic/racial identities, mainline churches help Asian Americans to be "fully accepted as they are," as the minister in the opening quotation recommends. Mainline ministers want church members to accept themselves, identify with their Asian heritages, and acknowledge the goodness and truth found in their traditions. If the "heart of Christianity" is a moral code, then the ethnic values and racial experiences of their Asian American members are not necessarily antithetical to Christianity. Instead, Christ and culture may complement one another as sources of wholeness. One minister expresses why he places emphasis on Asian cultural practices, especially to his youth members. He legitimates the construction of a strong ethnic identity as part of "God's design":

> By exposing them to their own culture, their own roots, we also give them the sense that God is also God of the new immigrants, of the Chinese, as well as of the young [Asian] Americans. They have their own culture to keep as well as the people of their own roots—which is also a part of the design of God. That's the multicultural context which I would include in my ministry and my message to them.

This mainline pastor, who works with immigrants who have a stronger tie to Asian homelands, views ethnicity as a primordial attachment to roots, ancestral forebears, and culture that establishes a sense of peoplehood (Geertz 1973; Isaacs 1975; Swidler 1986). In contrast, other mainline ministers observe that later generations of Chinese and Japanese Americans have acculturated to such an extent that they no longer have such attachment. American host society initially sought to exclude Asian immigrants but later developed policies to assimilate the native-born generations (Chan 1991; Takaki 1987). As a result, Asian Americans may experience marginalization both in mainstream American society and within their own ethnic communities. Within mainstream society, the racial features of Asian Americans set them apart as outsiders. The Episcopal Church has an Asian American consultation for ministers to gather and address this marginalization:

> Why we have that [consultation] is not because we feel more comfortable, it's that we are all outsiders. We are not part of the American society. That's how we feel about each other and we try to help each other, try to support each other. Another reason for that is we feel that the programs, the ministries of the Diocese are mostly designed and intentionally or unintentionally for the [white] Americans. So the Asian church members either cannot participate or cannot fully participate.

Within Asian Americans' own ethnic communities and back in Asia, the lack of cultural and linguistic competencies also preclude them from full participation and authentic group identity. Another priest observes: "[Chinese Americans] feel they are afraid of being rejected. They are afraid they are looked down on because they are not American, not Chinese. They are called Chinese Americans but what are Chinese Americans? Chinese? American? They have to find what side they are on." Denied culture, language, and a sense of community in the United States, native-born Asian Americans have had to establish their own institutional spaces to feel accepted and at home. Within these congregations, ministers seek to reconstruct ethnicity to help acculturated Asian Americans regain ethnic pride. Ethnicity for these Asian Americans is not primordial, but an invented social construction or reconstruction to reclaim one's identity and community (Conzen et al. 1992; Nagel 1994; Sollors 1989; Yancey 1976).

Asian religious traditions and Asian American congregations provide resources, practices, symbols and space to construct new, invented ethnic and racial identities (Chong 1998; Warner 1994; Williams 1988; Yang 1999). The mainline ministers observe how the cultural practices that affect church life have been selectively transferred from previous generations. However, as one minister perceives, the traditional cultural values that are maintained may be both subconsciously and individually selected: "The Japanese American church has something in it that's Japanese but you can't predict what it is. The places where you stumble across some Japanese pattern, you can't tell where it's going to be. Because each individual kind of picks and chooses in terms of their ethnic stuff."

In the more conscious rearticulation of faith and congregational practice with Asian American elements, ministers tend to select core Asian values that deal with family and traditional festivals that represent ethnic community.[9] For example, a priest feels that respect for the elderly was an Asian value that needed to be maintained and retaught to Chinese Catholic youth: "I've always thought the Chinese take care of their elderly, that's their responsibility. In Chinese New Year, the prayer that we do in the tribute is that we're called to be dutiful sons and dutiful daughters. [You] have a responsibility to pay respects to your parents because who you are and what you have is because of your parents." Asian holidays that are often celebrated by mainline churches include the Chinese Lunar New Year and Qing Ming (Ancestral Memorial Day) and the Japanese Sakuramatsuri (Spring Bazaar) and Akimatsuri (Fall Bazaar). For example, this priest describes his parish's New Year's celebration: "At Chinese New Year's we have a very beautiful bilingual liturgy in Cantonese and English with Chinese and American music. At the end, we do the traditional ceremonial tribute to the ancestors. We build a shrine and at the conclusion of mass, we pay tribute to the ancestors." Red banners with "spring couplets" are hung to greet members with inscribed blessings. In this ceremony, oranges for good fortune are piled in a pyramid to construct a shrine and incense is lit. People bow before the shrine to demonstrate their respect to their ancestors, as well as to God.

Besides upholding and celebrating core Asian values and practices, Asian American mainline ministers infuse regular Christian rituals with Asian American meanings, symbols, and elements. The host and the wine of Eucharist may utilize different breads or drinks to give new meaning to communion. Liturgies and prayers may acknowledge ancestors or incorporate Chinese or Japanese language in an effort to speak more directly to the hearts of Asian Americans. A minister of a multiethnic mainline congregation explains that he wanted a multicultural worship experience for his members to be more relevant and to integrate their family, ethnic life with their church one:

> I played with doing communion with bao and tea and doing some kinds of those things. We've integrated some more language things within our worship services and prayers because our youth that are coming in, a lot of them are immigrants and so speak two different languages.
>
> What we allow here is to do some thinking about what are social rituals that we do with our families and what are religious rituals. What are faith rituals? Does that conflict with what we do here [at church]? . . . If somebody is not preaching about ethnicity or diversity and how that affects you and your Christian life and how you act, then you're not being in touch with the community.

Evangelicals may fear and reject old religious practices, but the mainline ministers embrace and reinterpret traditions to develop broader views of God. This minister argues,

> We are one people of different races, different cultures. Each one has their own rich backgrounds. The fundamentalists, they are more radical about it. I'm not just speaking of the Episcopal church, but we accept ancestor worship as part of our own culture that we need to respect. So we actually encourage people to have them. We conduct and even promote a service for Qing Ming, which is predominantly ancestor worship. Ultimately, ethnic culture like ancestor worship can be a way to draw the children of God to Christ culture.

Besides making use of Asian religious and cultural traditions, mainline ministers also look to Asian American history and community as sources to establish group solidarity and help their members become more integrated with their spiritual, ethnic, and cultural identities:

> The whole idea of coming together and affirming the fact that you are a child of God, you're really human, is to recognize who you are in terms of your background, your history and heritage and culture. All the church

plays a real part in that. It's not what you would call a pluralism in which you just come together for self-support and security, but coming together to affirm the richness of your own culture and identity and background.

Ties to the Community: Historic and Geographic Connections

The second characteristic of Asian American mainline congregations is that they maintain institutional ties to their respective denominations and to their geographic communities. This sense of establishment and tradition provides an identity for a mainline congregation as well as a role to play in its specific location. Mainline liberal ministers believe that community involvement is precisely the call of the church. A Catholic priest connected ethnic heritage with a social responsibility and Christian witness to serve the community. He explains about his work with youth:

> One of the things we want to teach them and try to instill in them is that if you take from the Chinese heritage, you have to give back to the community. What we try to do is encourage them to have a sense of social responsibility. Through their witness and the fact that they come back to the community, kids will see that when they leave Chinatown, they do have a responsibility to the culture and the tradition.

Similarly, Methodist, Episcopalian, or Presbyterian ministers also see themselves connected to a wider establishment of believers that facilitates a universal Christian identity and a specific ethnic tradition. Because these congregations were established originally to serve Chinese and Japanese immigrant communities, they remain situated in geographic locations usually within ethnic enclaves of Asians. These churches have historical legacies of serving ethnic communities that have faced segregation and severe discrimination in the past. Having a denominational tradition and a historic role in the community makes congregations more aware of their roots and their ethnic experiences in the United States. These roots frame the ministers' understandings that members have multiple, intersecting identities of ethnicity, race, and religion. With less emphasis on evangelism and more focus on creating communities of sanctuary, mainline congregations emphasize the reconnection of families to the past. These mainline ministers see that the role of the church is to affirm its members as the people of God with specific ethnic and cultural heritages. Also, ministers use this historical perspective to draw connections between the experiences of the different Asian ethnic groups in America and to develop a Pan-Asian, racialized perspective. Specifically, Asian American ethnic groups need to establish community institutions to resist the racism experienced by their members. Pan-Asian congregations can build upon the solidarity of having faced common oppression and upon their similar situation as minorities in the United States.

As stated previously, churchgoing members of mainline congregations see themselves as belonging to old, established denominations (Smith 1998). As part of the older establishment, they tend to value a faith tradition and the religious heritage of those who have gone before them. Not only does their denomination provide a certain church government structure and worship style, but it provides an institutionalized means to serve the local community and to do global missions (Marty 1981; Warner 1988; Wuthnow 1988). Recent research does highlight the declining significance of denominationalism in the American religious scene and the increasing diversity in local congregationalism (Balmer and Winner 2002; Jacobsen and Trollinger 1998; Warner 1994). However, mainline congregations, much more than the new paradigm evangelical churches, have longer-standing ecumenical arrangements and institutional ties within their communities that encourage a sense of the past.

The mainline ministers in this study maintain a historical perspective of their church roots and faith tradition. In contrast to their evangelical counterparts, who mobilize people around a common mission and look forward toward church growth, mainline ministers reconnect their members to the past and see that their solidarity is rooted in history and tradition. One minister believes that

> people in America today really do want to be in touch with some spiritual stuff. And they want the stuff to be not just their personal stuff, but they want to somehow be connected to other people and connected in a way that surprises me. And connected with a tradition, some kind of church. There's a longing for that.
>
> So churches are in a position to meet that need if we can respond to that. So I think that these young families do want their children to have a sense of who they are as a human being and who they are as a person connected to a larger community. The parents are really motivated to provide that for their children. Because they feel the need for that themselves, obviously.

As young families raise their children, they look to the church to provide them with a sense of identity and a bond to a religious tradition.

Although the churches in this study do not work much with denominational structures, they do see themselves aligning with their faith traditions and being a part of reworking them. One minister argues that even though religious traditions are irrelevant to Asian Americans in the 1990s, the denominational identity should be maintained as it is reworked to fit and connect with Asian Americans:

> To take the religious tradition in the Methodist church and try to make that fit in your own spirituality, it's going to be a no fit. . . . If religious

traditions are going to be of any value, there has to be major reworking of those traditions. So it's kind of looking at the stories of Jesus and trying to figure out what those stories meant and how does that story strike you today? The requirement is that you feel free to play with those stories.

Another minister sees that his new ethnic congregation, under the umbrella of a host white church, helped the denomination and this individual church become more multicultural:

> In our diocese we have close to ninety churches. I'm responsible to the bishop and the church saw the need to do Chinese work. Christ Church is a white church but demographics are changing. They were enthusiastic about doing something non-white. So I started this experiment. As long as there's a Chinese service in the chapel, it's a symbol of diversity and unity.

Both faith tradition and a loose denominational affiliation remain parts of a congregational mainline identity. They in turn influence the people's sense of connectedness.

Asian American mainline ministers are conscious of their congregation's institutional role in the ethnic community and their members' ties to specific neighborhoods as well. A minister recounts that the local Presbytery offered his congregation another building in a suburb outside of a Chinatown.

> The decision was no, we want to serve the people who come to Chinatown. That is the goal. Chinatown is their goal. They're fixed. They see a meaningful ministry here. They want to be a part of serving the community. They want to come back here to meet their friends, with everybody coming back as a family gathering.

While evangelical church plants seek to draw in networks of Asian Americans who might commute to church, the mainline churches tend to be more based on locale.

Older, first- and second-generation members of mainline congregations felt close ties to their ethnic neighborhoods because they grew up in those settings that served all aspects of ethnic life. Facing discrimination outside the ethnic enclave, they forged strong bonds with co-ethnics inside their tight communities. One minister described how the second generation wanted their congregation to remain in Chinatown, while the younger ones wanted to move the church to a neighborhood with easier access. The former generation wanted to retain their associations both with each other and with their neighborhood. Their minister claims: "There's a strong emotional attachment here. Many of these people grew up in Chinatown. They look around and see some of their friends who said they wanted to stay, so they're going to stay." To capitalize on this local identity, ministers like this one encourage their members to serve the neighborhood where the church is planted:

> I think members are being challenged to look beyond as well and to see how we can really be a ministering presence in the community. We're in a great place! This [is] Japantown! The Japanese community is right here and the businesses are, too. There's also a great Asian community that I think people feel akin to.

Even the new church developments of the mainline denominations that are outside ethnic enclaves remained targeted toward a geographic, parish-based orientation. One multiethnic church plant located itself in an area with a growing second- and third-generation Asian American population and wanted to reflect the population of the community: "The vision is eventually to serve many of the elementary and middle school children in the area, most of those being Asian. We're not looking at becoming a commuters' church. Seventy-five percent of our members are within a three-mile radius." The roots of mainline churches in a particular faith tradition and in a geographic location facilitate connections with ethnic heritage and racial background. As "communities of memory" for Asian Americans, mainline churches integrate faith, history, and ethnicity.

For Asian American mainline members, one's heritage is not only religious but also ethnic. In a primary mainline articulation of Asian American theology, *Out of Silence: Emerging Themes in Asian American Churches,* Fumitaka Matsuoka (1995, 30–31) writes the following:

> It is practically impossible to talk about Christian faith without acknowledging the deep spirituality that has been nurtured by our memories of the past, both ethnically and culturally. . . . Just as European Christians did as they built their tradition from before Nicaea and Chalcedon, Asian Americans are doing by forging expressions of faith within our own ethnic, cultural and historic context.

The church continues to be a site for group socialization for third-, fourth-, and fifth-generation members. One minister asked her members why they drove long distances to attend her congregation: "They say they want to come to an ethnic church. We want our children to grow up in ethnic community. I think there's a want to be—and some kind of tie—with Asian people. Maybe some people think they'll lose that stuff, whatever that stuff of ethnicity, unless they keep a hold of some community involvement. And maybe their involvement is with the church." Likewise, this pastor says that families bring their children to keep in touch with the older generation: "Church is one of the few places in actual experience where the different generations come together. Where the normal work pattern is multiple generations." Because so many of his members live in suburbs where the children attend schools that are primarily white and their activities are age-specific, the church purposely promotes opportunities for intergenerational contact.

A sense and knowledge of history not only encourages ethnic identity but also creates new Pan-Asian solidarity. Mainline ministers draw parallels among the Pan-Asian ethnic experience historically. In particular, they note that Chinese, Japanese, Koreans, and Filipinos in the United States have experienced similar discriminatory policies, economic underemployment, and residential segregation. One minister of a mainline church development explains why his church formed along Pan-Asian lines: "The need we were trying to meet was to create a place where Asian American experience would be a regular part of the life of this community. That history, field trips, activities, programs were a regular part of it." To remember and celebrate that experience, the church took visits to Locke, an old rural Chinatown, and to Angel Island, the site where Asian immigrants were detained while being processed for entry to the United States.

Another minister of an Asian American congregation explains that Asian Americans have a shared story that comes alive and becomes renewed whenever the congregation meets. Although continually being written, the Asian American story consists of groups with common beginnings in ethnic communities. He speaks of the pride that some members had for their previous church:

> I don't think if you ask people, they'd say ethnicity is a live issue. But when you spend time with them, it's not hard to see that it is. And that's what people talk about. That's what they get engaged in. Get them talking about some shared experience they had in the past, that's when they come alive, when they remember that story.
>
>   For instance, there's a great deal of affection for the former pastor. They're pretty proud of what he did and very proud to be associated with that role. He got Asian Health Services started, he got the Asian Cultural Center started, and so on and so on.

To sum, mainline congregations have a greater sense of tradition, history, and space than their evangelical counterparts. This historical perspective translates into an appreciation for the ethnic church's traditional role in the community and for the need to assist members in reconnecting with their pasts. Thus mainline congregational identity has roots in the ethnic enclave and has the function of ministering to that particular locale. Even for the Pan-Asian and multiethnic mainline congregations, bridging different ethnic heritages becomes a focal point for building church unity. The historic institutional role of mainline congregations in the ethnic community continues today as the churches work ecumenically to address the needs of their neighborhoods.

A Social Justice Frame and Ethnic/Racial Issues

The third organizational logic of mainline congregations is that Christian teachings call for a commitment to service, peace, and justice. These ministers believe that more than just preaching the gospel, the church is to embody the values of the faith by living out Christ's teachings. In contrast to evangelicals who stress personal salvation, this pastor emphasizes a broader concern for the community:

> Where Scripture leads me, my focus is on service and justice issues. Some people concentrate on salvation—that's their big part of Scripture they'll concentrate and preach on. If you were to hear my sermons, mine are really on justice and what that means for us and how to act that out. I preach a lot on issues of homelessness, preach on youth and empowering people.

With this frame of social justice, ministers examine the lives of their congregational members and the injustices that they experience or their community experiences. The racial situation of Asians in America clearly becomes the issue around which these ministers mobilize. To empower the Asian American population and address justice issues within it, mainline congregations organize their ministries by claiming rights as minorities in the United States.

Since the fundamentalist-modernist split in American Protestantism from 1917 through 1925, mainline Christianity has been characterized as being more engaged with and mediating toward the modern world than fundamentalists (Albanese 1992; Marsden 1980; Marty 1971). This engagement included ecumenical efforts to address social ills, urban problems, and world peace. As Roof and McKinney (1987, 227) explain, "In ethical stance the liberal Protestant tradition still bears the legacy of its historical concern for social and political issues, making the 'cure of the souls' almost a lost art within the tradition . . . in public affairs the thrust is more activist and absolutist, motivated by strong reformist impulses." The civil rights movement and Vietnam War in the 1960s and early 1970s divided the mainline and evangelicals even more. Mainline liberal churches oriented themselves around direct action and social justice while evangelicals concentrated on individual soul saving. Robert Wuthnow (1988, 149) asserts that "those who began questioning the connection between values and behavior, who saw direct action as being more effective than good intentions, increasingly focused their attention away from personal salvation and evangelism toward engaging religious people directly in acts of love or in acts committed to bringing about social justice." He characterizes this polarization, falling largely along educational lines, as the religious realignment of America into conservatives and liberals. Controlling for social background (education, age, and region), Roof and McKinney (1987) found that liberal Protestants and

Catholics are much more likely than conservative Protestants to be committed toward racial justice and minority rights.

Since the 1980s, evangelicals have risen in educational attainment, become more liberal in racial attitudes, and have become even more active in politics than mainline liberals (Smith 1998). However, evangelicals generally seek societal change through individual moral conversion. In contrast, the theology and denominational influences of the mainline encourage social change efforts through the public sphere. Roof and McKinney (1987, 241) conclude that mainline churches have a heritage as "bridging institutions—concerned with public well-being and the larger social order." Furthermore, Robert Wuthnow (1988), Steve Warner (1988), and Martin Marty (1971, 1998) assert that liberal Protestantism emphasized a social justice platform of public responsibility.

In analyzing the issues of injustice that Asians themselves face in the United States, mainline ministers in this study often named racism, both institutional and individual, as the major cause for the social inequities and marginalization that they and their members experienced.[10] On a broad level, racism creates barriers for Asian Americans in gaining acceptance and power within American corporations and institutions. One minister discussed how his church members felt insignificant because they were segregated in the past and lacked access to authority and resources within the United Methodist denomination. Even though Chinese and Japanese American churches joined larger denominational structures in the 1960s, they remained largely powerless. The creation of separate Asian Pacific Islander caucuses within mainline denominational structures in the 1970s stemmed from a need for greater voice (Chang 1991).

Another major complaint regarding exclusion from mainline denominations is that Asian Americans are often viewed as outsiders or foreigners. One minister shared how an Asian American congregation sought the use of the facilities of a larger white church. However, the Asian Americans objected that the U.S. flag was an inappropriate symbol to be raised within a sanctuary. The minister recounts the response they received:

> And when the issue came up that we were going to have an Asian church share the facilities, this one elder commented, "Oh great. They're going to have their flag in there now." Which for us, points to the fact that they still don't see Asians as Americans. And that's the kind of experience that hurts Asian Americans.

In the provision of services to Asian ethnic communities, institutional racism may lead to culturally insensitive approaches toward ministry. This insensitivity may be unintentional, but it still affects how Asians respond to the Christian church. One minister suggested that Southeast Asian refugees did not join mainline congregations because of major cultural differences. He told one story of how a Vietnamese Chinese woman wanted to commit suicide because she had so much trouble adjusting to her host white American family:

> Even in the Episcopal Church, the old generations of the American society, the old members are still very naive about Asian ministry. I was called upon to counsel this couple because the wife was trying to commit suicide. The reason was that the host family—with very good intentions—wanted this couple to eat together to make them feel a part of the family. But they wanted their own meals and that offended the Americans.

In this particular case, this minister thought that the host family was too insistent on expecting gratitude and conversion to Christianity for their patronage.

Mainline ministers express that on an individual level, racism affects members' self-esteem and interpersonal relationships. For example, Pastor Rod, who was introduced in the beginning of this chapter, discussed the lack of positive media images for Asian American youth, especially the boys. He explains

> It's very clear to the high school students, the perception of Asian women versus Asian men in our society, particularly from the media. And the notion in the movies, it was always the white guy that got the Asian woman and the Asian guy never did. They are conscious of it. For some guys, it's a real source of anxiety. There's a fair amount of anger there.

He also shares experiences of Asian church members who attempted to join local white congregations but felt invisible:

> Others would share stories about how they would go for a couple of months and people were still coming up to them and saying, "Oh, is this your first time here?" Others would say they've been at a church for a long time and nobody ever invited them or included them in certain activities. They felt excluded. Maybe not unconsciously or not inadvertently—some of them felt it maybe was advertently excluded, left out.

Seeing that racism on both an institutional and individual level is a major issue confronting Asian Americans, mainline ministers felt that the church's role was to provide a sanctuary and spiritual home where ethnic people could feel comfortable, to provide an institutional space where Asian and Asian American culture was valued, and to advocate for greater inclusion of Asian Americans within society. Ministers believed that the comfort Asians feel among each other within the ethnic and Pan-Asian church is partly attributable to reactive solidarity. Being made to feel they are different from mainstream society, they come together for relief from that stress. One pastor believes:

> I really like thinking of the church as sanctuary, a place that is safe and free [where you can] be who you are and think what you think. For an ethnic person, there's a lot of stress with being ethnic in this world, in

this time and place. I think racism is so oppressive. And the whole inner stuff we have sometimes about not feeling good about who we are and who we are created to be. And a sanctuary helps you look at yourself again and say, "It is a good thing to be who I am."

The ethnic programs and cultural activities of mainline congregations aim as much toward establishing a healthy self-identity as toward seeking to really transmit culture. Often, parents just want their children to be in the context of other Asian American youth so that participation in a basketball league is as good an Asian American activity as Japanese *taiko* drumming or Chinese gung fu lessons. The above pastor goes on to explain the focus of youth camps: "One of the big things of summer programming is Asian American camp. It works a lot with kids growing up and understanding their identity. Yeah, it's church camp, but as well it's working with knowing who you are. And growing strong with your Asian identity." Being Asian American, then, may not involve having a distinctive culture, but having a racial identity that acknowledges and affirms one's status even as a minority.

Beyond supporting individuals, the mainline church's thrust toward public engagement leads these congregations to deal with societal issues affecting Asian Americans. Asian American evangelical ministers, when asked about the community or political issues that concerned them and their congregations, identified homelessness, abortion, and gay rights. In contrast, Asian American mainline ministers mentioned issues that directly affect ethnic communities or Asians as minorities. Mainline congregations both served the community and advocated for change.[11] For example, one minister notes

> The group was very concerned about living out its Christian faith by serving others. Doing that, whether it was soup kitchens, Second Harvest, serving a meal at the armory. We wanted to serve Asian Americans. There was a group called Asian Americans for Community Involvement. They started a women's shelter, a safe home and we got clothing and food to help them out.

Besides direct service to the ethnic community, mainline churches worked for justice by supporting different nonprofit organizations or organizing around political issues. Ministers feel that their members, as racial minorities, were sensitized to issues of oppression:

> I think there's a sympathy for people that have been treated unjustly. It comes right out of a memory of unjust treatment. A heightened sense of that because of the camps. There's something particular in this congregation about how they respond when they feel like someone has been treated unjustly. And that's different—in addition to human compassion, there's a willingness to bereave when someone's been actually mistreated.

If church members were not educated about community issues, ministers believed it was their responsibility to mobilize them to become involved. One minister supports political reform efforts by his members, especially regarding issues facing immigrants: "We encourage them to be involved, to bring their attention more to the care of the new immigrants. The laws related to the new immigrants, the benefits, the social reforms, as well as anti-Asian violence. Racism is another issue." In his preaching, another linked the economic exploitation of Asian factory workers by a multinational corporation with his members' own minority experiences of discrimination:

> I just preached a sermon on what it means for us, the things that we buy and what Nike does and the whole stuff in Malaysia and how that's affecting people. For Asian folks, that ties into their grandparents' experiences and then now, how do they spend their money and how they spend it on their kids. How do I affect that? How do I cause it? How do I change that?

Oriented toward mobilizing their congregations around issues of social justice, Chinese, Japanese, and Asian American mainline pastors focus on the inequities and marginalization that Asians themselves face and develop a "theology of struggle" (Matsuoka and Fernandez 2003).[12] This heightened consciousness of Asian Americans as racial minorities who are oppressed both individually and institutionally shapes the ministers. They see the roles of their churches—as sanctuaries for people facing discrimination, as community institutions facilitating positive identities, and as congregations working for societal change—as responses to their minority status.

Conclusion: The Mainline Definition of Asian American Panethnicity

The organizational logics of mainline congregations influence how ministers generate their definition of Asian Americans and their church's role in serving them. First, mainline theology is liberal and tolerant so that Asian cultural and religious practices are accepted and even promoted in Asian American mainline churches. Second, these congregations also see themselves as having an institutional role as "communities of memory," and they seek to reconnect members with their religious, ethnic, and family heritages. And, third, because the mainline has historically been concerned with social issues of the day, ministers in this study tend to address concerns regarding racial injustice and community development.

These discourses on Asian heritage, reconnection with the past, and marginalization as minorities frame how ministers view the group boundaries of Asian Americans. The symbolic markers that Asian American mainline liberals use to distinguish Asian Americans are the racialized experiences that have disparaged the group's identity. Thus, the formation of mainline Pan-Asian congregations serves to prevent acculturation or assimilation into the mainstream American religious landscape. Instead, they help to establish a group identity that integrates one's faith and one's heritage. One pastor agrees with the minister who was quoted in the beginning of this chapter. He sums up the Asian American experience that tends to be based on racial categorizing:

> If you're Japanese American or Asian American, that has some particular shapes to it. There are some things that are common, there are some common issues with respect to self-definition over against the definition of American. It shows up in lots of common ways: "Where are you from?" And you say, "San Francisco." And they say, "No, really. Where are you from?" There are a thousand little things that Asian Americans are accustomed to experiencing that reveal the need to be clear yourself about who you are as a person, as an Asian American. I think that's primary in terms of being the most intense thing that surfaces early as to character formation. It's entirely physical.

The ministers argue that Asian Americans have a shared racial experience as a group. Both historically and currently, Asian Americans face marginalization in both immigrant communities and mainstream society; need a sense of their heritage and identity; and should celebrate their collective identity through spiritual, cultural, and social practices. Yet this emphasis on the social concerns of their members leads to criticisms that these churches are not "spiritual" enough. Instead, they may be too broad in their theology and too liberal in their teachings, so that they are not distinguishable from secular organizations. Without a distinctive identity and calling that requires commitment and spiritual discipline, these churches find growth difficult.

Because the formation of these Pan-Asian congregations is so new, the establishment of an authentic, Pan-Asian culture or expression of faith has been limited. Barriers to panethnicity include the dominance of one ethnic group over the others, the narrow definition of Asian Americans around Confucian cultures, and the difficulty in imagining panethnicity or reinventing ethnicity. In most congregations, one ethnic group predominates because a church usually begins with a single, core ethnic group. Transition into panethnicity results as members out-marry or newcomers join because of the social and spiritual agenda of the church. However, the history and practices of the congregation tend to remain largely based on the original members of the church. While members of different Asian ethnic groups may participate in festivals or rituals, they may not be able to authentically claim these practices as their own.

Furthermore, the diversity of Asian Americans makes panethnic boundaries difficult to demarcate. Organizing around a common Confucian culture, such as ancestor reverence or family obligation, limits some congregations who claim to be Asian American. Asian Americans who hail from South Asia or Southeast Asia may not relate as much to this understanding of Asian American cultural practices. Similarly, not all Asian Americans have similar racial experiences. For some, the question "Where are you from?" is quite reasonable since almost 80 percent of Asian Americans are foreign born.

Even as Pan-Asian Christianity is invented with the hybridization of Asian cultural resources and Western religious practices, the symbols employed may not immediately resonate with Asian Americans or represent a collective consciousness. Engaging in an ancestor ceremony may seem foreign to a fourth-generation Asian American who does not know his or her roots. Feeling a sense of marginalization might not be the experience of a 1.5 generation person who has grown up affluently and works well transnationally. Symbols of Asian American panethnicity may be artificial and synthetic creations to which few can relate, or they may be deeply felt, strongly durable boundaries that instill a sense of pride.

6

Asian American Panethnicity at Grace Faith Church

When I parked at a plain stucco building in the Oakland hills, I knew I had arrived at an Asian American church. The lot seemed like an auto dealership for new and used Hondas. If the car was not a Honda, it was at least a recent Japanese make: Toyota, Acura, or Isuzu. In addition, every third car had a license plate cover proclaiming the owner's alma mater: UC Berkeley, UC Berkeley, UC Davis, UCLA, UC Berkeley, Stanford. Clearly, these educated people earned enough to purchase new, fast cars.

As I entered the lobby, smiling greeters welcomed me and handed me a program for The Open Door, a congregation of Grace Faith Church. The front page of the program had the logo of The Open Door, a black silhouette of a house. The door, in the shape of a cross, opened to let out light and to invite in guests. In bold words were the mission of the church: "To introduce ever more people to the wholeness and vitality of Jesus Christ." Underneath was a welcome statement that read, "We're glad you've come to share with us in this special time." In yet another greeting of hospitality, an italicized message under the sermon title said, "Everyone is invited to stay for refreshments following today's service."

In the church lobby, I had to write out a name tag. People who have attended GFC before can pick up their pretyped name tag. This way everyone can get to know one another. I stuck mine on my shirt and carried my program, full of inserts, into the auditorium. Under the one basketball hoop, which was elevated to the ceiling, diligent young men set up the sound and audiovisual equipment. Potted plants lined the stage, giving it a natural and simple look. Behind a riser was a huge screen where the words to songs were projected. Without any other symbols or religious adornment, the room seemed arranged more for a folk concert than a sanctuary where sacred rituals are practiced. People sat scattered about in the rows of padded chairs. In this airy room, everyone had enough space to spread out and still feel like they were part of a larger crowd.

After huddling for a short prayer in the corner of the room, members of the worship team climbed on stage. They included four Chinese Americans, a Japanese American, and a Korean American, all in their twenties or thirties. The worship leader, who was male and played guitar, stood in the center and wore a T-shirt and shorts. The female singers stood on the side, and the musicians—a drummer, a keyboard player, and a bass player—positioned themselves in the back. When they began playing and singing over the big speakers, they sounded polished and rehearsed.

After a short prayer thanking God for his love and for inviting us to his celebration, the audience stood to join the worship team in the singing. Many of the 150 people closed their eyes, and 6 to 10 people raised their hands over their heads. The worship part of the service was lively, upbeat, and focused. We sang the same simple song three or four times before the worship team transitioned into the next song, which was also repeated three or four times. These contemporary praise songs spoke of God's love and power available for us. At the start, the worship team energized the audience with the raucous, lively music, but by the end they had led us into a more serious, contemplative mood with slow and reverential songs. As they ended their set, the pastor silently moved to the podium platform in front of the stage.

The pastor, dressed in the crew shirt and jeans that every other guy there seemed to be wearing, delivered his sermon in only twenty minutes. He started with an amusing anecdote found on the Internet, read a scripture passage, and then related his topical sermon on relationships. The Bible story provided general principles that one can follow. At one point, he addressed the nonbelievers in the audience and noted that they, too, can gain happiness in their lives and relationships if they follow Jesus. People listened attentively, with a few entering notes on their personal digital assistants. He closed with three clear-cut ways people can apply the sermon to their own lives.

After a few announcements about upcoming programs, done in commercial format to entice the members, we adjourned for fellowship time—a time to enjoy refreshments and hang out with friends. During the closing of the service, ushers set out snacks. Expecting Pan-Asian treats, I was disappointed to find mass-produced Costco products. People took

tortilla chips from ten-pound bags and dipped them directly into gua-
camole served from its original plastic container. For drinks, we had juice
in big plastic red cups. When I asked a stylish young woman who had
driven thirty minutes from the next county why she was attending this
church, Jeannie replied, "It fits my lifestyle."

This description of a Grace Faith Church (GFC) service provides a blueprint for
the prototypical Asian American evangelical congregation. The cars of the worship attendees symbolize the demographics of the targeted spiritual market
group. GFC plans to grow numerically by reaching out to people "like themselves"—that is, young urban Asian American professionals. The informal
church atmosphere—as evidenced by the church's greeters, its printed materials, the functional utility of its worship space, and the dress of its leaders—is
strategic. To attract members of their target group, who dislike hierarchy and
meaningless rituals, the church offers authenticity, emotional uplift, and rele-
vance. The contemporary worship focuses on experiencing God in an intimate
and relational manner. Sermons are always direct and applicable so that people
can live by the scriptures. And the bond of fellowship centers on individual
spiritual development, fun, and friendships. Together, these church practices
aim to introduce people to the contemporary evangelical experience of salvation, understood as "wholeness and vitality of life in Jesus Christ." GFC's congregational life reflects one subculture of Asian America while at the same time
it helps to define it.

The previous chapters traced how the theology and organizational logics of
Asian American evangelicals and mainline Protestants dictate the use of specific symbolic boundaries to define Asian Americans. For evangelicals, the
organizing commonalities assume that Asian Americans have a shared family
upbringing, psychological orientation, and personal networks. The Pan-Asian
church subculture that emerges is goal oriented, selectively hybridized, and
professional. These characteristics can be seen throughout the organization,
worship, teaching, and congregational life of one evangelical Pan-Asian church,
GFC. To understand how GFC relates its Asian American constituency to its
evangelical beliefs, one must start with its history.

History of Grace Faith Church

The calling of Bruce Nakamura to the pastorate of GFC in July 1983 marked the
transition of Grace Faith Church from an elderly to a young singles congregation, from a neighborhood church to a commuter church, and from a network
of families to a seeker-sensitive voluntary association. These transitions each
relate to the church's transformation from a Japanese American church to a

Pan-Asian one. Founded in 1922, GFC began its services in private homes after seven Issei Christians left another Japanese American congregation because it was theologically too liberal. The church grew as members invited local neighbors or friends from the same *ken,* their districts in Japan. During internment in World War II, members attending joint services enjoyed hearing sermons in English for the first time, and, as a result, the second generation hired its own English-speaking minister. Eleven different ministers served the church from 1946 through 1982, but over this time church numbers dwindled.

When Nakamura became pastor, the church had a small Japanese American congregation of thirty-five people. His first sermon, "I Am Not Ashamed of the Gospel," based on Romans 1:16–17, emphasized the need for evangelism and his vision for the church's growth. His own experiences with Asian American campus ministry at the University of California, Los Angeles, instilled a desire to establish a Pan-Asian congregation in the San Francisco Bay Area. But when he first arrived in 1981, the congregation, one-third of whom were elderly Nisei, was discouraged and shrinking. Pastor Bruce reports:

> I really felt when I moved up here that my calling was to do Asian American ministry. I told Grace Faith Church that when they interviewed me. Everybody said, "Oh, that's fine, that's fine." But I don't think anybody knew back then what that meant or what kind of changes that would bring.
>
> To me, I was kind of drawing on some of my own experiences with Asian American Christian Fellowship in Southern California. The way I had seen some of the historically Japanese churches become more Asian American, with Evergreen and Cerritos.[1]
>
> Part of it was that I was at UCLA in the early to mid-seventies. I just saw Asian American Studies, Asian American ski clubs and volleyball leagues and bowling leagues and fraternities and sororities. But I didn't see any churches that were Asian American. So I began to see this emerging people group and there weren't ministries targeting them.[2] There's just kind of this whole Asian American subculture in the dorms. When I moved up here, that's what I hoped would happen, that our church would become an Asian American church.

That fall 1983, students and campus ministers founded an Asian American Christian Fellowship (AACF) at nearby University of California, Berkeley. GFC's growth came mostly from these Chinese American students. Pastor Bruce explains:

> I wanted to be intentional [about being Asian American] but I didn't really have a strategy for how that would happen. Coming to a bilingual church, bilingual worship service—I think I was naive. I thought that the bilingual service wouldn't last very long, but it lasted ten or eleven years.

The thing that happened right away was that I was asked by JEMS to help start AACF at Cal.[3] There were three students who were really interested in starting AACF at Cal. They were all American-born Chinese from Sacramento and they were all seniors at Cal who had some InterVarsity background. But they had friends in AACF on other campuses and they had gone to some of the JEMS college camps. They were really motivated to start AACF. I just helped them to get started the fall of '83.

Immediately it was a pretty big group, a group of sixty to eighty students almost overnight. Almost all of them were American-born Chinese. So some of them started coming to our church.

The influx of Chinese American AACF students radically changed the church. By 1989, the church grew to 115 members, with Chinese Americans making up 68 percent of the congregation, and Japanese Americans, the remaining 32 percent. Its mission statement now read:

> Our vision is to spur a dynamic movement of spiritual renewal especially among Asian Americans throughout the Bay Area by turning unchurched, English-speaking, Asian Americans and others into fully devoted followers of Jesus Christ. (GFC 1998a, 4)

To accomplish this vision, in 1989 the congregation launched The Open Door (TOD), a contemporary worship service "especially for those who may have given up on traditional services." This second service complemented the first morning service, which retained the older members. Along with a new worship style, leaders wanted TOD to be an informal, casual service that would appeal to West Coast baby boomers. Pastor Bruce notes:

> So in '89 we started The Open Door. Part of it was facilities—we needed a new service to reach more people.[4] But we also wanted to target it very differently. We wanted to say it was all-English speaking, all contemporary worship, and casual-dress.
>
> We said, "We are a ministry designed especially for those who may have given up on traditional churches." We wanted to be a "come as you are" kind of place. We said we wanted to welcome everyone that wanted to come, but we felt especially called to reach the vast population of Asian Americans born since World War II.

Indeed, the new ministry proved to be so popular that in three years TOD grew from 25 initial attendees to 150 worshippers.

GFC had difficulty assimilating new members into the life of the congregation and growing from a small church to a larger one, but the transition from its ethnic identity to a Pan-Asian one was fairly smooth. The elderly Nisei maintained their own Bible study, but as they became less involved the morning service also phased in a more casual, contemporary, and English-only service. Pastor Bruce thought that the elderly were encouraged by the influx of new people, and, at the same time, the church leaders were sensitive to the needs and participation of the elders. They maintained a bilingual form of worship service until 1993.

> It wasn't too much of an issue, [Pastor Bruce continued,] as far as the ethnic diversity. One thing that I was trying to do gradually during the eighties was to cut down the amount of Japanese translation. So by the late eighties we still had bilingual service but only 20 percent of the service was actually translated into Japanese.
>
> We phased it out really gradually. By the time we got to 1993, our translator wanted to step down and so we let her step down and we didn't try to replace her. Also, our organist wanted to step down so we didn't replace her. We had a very blended service in the morning, some bilingual hymns and some contemporary music. At that point, the worship started getting very contemporary and a drummer started playing drums in the morning service.

By 1994, the church had 135 Chinese American members, 40 Japanese American members, and a few others from different Asian ethnic backgrounds. Pastor Bruce acknowledged that The Open Door model of worship style and philosophy of ministry had influenced Asian American churches throughout the Bay Area.

The church's ethnic and racial composition now shapes its ability to reach more people. A 1998 census of 206 GFC attendees conducted over three weeks revealed that 73 percent of GFC is Chinese American and only 13 percent is Japanese American. Despite the growing numbers of Korean American Christians in the area, only 5 percent of the church is Korean, and 2 percent is Southeast Asian. "Reaching more people" seems limited to Chinese and Japanese. In other evangelical Pan-Asian churches, the majority are Chinese and Korean because they started from Korean congregations. Filipinos and South Asians, the other large Asian groups in California, are less likely to be evangelical Christian and join churches like GFC. Southeast Asians, because of their refugee status, are also less likely to join this type of congregation. Because Asian American social networks are partially founded on social class, this church tends to attract educated and professional Asian Americans. Among the 206 church census respondents, only 6 persons did not attend college. Instead, 46 percent completed their undergraduate degrees and another 40.6 percent obtained graduate or professional degrees. The racialization and class of these particular Asian groups, along with the church's evangelical roots, intersect in this church's unique organizational mission and vision.

The Mission and Vision of GFC

GFC often repeats its mission—"to introduce ever more people to the wholeness and vitality of life in Jesus Christ"—to its members in its printed materials, promotional flyers, and sermons. Guided by evangelical church growth models, the leaders' intentional rehearsal of the mission is an effort to unite members around a common purpose. The mission of GFC includes a ministry focus and target group: "to make disciples especially of unchurched, English-speaking, Asian Americans throughout the Bay Area and others" (GFC 1998b, 4). Paradoxically, the use of contemporary evangelicalism to articulate the church's Pan-Asian vision has the unintended consequence of making its members even more American.

Two main characteristics define the Asian Americans who make up GFC's target group. They are *unchurched* and want a new type of spiritual experience, and they are *English-speaking* and uncomfortable in Chinese or Japanese language contexts. The unchurched are adults who either did not grow up in a Christian church or left their parents' churches. Terry Woo, a pastoral intern at TOD, explains:

> The original purpose was to be a ministry designed for those who had given up on traditional churches—what they call the Silent Exodus, where a lot of Asian Americans are leaving their ethnic churches, seeking more of a contemporary worship environment. In my opinion, part of it is cultural, ethnic, and part of it is age and generational differences.
>
> We're open to different ways of running church, different ways of living church. It doesn't have to be so structured. Church is more for the people and not for the leaders. Things don't have to be so formal here, so rigid.

With this understanding that many had left the church because the old ethnic church was no longer relevant to them, GFC leaders sought to make their congregation more vibrant, vital, and contemporary. For the other segment of the unchurched, those who did not grow up in a church, efforts are made to make Christianity less daunting and formal.

GFC leaders thus establish a panethnic identity for Asian Americans by differentiating them from those in ethnic congregations. Terry said that Asian Americans prefer a different style of worship with praise songs instead of the hymns used in ethnic services. Use of language also affects how comfortable people feel about a congregation. Pastor Bruce notes that Asian Americans "zone out" during bilingual, translated sermons but that they stay more involved when the sermons are topical, relevant, and in English. Furthermore, those attracted to Pan-Asian congregations have a different view of structure and authority. According to Terry, attending and participating in church seems more authentic for

Asian Americans when they go voluntarily, when their spiritual needs are met instead of those of immigrants', and when the leaders serve the laypeople. In contrast, he intimates that Asian Americans' needs are not met in ethnic congregations, but that these churches only serve to provide status to a few elderly men who claim leadership roles.

GFC also differentiates Asian Americans from the white mainstream of American society. Pastor Bruce identified three reasons for establishing an Asian American church. First, he felt that "as long as Asian Americans affiliate with each other outside the church and find some affinity, it seems to be valid to have Asian American ministries." Asian American Christians may have relational networks with other Asian Americans who are unchurched and be better positioned to evangelize them.

Second, he noted that in terms of discipleship and Christian nurture, Asian Americans may possess cultural differences from whites that affect their Christian growth. As an example, he suggested that Asian Americans might not be so open or receptive to direct, confrontational evangelism techniques that other ministries employ:

> In terms of discipleship and spiritual maturity, a good example would be if we expect every believer, if you're really faithful to Christ, then you're going to go out door-to-door witnessing or cold turkey evangelism. Very few Asians are going to do that. So I think we need to be involved in evangelism, but are there ways that are more culturally appropriate?

Other differences that he mentioned included psychological issues or family patterns that influence one's relationships:

> I think that this whole issue of dysfunctionality is really big with Asians. Some of that has to do with being immigrants and having communication barriers with our parents. Part of it is that and there's a lot of values conflict between people who are born and raised in Asia and their children who are born and raised here.
>
> I also think that there are some cultural issues about the typical Asian father being the strong, silent type. [They are] not very emotionally involved with their children, maybe not very verbally communicative. I think those things are huge factors in the kind of people that are in our church. Not to say it's not in the general American culture as well, but some of those things are huge.

Again, these understandings of Asian Americans stem from the evangelical emphasis on therapeutic concerns and healing.

Third, Asian Americans in Asian Americans churches have the opportunity to develop leadership skills. Pastor Bruce affirms, "People who are Asian American need to see Asian American leaders." Asian Americans, who need role models of Christian maturity, are more likely to identify with and learn from other Asian Americans. Pastor Dan, an associate pastor at GFC, elaborates: "Where [the Asian American church] affects their identity is when they can see role models as far as Asian American people in leadership—pastoral leadership, board-level leadership."

While this vision differentiates Asian Americans from ethnic immigrant groups and from the white mainstream, GFC's use of a rational, corporate church model assumes a very American and very contemporary evangelical discourse. GFC is a church that finds commonality in purpose. As corporate professionals, GFC people believe that having a mission statement and congregational slogans are very important to the church. For example, GFC has adopted the purpose-driven model of Saddleback Community Church in that it seeks to build solidarity and unity through a common mission of evangelizing Asian Americans. It also incorporates elements of the seeker-sensitive Willow Creek Church model that aim to make the church a welcoming and growing voluntary association that people choose to join.

Rick Warren's model of a "purpose-driven" congregation, based on his Southern Baptist Saddleback Community Church, aims to give "everyone a common focus, a biblical understanding, and language for knowing how they can be engaged with their own growth and the church's overall growth" (www.purposedriven.com). Claiming to have trained more than 200,000 church leaders in twenty-two languages, this evangelical church-growth model orients church staff, structures, and activities around the core purposes that the church self-identifies.

This understanding of the church as a rational organization oriented toward measurable ends has two consequences. First, the church organizational structure, programs, worship style, and setting become tailored to fulfill the utilitarian mission of introducing more Asian Americans to God. Instead of having programs that may meet the cultural needs of ethnic members or the political concerns of transnationals, the church implements only ministries that build up the spiritual discipleship of its members or evangelizes the unchurched. For example, official participation in Japanese basketball leagues was dropped, but the church encouraged participation in many evangelical training workshops.[5]

Second, this particular evangelical understanding of church as a rational organization affects the church's idea of individual membership. The church views Asian Americans as autonomous individuals who have the option of whether or not to join the community. As spiritual consumers, Asian Americans are expected to look for a church home that will suit their private needs, such as providing friendships, teaching good values to their children, and playing music tailored to their tastes (Berger 1967; Warner 1994). They will later join as official members if they "buy in" and agree with the church's rational objectives. In an article in the *Challenger,* a monthly publication of GFC, John Wong suggests this type of commitment, based on subjective and rational criteria, when he explains why he became a member: "I became a member of the GFC family because I believe that the Lord wants me to be part of the vision of introducing ever more people to the wholeness and vitality of life in Jesus Christ. If this is also on your heart, I encourage you to join the supportive family" (Wong 1998, 1). Unity as a family, solidarity as a community, and commitment to the body are found in common mission, not shared heritage, family ties, or cultural similarities. Although immigrant churches rely more on duty and filial responsibility to retain members, American evangelicalism introduces to Asian Americans the idea that commitment is secured through building a common vision among autonomous individuals.[6]

The Worship Style of GFC

Perhaps the most novel characteristic of GFC that made it a distinctly Asian American church and not an ethnic one was its worship style. Since 1989 when GFC introduced a more contemporary worship form in its afternoon service, many other Asian American congregations have also adopted it.[7] Pastor Bruce wrote about how the new worship style was intended to bring people into the presence of a living God:

> We're finding that members of these generations are often receptive to the good news of Jesus when they can learn of Him in language they understand from people with whom they can relate. That when they come to know the Lord in a personal way, they will engage joyfully in worship that utilizes music they enjoy to express love and devotion to God. That worship touching both the mind and the heart, and involving not only our voices but our whole selves, can be life changing and liberating. (GFC 1997, 8–9)

GFC's worship teams hoped the language, music, and heartfelt experience of their own worship style would "touch" and "liberate" Asian Americans. Yet the songs and music came from large, evangelical music publishing houses, so what made their worship any different? GFC leaders would argue that because the worship was led by "people with whom [Asian Americans] can relate," the worship represented a more uplifting and meaningful expression of their faith. While the worship of GFC Asian Americans is sincere, "the language that they understand" and the songs that they sing seem limited to their personal relationships with God—again, a very American evangelical theme.

To help Asian Americans worship in a more meaningful and heartfelt way, the GFC worship team took training from Vineyard Christian Fellowship worship seminars and utilized songs that were primarily written in the 1980s and

1990s. In fact, GFC adopted many of the ideas, values, and lyrics from the very American evangelical megachurches that Donald Miller (1997) coined "new paradigm churches." These churches have responded to therapeutic, individualistic, and anti-establishment themes of the 1960s counterculture and have become the new "face of American Protestantism."[8] GFC wants to create a worship experience where an individual could enter and feel God's presence and respond joyfully to God. Pastor Bruce elaborates:

> I think basically what we were saying was that we could reach people that were like us, which is primarily American-born, English-speaking Asian Americans who liked contemporary music and weren't interested in a very liturgical, high church kind of experience. We were very influenced by movements like the Vineyard, Calvary Chapel, Hope Chapel. We were doing their music.
>
> The things that were meaningful for us in terms of style of teaching and music, that's what we tried to go for. We felt like we were doing something distinct. We took this attitude that we wanted to learn from any ministry that God was blessing.
>
> Part of it was using their songs, getting their training. A lot of it was their values—the value that worship should foster intimacy with God. That we don't sing about God but we sing to God. While doctrine is important, the primary purpose of singing songs was not to reaffirm doctrine which seemed to be the primary purpose of a lot of the hymns. But a lot of it was the spirit of things. Do we really expect God to be there and to work among us?

To establish a meaningful worship experience, simple songs are sung repeatedly for twenty to thirty minutes so that people could memorize the words and focus on singing to God. In this adoration of God, people hopefully enter a different disposition that enables them to transcend their immediate circumstances.

The songs used at GFC are basically love songs. These songs are either songs of praise for God's love, power, and worthiness or they are songs of supplication asking God to purify the members' hearts. Over the two years I visited GFC, the top titles sung include "Arms of Love," "In the Power of Your Love," "I Could Sing of Your Love Forever," "I Will Celebrate," "Shout to the Lord," "Pure Heart," and "Undivided Heart." Again, the songs are not theologically complex or even that lyrical. Rather, their simplicity helps evoke a mood. Without being bound to the hymn structure of verses and choruses, the use of these songs allows for more freedom of movement. As GFC's pastoral intern observes:

> [The songs are] easy to sing, easy to remember, easy to focus on God. My perspective is people feel they can express themselves more and move into a more reverent mood if there's a contemporary type of worship

service where everything's not so structured. People can sit and stand at the same time and not feel awkward about it.

Thus, the worship singing at GFC is American in both the music and the themes of the lyrics. They promote intense and intimate love, freedom, and healing. Contemporary worship songs do not relate the individual to church traditions or to their ancestral heritages. Instead, worship is to facilitate the relationship between the individual and God.

Although the worship style at GFC is very American, the fact that Asian Americans are physically worshipping together does represent a very symbolic and meaningful racial experience for members. The sight of Asian Americans up front in church and the fact that they can sing and perform well does provide visible symbols of "excellent worship." Because many of these Asian American Christians come from ethnic churches with mediocre or listless singing to organs, the professional and highly participatory worship at GFC helps members feel good about worship and about themselves. Pastor Dan believes

> it's maybe a feel-good thing or it's a feeling that here's a church that has high quality teaching and high quality music from Asian Americans. So maybe it does make a difference who's on the staff. It does provide a sense of an Asian American role model. That our church is a very dynamic and exciting place to be.

As a Pan-Asian congregation, members can simultaneously sing of the American Christian values that are integral parts of their Asian American experience and see themselves as racially distinct. The very fact that they are singing American Christian songs—and performing them well—in a Pan-Asian context signifies to members that they are authentically Christian without having to assimilate into white mainstream churches.

The lack of a clear, distinct Asian American worship style reveals the relatively nascent development of Pan-Asian churches. Asian Americans have not yet created their own cultural forms of expression in the way that African Americans have developed gospel music or that Latino congregations have used Spanish songs. Finding a unifying experience or even language is difficult when dealing with several different Asian ethnic groups. Instead, the work of contextualizing the Christian gospel to the Asian American experience and the subsequent expression of that faith through worship still remains to be done. The first Asian American worship conference was held in 2003 because, as one organizer put it, Asian Americans need a "deeper incarnation of the gospel in Asian American expression, especially in terms of worship forms and music."[9]

The incorporation of more ethnic or Pan-Asian elements in the worship is also limited by both the evangelical understanding of worship and the cultural resources available to Asian Americans. Currently, worship at new paradigm evangelical churches tends to be understood as an experience of music and singing. Because most Asians born in the United States have not been trained in traditional Asian instruments, developing and employing hybrid forms of Asian American music is unlikely. The use of English songs is necessary because it is the common language spoken among the Asian American ethnic groups. Other forms of worship expression, such as dance, art, and ritual are seldom employed during evangelical services.[10]

Along with the relatively recent emergence of Pan-Asian churches and their limited cultural resources, the teachings of evangelicals about ethnicity and race do not encourage the creative development of an Asian American worship style.[11] While they acknowledge that God affirms the ethnic heritage and racial backgrounds of all groups, they preach a more universal understanding of identity and community. How these ministers negotiate the seeming contradictions of ethnicity, race, and evangelical theologies of diversity can be seen in the sermons at GFC.

The Teachings of GFC

As an evangelical church, GFC places a heavy emphasis on the correct teaching of the Bible with topical sermon series.[12] According to church annual reports, none of the sermons or sermon series from 1987 to 1999 dealt directly with issues of race and ethnicity. Being Asian American was an assumed identity but not an issue significant enough to warrant teaching from the pulpit. However, to make these topics relevant, the speakers often did address concerns about identity and community and thereby instructed church members about the true nature of one's identity and community. In these teachings, speakers alluded to how race and ethnicity fit into these spiritual concepts and how members might want to understand their ethnic and racial backgrounds.

Identity

At GFC, a person's identity is understood in terms of one's relationship to God. An individual does have a racial identity and a cultural background, but these characteristics are not as primary as one's true self—that is, one's inner, spiritual identity. The church sees a person constituted essentially of spiritual needs and wants, expressed as a need for happiness or health. Only salvation through Jesus can meet these needs through his love and power. Having accepted this love and power, a Christian has a secure identity as God's child.

Speakers at GFC use examples of ethnicity not to illustrate difference, but to demonstrate that all people have a common basic need and spiritual identity. In a sermon on "Being a Caring Family," Pastor Dan taught that one characteristic of a caring church is that people "support each other and let go of differences by focusing on what's common—their mission in Jesus Christ." He shared that as a Chinese American he was initially apprehensive about leading a Bible study for Japanese American elderly. He said that he "began working with Issei and Nisei and thought they were foods!!!" Months later, he saw a breakthrough moment when the Japanese American seniors talked about inviting their Chinese American senior friends to church. Previously, these elderly had thought of their church as a Japanese American one, but now they had let go of differences and focused on a mission of introducing other people to Jesus Christ. Their spiritual identity, based on the mission focused on reaching out to Asian Americans, was to supersede one's ethnic identity.

One's interior state is the source of one's true identity. "Get Real: A Seminar on Relational Health with God, Self, and Others" was a GFC-sponsored conference that affirmed this teaching. Attended by 170 church members, this seminar acknowledged the Asian cultural background of people but saw it as a barrier to gaining one's real identity and wholeness. The promotional brochure explains how the shame-based culture of Asian Americans affects how people view and present themselves:

> Many of us have grown up with the pressure of perfection. At times we all feel insecure or struggle with shame. We push our strengths to the front, hoping others will love and accept us because we *appear* perfect. But inside, we know our weaknesses well. How often do we wander away from His love as we invent and reinvent ourselves, trying to earn the worth we have already been given by grace?

This inventing and reinventing of one's identity is an attempt to please others and gain acceptance that may have been withheld by Asian parents. Yet an Asian American identity, based on accomplishment and perfectionism, is a false front that needs to be unmasked. The conference encouraged people to "get real" and "get free."

The teachings of GFC thus recognize an Asian American identity as legitimate and as a valid basis for church mobilization, but they also state that a more authentic identity can be found knowing Jesus Christ. These two identities are sometimes contradictory but usually coincide as parallel identities. Being Asian American is a cultural background that is associated with family patterns, a lifestyle, and a social set of relationships. Being Christian is an interior and spiritual state of being that should influence how one relates and behaves in this world.

Community

Just as GFC teaches that true identity is not necessarily based on ethnic or racial background, true community is not based on cultural ties, a shared history, or a common experience. Instead, it is based on continuously experienced, personal relationships of intimacy. These notions of community do not stem from

Confucian ideals of social responsibility but a therapeutic model of Christian fellowship related to authenticity, self-disclosure, and mutual support. Group solidarity and unity, then, are gained when individuals voluntarily choose to participate, give up time and resources, and communicate to each other care and concern. In this exchange relationship, individuals receive emotional health, wholeness, and vitality. One speaker defined community as "the experience of knowing and being known, loving and being loved, serving and being served, celebrating and being celebrated."

In a sermon entitled "The Pathway to Authentic Relationships," Pastor Bruce said that he heard about a practical joke on the *Candid Camera* television show. An actor sitting at a lunch counter would reach over to another customer's plate and take his french fries. Nine out of ten victimized customers would not say anything to the thief. Pastor Bruce asked, "Does that surprise you?" After a pause, he reflected, "Not if they're Asians, huh?" and the congregation laughed because Asians are known to avoid conflict and direct confrontation. He continued to discuss the Asian desire to save face and its attendant problems:

> When we submerge our true feelings in order to preserve harmony, we undermine the integrity of the relationship. We preserve peace on the surface, but underneath there are hurt feelings, troubling questions, and hidden hostilities waiting to erupt. It's a costly price to pay for a cheap peace and inevitably leads to inauthentic relationships.
>
> It's human nature to prefer peace-making over truth. We'll never experience true community and authentic relationships until we learn to speak the truth in love to one another.

In this sermon, Pastor Bruce investigates an Asian American cultural pattern under the light of both scripture and American therapeutic discourse. He makes light of an Asian stereotype of nonconfrontation but then goes further to diagnose it as possibly an inauthentic and unhealthy pattern of relating. Instead, Asian Americans are to aspire to authenticity, health, and true community in which people speak the truth in love. Pastor Bruce referred to self-help techniques of best-selling psychologist M. Scott Peck and his book *The Different Drum: Community Making and Peace* to provide models for how this scripture can be applied in life situations. Not only is speaking the truth in love a commandment from God, but it also benefits the Christian believer by offering a path to deep and satisfying relationships.

In GFC's understanding of both identity and community, traditional ethnic understandings of these concepts have given way to more contemporary, American ideals of selfhood and relating. As therapeutic language and values have seeped into American evangelical discourse, so they have entered the Asian American evangelical church. GFC teaches its Asian American members that their identities and communities should be spiritual in nature. Their identity is that they are the beloved children of God and their community is the family of Christ. In this world, however, these identities and communities are to be expressed in very American ways. A person is understood in terms of his or her individual needs, value, and potential. A community is based on group communication and intimate relationships. Given these assumptions, GFC aims to draw in people to its family by fostering the individual's growth and creating group atmospheres of trust and comfort. People thus make commitments to the church and each other if their needs for intimacy are met, their potential is realized, and they encounter a living God.

Although the therapeutic orientation of evangelicals has permeated the thinking of Asian American ministers, they assert that race still matters, especially in symbolic terms and in church growth. The GFC believes that having an Asian American church, with Asian American speakers and Asian American musicians is visually important for its members and guests. Those who react against historically ethnic churches equate Christianity with the irrelevant, tradition-bound perspectives of their parents. At GFC, however, attendees can see positive Asian American Christian role models with authentic and vibrant faiths. For those who do not feel comfortable at white congregations, the sea of faces at this Pan-Asian congregation enables people to feel at home. Also, the regular references to Asian cultural or family patterns in the sermons reinforce a comfortable social setting for Asian Americans. Race is not a barrier to evangelism and church growth but an asset for group mobilization.

The Congregational Life of GFC

The programs and ministries of GFC reflect its mission and vision as well as the lifestyles and concerns of their target population. Structured as an efficient organization, the church has five main ministry areas.[13] Along with programming for children, the most popular programs of the church are the home fellowship groups and the church-sponsored seminars and conferences. While the church is Pan-Asian, the professional background of its members also heavily influences the church's congregational life. The resulting church subculture is a religious "ethclass,"[14] in which American evangelicalism, Asian Confucianism, and corporate professionalism intertwine to shape the form and content of the church's activities.

Defining a Target

GFC's aim to reach out to professional Asian Americans leads it to be concerned with excellence and effectiveness, two values borrowed from their target group's occupational world.[15] What is considered "excellent" or "efficient" has much more to do with the professional tastes Asian Americans developed in college and in the workplace than their ethnic or cultural sensibilities. From the way events are announced to the scheduling of activities, GFC takes into account the lifestyle of its members and their social networks.

Each week, a worshipper receives a church program stuffed with inserts that announce upcoming events and programs.[16] These inserts, along with the announcements in the church program and the monthly church newsletter, advertise the benefits of attending these events. GFC also employs multimedia, video, and drama to complement their slick marketing publications. Prior to an event, members usually put on little skits at the service to advertise the function. The overall mood that is conveyed to newcomers is that church can be fun, hip, cutting edge, and entertaining.

Beyond marketing events as fun and spiritually enriching, GFC leaders strategically schedule programs to assist time-strapped members who work overtime, have family functions, and need to commute long distances. Adult Sunday school is not offered because teachers are difficult to find and students might not commit for long periods of time. Instead, GFC trains its members using periodic seminars and conferences when people can commit to a limited block of time. Pastor Bruce admits that the church tailors its schedule around the needs of its members:

> That's part of the reality of the Bay Area—the traffic, the long commute. It's better to sometimes get people for a big chunk of time, a half a day thing. Whenever we try to do a come-back for five sessions in a row, the attendance is so inconsistent. Our membership class, we do all in one day— that works better than trying to get people to come four weeks in a row.

A result of marketing and scheduling to meet the needs of a target audience is that people become accustomed to being fed as spiritual consumers. GFC members attend and commit to church if it meets their individual needs and if they are continually enriched and satisfied. The voluntary nature of congregation life limits the church in that it cannot demand too much from its members. Thus, one difficulty the church faces is finding volunteers to facilitate home groups. Leadership involves too much of a time commitment and responsibility. Another example of this limited commitment is the priorities that individuals hold. In the 1998 church survey, members planned to commit more time to personal development than to community service, evangelism, or church attendance.[17] While GFC members are consistent with their personal spiritual practices in that they pray and read the Bible often, they find taking responsibility in the church to be more difficult.[18]

Home Groups

Many people, however, are able to commit to attending and participating in home groups sponsored by GFC. From just one young adult fellowship group in

1983, GFC has grown to hold thirteen home groups in San Francisco, the East Bay, and the South Bay.[19] Meeting at members' homes in the middle of the week, these groups range from ten to thirty participants. The stated function of these groups is "to connect people relationally for the purpose of growing in Christ-likeness" (GFC 1996, 28). Groups gather to sing, pray, study a scripture passage or a Bible study guide, eat, and "fellowship." The home group's purpose to connect people in small face-to-face meetings is representative of an overall American religious trend. Sociologist Robert Wuthnow (1994, 3) notes that four out of ten Americans now participate in small groups and asserts:

> Community is what people say they are seeking when they join small groups. Yet the kind of community they create is quite different from the communities in which people have lived in the past. These communities are more fluid and more concerned with the emotional states of the individual. . . . God is now less of an external authority and more of an internal presence.

In a like manner, GFC members want community mostly to help themselves rather than to submit to a greater good or to further the purposes of the church as a whole.

The discussions at home group meetings illustrate how the community serves the individual instead of how the individual serves the community. Home groups may spend forty-five minutes conducting a Bible study, but they also make a point to have people share personal concerns. People enjoy sharing stories about their careers, relationships, and stressful circumstances and then having others pray for them about these issues.[20] Rarely do the meetings revolve around churchwide concerns, community issues, or global topics.[21] Instead, people seek God's presence and intervention in their immediate situations.

Fellowship is now understood as enjoying Christian friends in any type of context. After the formal home group meeting, GFC members spend an extra hour eating refreshments and chatting with one another and planning upcoming events. At church, one can meet friends of similar backgrounds who enjoy common pursuits—skiing, basketball, eating out. Asian Americans here can also join other parents who want to raise their children with the same class aspirations as their own. As Jeannie, the woman in this chapter's opening vignette, explained, the church "fits her lifestyle." One home group, on successive weekends, went skiing, biking to Angel Island, skydiving, and singing at a karaoke club. These expensive pursuits of Asian American Christian professionals seem to indicate a comfortable engagement with the world rather than a separatist battle against worldliness that fundamentalists might articulate. Members, even home group leaders, believe that they can miss an occasional worship service if they take a trip with other Christians. These fun, social outings are fellowship opportunities to build community oriented around the individual's wants and lifestyle.

Asian American churches sanction these lifestyle affinities because they see them as an opportunity to infiltrate a target group and reach out to the unchurched. Ministers do not promote these lifestyles and aspirations, but they do mobilize around the leisure events that Asian Americans enjoy. Rather than viewing Asian Americans as a racial minority group dealing with broader, structural issues of discrimination or as an ethnic group with traditional cultural commonalties, these groups reinforce the notion of Asian Americans as a group with lifestyle affinities. By promoting fun but expensive fellowship opportunities, they unfortunately exclude other Asian Americans from different class backgrounds.

GFC Conferences and Seminars

Another popular part of congregational life at GFC are the periodic conferences and seminars. The events hosted by GFC tend to be generic for American Christians and are not particularly related to Asian culture. GFC has no adult Sunday school or regular theological training for its members. Instead, people attend small groups and conferences tailored around interests or populations of need. Just as church teaching, marketing, and home groups reinforce an Asian American congregational identity with a very Americanized value system, the conferences also demonstrate how GFC helps transform people from ethnic patterns to Asian American ones. During my time at GFC, church leaders encouraged its members to attend two weekend conferences that were only two weeks apart from each other. These two conferences both focused on the individual and the individual's intimate relationships.

The first focused on "resolving personal and spiritual conflicts." In the introductory session, the speaker asked how many in the audience struggled with "worry, anxiety, depression, feeling insignificant, rejected, and insecure." After noting that fifty-nine out of sixty seminary students feel all of these emotional issues, he said that the "answer" to these issues is a new identity in Christ.

This new identity in Christ, according to the speaker, can provide a sense of significance, acceptance, and security that the audience members felt they lacked. To experience the freedom that God provides, Christians need to renounce old lies and claim the truths of the gospel. The first step is to "renounce your previous or current involvement with satanically inspired occult practices and false religions." Experiences to renounce include fortune telling, magic eight ball, New Age activities, spirit worship, Buddhism, and the religion of martial arts. The latter three "false religions" are traditional Asian beliefs that the families of GFC Christians hold.

Embracing a Christian identity, in this case, entails a renunciation of one's ancestral heritage and, perhaps, the practices of one's immediate family. Ethnicity then gets distilled down to maintaining general Pan-Asian values that mesh with evangelical Christianity. These values of family, education, and hard work may be found both in Confucianism and Christianity. Paradoxically, the members' new identity in Christ also helps the distillation process of ethnicity and the racialization of Asian Americans.

The speaker from Louisiana made some remarks about Asian passivity, for which he later apologized because he recognized his cultural insensitivity. He also took a photograph of the conference attendees to show his wife, who had never been with so many Asians. Despite his insensitivity and ignorance of Asian American issues, the audience embraced his teachings and wanted to incorporate the principles of the conference into their small-group formats. Through these kinds of conferences and retreats, Asian American evangelicals adopt the identities and practices that assimilate them into the broader evangelical world and discourage them from maintaining certain traditional ways. In fact, these ways are considered sinful and detrimental to their spiritual and emotional health.

Two weeks earlier, six hundred Asian American men joined together for a conference modeled after Promise Keepers conferences. Again, GFC sponsored this event, whose theme was unity. Chinese, Japanese, and Filipino pastors, all of whom were highly entertaining, spoke on unity with God, with one's own personal integrity within the church, within the home, and within the workplace. Their illustrations and examples were so generic that I believe non-Asian men and evangelical women probably could have heard and embraced these messages just as easily as these Asian American men. The use of the Promise Keepers format again illustrates how Pan-Asian congregations utilize and accept teachings and trends from the broader, American evangelical subculture.

So what made an Asian American men's conference distinct, and, for that matter, what made panethnic congregations uniquely tailored to serve Asian Americans? The conference's workshop topics provide insight on this matter. Like the GFC home groups, these conferences are highly therapeutic and oriented toward meeting the emotional and psychological needs of individuals. The workshops, led by Christian psychologists, counselors, and pastors, included "Perfectionism," "How to Keep Your Cool," and "When West Meets East: Connecting with Our Fathers."

Unlike other Promise Keeper events, this one did not emphasize racial reconciliation with other racial groups. Unfortunately, the positive role of what Asian American Christians have to offer to the broader Christian community, such as biblical understandings or cultural expressions of worship, was not discussed either. Instead, an Asian American background is more of a negative past from which one has to be healed and a culture from which one needs to be transformed. By categorizing ethnic traditions and values as, at worst, "satanically inspired" and, at best, "unhealthy patterns," Pan-Asian congregations discard cultural resources and experiences that might make them distinct from other evangelical Christians.

Conclusion

Evangelical thought intersects with East Asian ethnicity and American corporate culture in shaping how panethnicity is constructed and lived out in this Asian American congregation. Evangelizing unchurched Asian Americans affects how the church understands its history, develops its organizational structure, creates its worship style, and orients its teachings. The resulting congregational activities and programs thus focus on Asian Americans as a racial social network, yet they express the Christian faith in American cultural terms. In particular, American values of therapeutic health and organizational efficiency permeate what is said and how things are done.

In many significant ways, the panethnic evangelical church helps to acculturate Asian Americans. In contrast to ethnic congregations, it values identity as a primarily spiritual concern and understands community as building emotionally enriching friendships. Instead of binding people with ethnic or generational obligations, it draws people together on the basis of individual interest in spiritual matters. The songs, the sermons, and the seminars utilize a discourse of authenticity, intimacy, and personal freedom as means to know God and relate to others. The church identifies needs of the Asian American community as social, emotional, and spiritual issues, but very seldom do they understand them with racialized language of discrimination, lack of rights, injustice, or colonization.

The demographics of the church reveal that it reaches one class segment of the Asian American population, the educated professionals. The format, scheduling, and topics adopted by the church target this subgrouping so that they might feel more comfortable and committed to choosing this congregation. While the ministers do not condone the affluent lifestyles of their members, the people are not particularly challenged to repent of them or to identify with other social groupings. Instead, the social life and recreational activities of the GFC Christians are considered fellowship opportunities. They do not discuss community issues of a political nature but seem insulated within their middle-class lifestyles.

Integration into the middle class and acculturation into an American evangelical subculture do not necessarily entail structural assimilation. As Asian American Christians bring friends who are similar to them, the church provides an institutional space where racial networks can meet and have their needs addressed. Asian American evangelicals do want a racial identity that is symbolic. They see the need for Christian role models and leaders with whom their members can relate. They continue to value their ethnicity and racial background and acknowledge their differences from whites. The Pan-Asian congregation thus legitimates Asian Americans as a valid spiritual target group, creates an institutional space for networks to meet, and offers roles to which Asian Americans can assume leadership. Mainline liberal congregations, however, construct Asian American panethnicity in much different ways.

7

Asian American Panethnicity at Park Avenue United Methodist Church

In the middle of a residential street with A-frame wood homes, a concrete building with stained-glass windows stands with a small, well-manicured Japanese garden in front. A sign next to the lantern proclaimed, "Park Avenue United Methodist Church Worship Service: 10 a.m." The same information was written in Japanese.

Upon entering the side entrance of the building, I received a worship bulletin with four faces on the cover. It read, "Where Two or Three Are Gathered in My Name, There Am I." One face was clearly that of an Asian woman, and the other was an African woman. Behind them were two Pacific Islander faces, one wearing a lei.

Directly opposite the front door, photographs of the regular members of Park Avenue United Methodist Church lined the wall. These faces ranged in age from schoolchildren to seniors, but 90 percent were Asian. Surnames identifying the faces were mostly either Japanese or Chinese.

People entered during an organ prelude. Inside the small sanctuary with seating for about eighty persons, the pews fill according to age groupings. Elderly women sat in the back rows on the right side. Children unescorted by their parents boldly took the front rows on the left side, with the teenagers behind them. Parents with their younger children sat free-for-all in the remaining pews.

Following the lighting of altar candles and a responsive call to worship, the congregation stood to sing from the United Methodist hymnals. The church's choir performed only for special occasions, and the singing was slow and tepid at best. The church usually had an opening hymn, a hymn of preparation, and a closing hymn with a chorus and doxology interspersed through the service.

The pastor, dressed in a robe with a collar, took fifteen minutes to deliver his sermon. During this Lenten season, the church's theme was

Environmental Justice. In challenging his congregation to be "a community of praise and repentance," the pastor exhorted them to acknowledge the "life force of existence." In repenting, they were to recognize that they "fail to be good to themselves, to others, other living creatures, and to creation."

This first Sunday of the month was Memorial and Communion Service Sunday. Near the organ in the front sat a table with a vase. During the memorial remembrance, names of church members who had passed away were called out. When a name was announced, a child went up and placed a flower in the vase in their memory. The child then joined the deceased's family or widow in the pews. A moment of silence was observed and then the next name was called out. After the pastor spoke a little about these members, a memorial hymn closed this portion of the service.

After being dismissed, the congregation filed to greet the pastor and the liturgist. I followed the congregation and entered the social hall to celebrate the annual ethnic potluck. Grandmothers in aprons set out the homemade dishes: sushi, chicken salad, chow mein, and lasagna. We drank green tea poured from brass teapots. When asked why he chose to bring his family to this church, Eric replied, "The pastor has a passion for social justice and it attracted me."

Park Avenue United Methodist Church (PAUMC) is an Asian American mainline congregation that integrates various Pan-Asian elements into its worship and actively participates in racial justice issues. Only four of twenty-two of the Pan-Asian congregations in this study belonged to mainline denominations. This church is even more atypical because it is more of a social activist church than others. Yet PAUMC serves as an excellent case study because it demonstrates the clear relationship between church discourse and racial/ethnic practices. While PAUMC's worship liturgy is standard for the Methodist denomination, evidence of its Asian American identity is present in its architecture, rituals, programs, and ministries. Ethnic reinvention, the rearticulation of ethnic practices and values that may have been lost, is most clearly seen in the monthly memorial service (Nagel 1994). The aim of the memorial is to acknowledge the presence of loved ones who have gone on before the congregation, to connect the children with the elderly, and to respect the Asian practice of ancestor reverence. Racialization of the members, the heightened awareness of racial difference and similarities, occurs as the congregation organizes around issues of social justice, multiculturalism, and even sports (Omi and Winant 1994). This church's understanding of panethnicity is that Asian Americans constitute a racial minority grouping that needs to reconnect with its cultural identity and heritages.

Panethnicity at PAUMC, which celebrated its centennial anniversary in 1998, reflects the history of its members in the community and the vision of its pastor for the church's future. In contrast to evangelicals, who define Asian Americans as people with shared family upbringing, psychological issues, and personal networks, mainline ministers understand Asian Americans as people with a common racial history and a shared minority experience in the United States. Drawing group boundaries around different symbols results in the generation of a very distinct Pan-Asian congregational subculture. By seeking to affirm and even reinvent ethnicity, the church looks to its past and employs elements of its members' own cultural heritages. And by addressing the racial struggles that Asian Americans face, it promotes Pan-Asian political solidarity. In its mission, liturgy, teaching, and programs, PAUMC creatively draws together Christian, ethnic, and racial discourses to serve an increasingly multicultural community. Its own history exemplifies how mainline congregations have followed the multicultural ideology of today.

The History of Park Avenue United Methodist Church

The early history of PAUMC is similar to that of Grace Faith Church's in its development from an immigrant church to a family-centered church and the subsequent numerical decline in its third generation. It first started as a mission outreach by the Methodist Episcopal Church, South, in 1898 and officially organized and received its first full-time minister in 1903. At the turn of the century, in response to the regional racism and segregation, PAUMC established its own full-time accredited school that taught in the Japanese language. As the Japanese American community grew in size during the 1920s and 1930s, PAUMC became the unofficial community center and sponsored musicals, sporting events, and picnics for Christians and Buddhists alike. Internment during World War II dispersed church families across half a dozen camps. Despite efforts by the denomination to prevent its reopening, PAUMC reestablished itself after the war. With the postwar baby boom, membership grew to ninety-one by its sixtieth anniversary in 1958. Unfortunately, the church would undergo a period of decline starting in the 1960s. By the late 1970s, the church considered merging with two other Japanese American Methodist congregations in the East Bay. PAUMC decided to remain separate but still faced an uncertain future.

The official appointment of Pastor Bill Ono in 1988 marked a turning point for PAUMC. Like Pastor Bruce's work at GFC, Pastor Bill's dynamic leadership and the timing of his appointment helped to revitalize his congregation and direct it toward a new vision. When Pastor Bill arrived at PAUMC in 1986, the church was made up of mostly Japanese American seniors, with fewer than twenty-five people attending worship service. The church primarily wanted him to revive the congregation and to meet the needs of the older people, but they were also open to new ideas. First hired to work with youth, he recounts the following:

> When I came in '86, part of my task was to work on the youth participation and younger families. One of the issues for me coming here is obviously I have a real bent for justice ministry and particularly, racial justice issues.
>
> I remember talking with our Administrative Board about that, to say that racial justice was something that was moving me. I didn't want to impose it on them. And they said you do what you do and if it causes some problems, then we'll tell you if it's an issue. In some sense, there was some flexibility from people.

Pastor Bill's ability to develop family programs, meet the needs of the elderly, and continue his activism has enabled PAUMC to grow in number and influence.[1]

One of his first projects that brought community concerns to the congregation was the Sansei Legacy Project. This project examined how racism and internment had psychologically impacted later generations of Japanese Americans. Pastor Bill's aim was for the church to become involved in a major community issue:

> It was very clear when you put out an invitation to the community, it's not for the church that people are coming. It's for the issue. And given the history of the Christian church in the Japanese community, we cannot be pushing the church. We cannot be pushing Christianity. And also, we're dealing with a mixed religious community. We have Buddhist folks that we wanted to include and invite in.

Later efforts to engage the outside community included dealing with local racist incidents and founding the Organization of Asian Americans. This emphasis on justice and Pan-Asian racial issues slowly began to attract other members, including Chinese Americans and Filipino Americans, who value this commitment to social change. Pastor Bill observes that this involvement is the right thing to do and church growth is only a by-product: "At times, it's caused trouble with the church in terms of people asking, 'Well, what does this have to do with the church?' But as a by-product, a family joined the church. A woman who came to one of the initial meetings was looking for some religious community for her family, too." While engaged in the outside community, the church developed more programs for church members as well.[2]

The transition from a Japanese American to an Asian American congregation has taken some adjustment. According to Pastor Bill, some of the Nisei elderly privately expressed resistance to other Asians in the church. Nonetheless, Pastor Bill continued his advocacy efforts, and this work, along with the building of youth basketball programs, has drawn in other Asian Americans. The administrative council did not oppose his advocacy work but drew the line when he began to address gay rights. According to Pastor Bill, welcoming other Asians in the congregation is now much easier for the elderly to accept in comparison to openly embracing gay members.

Japanese Americans now make up about half of the congregation, and Chinese Americans constitute 22 percent of the congregation.[3] Whites, who usually join the congregation because they are married to an Asian American, make up 7 percent of the congregation. Persons with mixed ancestry, mostly either Japanese/Chinese or Japanese/white youth, compose 15 percent of the congregation. Indeed, attending a Japanese American or Asian American congregation is a significant factor of why members attend and stay at this church. At PAUMC, attending an Asian American church was the second highest scoring factor for attending that church. At GFC, it was only the fifth rated factor. This prioritization of its Asian American identity relates to the specific mission of PAUMC.

The Mission of PAUMC

PAUMC developed its mission statement in response to a denominational request to identify church goals and local community issues. With the development of new youth and community development programs, a planned physical rehabilitation of church facilities, and an uncertain funding future, the pastor recognized the need to develop a strategic plan. Specifically, he wanted to unify the congregation with a cohesive, clear vision of where the church would head for the next three years. The mission statement that the church adopted reveals the mainline roots of the congregation and its influence on how the church develops an intentionally Pan-Asian congregational life.

PAUMC's mission statement describes itself as a faith community with strong ethnic roots and a Pan-Asian composition. Perceiving itself as "historically rooted in the Japanese American community, Park Avenue United Methodist Church is a welcoming, intergenerational family of faith that continues to embrace Asian American cultural identity and values."[4] The team of individuals on the strategic planning team, a cross-section of members who varied in age and ministry, wanted to emphasize three aspects of the church's identity. First, they wanted to recognize the historic role the church played in the local Japanese American community and the significant presence of elderly Nisei in the congregation. The planning team included ethnicity and race as part of its core identity because these factors were important reasons for why people attended. Second, the planning team did not want to be exclusive in its ministry or closed to worshippers from different backgrounds. One of the church's objectives is "to nurture loving ties within this congregation that embraces family, heritage, and diversity." In embracing both heritage and diversity, the church attempted to balance ethnic solidarity with an inclusive attitude toward others. Third, the church affirmed its unique position within the multicultural politics of the Bay Area by claiming "Asian American cultural identity and values." Pastor Bill explained that their Asian American identity not only affected how they do church worship and programs but also described their particular role within the broader community. When outside denominational and community people expressed their impressions of the church, they noted that PAUMC was regionally known as a "social justice" church that focuses on Asian American issues.[5] The planning team therefore affirmed this role as part of the church's identity.

The portion of the mission statement that identifies PAUMC's six main beliefs reflect its mainline faith tradition. The congregation first claims a Christian tradition by observing "God's hope, love, justice and healing are embodied in the life of Jesus." The next two belief statements indicate the source of moral authority and faith for the church. Unlike evangelicals, who recognize the Bible as the ultimate authority for truth and the only revelation of salvation, PAUMC asserts, "our faith is deepened and shared through life's experiences." According to Pastor Bill, the source of strength that upheld members of PAUMC during periods of crisis, such as wartime internment, is not an outwardly proclaimed trust in some scriptural statement. Instead, it is an inner resoluteness that becomes communal when the congregation journeys through life together and perseveres. God is revealed through experience and other means. PAUMC members believe that "within each person and all of creation, God can be known through many traditions." The member who recommended this statement felt that each person and living creature is sacred and is to be valued. This sacredness may be recognized and acknowledged through different types of traditions, including Asian religious practices. These two belief statements are indicative of the members' religious pluralism and liberal understanding of scriptures, hallmarks of contemporary mainline beliefs.

PAUMC seeks to usher in God's kingdom by promoting peace and social justice. After surveying members about what they believe the goals of the church should be, the long-term planning committee agreed to emphasize three strengths of the church in the next three belief statements. As a healing community for "a growing relationship with God," the congregation seeks to "welcome, nourish, and receive members of all ages and backgrounds." Again, the church wants to be an inclusive congregation that brings people into its community. Another belief statement reiterated that the church was to be a voice for the Pan-Asian community. They believe "God continues to give us a unique role in the Asian American community and society." Finally, they asserted that the congregation was to take stands on social and political issues to be a light to the world. They wrote, "As a prophetic voice for justice, we will be an example and influence in our local community."

Of the different models of church that the congregation could adopt, PAUMC wanted to be an ethnic sanctuary for its families and to be an activist, prophetic voice in its public religious presence. As an ethnic sanctuary, they could continue to preserve and reinvent ethnic traditions, valorize heroic co-ethnics and church members from the past, and legitimate certain styles of relating and interacting as culturally appropriate. As a prophetic voice, they could mobilize staff, resources, and members around social and political issues confronting the Asian American community.

Paradoxically, while the church recognizes the racially marginalized position of Asian Americans, the members themselves, like those at GFC, are upper middle class. In terms of educational attainment and occupational status, the working adult members are college-educated professionals (37.5 percent have bachelor's degrees and 45 percent have graduate or professional degrees). The top occupational fields are accounting/finance (24.4 percent), executive/managerial positions (14.6 percent), education (12.2 percent), and health (12.2 percent). The mean income per working adult member is also extremely high at $95,000 a year. One of the reasons it takes progressive stances on issues such as affirmative action or affordable housing is that its members value their ethnic and racial heritage and the struggles that their parents and grandparents had. The liturgy of PAUMC illustrates how it operates as an ethnic sanctuary and community of memory.

The Liturgy of PAUMC

PAUMC utilizes standard Methodist liturgy, songs,[6] and the official church calendar, but its "Asian American cultural identity" appears in its worship style and practice. The usual Sunday worship service has four parts. These are (1) Bringing Forth the Light—introductory music and a call to worship; (2) Proclamation of the Word and Sacrament—the reading of scripture, message, and communion; (3) Responding to the Word and Sacrament—offering and passing the peace; and (4) The Sending Forth—the benediction and announcements.[7] While recognizably Methodist in the above elements, the church celebrates its ethnic and panethnic identity on ethnic festivals, such as New Year's Day,[8] through the introduction of Asian elements in its art and architecture, and primarily through its worship practices that incorporate certain Asian sensibilities, such as the use of memorial and silence.[9]

The monthly memorial service is probably one of the most singular aspects of PAUMC's worship. As described in the introduction of this chapter, the congregation takes time to observe the passing of its former members, to recognize their lives and their contributions, and to connect the different generations with the past. Pastor Bill describes the purpose of the memorial:

> If you look at Confucian culture, the whole idea of our relationship with people that have gone before us—others call it ancestor worship; I call that the Western way of describing what it is—is that we have relationships with the forebears that have gone before us. It's very important for us to be in touch with their presence and what their lives mean for us. For people to do memorial is the time to be in touch with people but it also helps with grieving and the grieving process.

The actual ceremony is fairly simple. Pastor Bill reads aloud the names of those who passed away in previous years during that month. He next says a short word about their lives and the children place flowers in a vase on the front altar in honor of the person. This involvement of the children within the memorial service aims to teach them about their community. Pastor Bill relates:

> It's for the kids to realize that there's a cosmology in which we are in touch with people who have passed on. We might translate it to Christian terminology of communion with saints. But I don't limit that to people who are Christians. If it was somebody who was Buddhist that passed away and we want to acknowledge our connection with them, then that's fine. The children grow in the community with a sense that tells us, "Yes, it's good to remember people who have gone on before us." And it does resonate.

In aiming to connect with an ethnic community of ancestors, whether Christian or Buddhist, this practice reinforces an Asian spiritual ritual. Often, Japanese and Chinese American families have private shrines at home or observe memorials at the cemetery on specific dates, but they do not usually have an institutionalized church practice of memorial. Pastor Bill feels that his church, as an Asian one, has the responsibility to uplift these practices as part of the members' spirituality.

> One member who's like, ninety years old, his parents always ate and did this little rice offering, which is I think Shinto. They had this miniature rice ball and in their tradition, you always—before you serve yourself—you put the rice in a rice bowl and put it up on the altar. He says, "Is it okay if we do that?" I said, "I think it's okay. And I think you know it's okay because that's why you do that."
>
> We need to say as Christians "that's okay." It has nothing to do with whether or not I can be a good Christian. It has everything to do, though, with what's important to me in terms of what I've been taught about my relationships with other people.

The church integrates the memorial, which is primarily seen as an Asian practice, with its Christian communion practice. Besides helping with the grieving process and connecting children with their ancestral heritage, this ritual has two other functions. It opens up possibilities for new Asian American Christian understandings of faith and it imbues Christian practices with meanings that resonate more readily with the congregation. Pastor Bill notes that his members were taught that Christian and Asian spiritual practices were antithetical. The incorporation of the memorial into the church service, on the other hand, is official recognition of the people's popular religiosity. Furthermore, the memorial expands their understanding of communion by likening it to an Asian memorial:

> I blend it in with communion. Because in a way, communion is like a memorial. And so when we blend, it's like we're just doing a worship service and we're not worshipping our ancestor, but we're remembering people and understanding that we have a paradigm that makes sense for us. It's saying that part of your life is part of your whole life and it's affirmed here.

Another example of the incorporation of Asian practices in church liturgy is the use of silence to "center" people. During the prayers of the people the pastor leads, much time is spent in silence so that people can focus their thoughts and energies. In one children's sermon on prayer, Pastor Bill had the children sit still in silence to become more aware and present to the moment. And before one committee meeting, a member led the group in a tai chi breathing exercise to help us relax and clear our minds. In contrast to the evangelicals, who seek lively, upbeat worship experiences, this congregation opts to employ an Asian cultural value, quietude, to integrate spirituality and communal faith.[10]

These liturgical practices demonstrate how Asian American subculture is a fluid creation in the making (Ng 1996). By creating hybridized practices that incorporate Asian sensibilities with Christian rituals, PAUMC has a very distinctive worship service that is both traditional and innovative. GFC has a worship style that seeks to mediate Asian Americans' individual relationships with God, while PAUMC had developed a liturgy that emphasizes the group heritage of the congregation. GFC has found a style that appeals to the tastes of Asian Americans developed in their professional world and popular culture, while PAUMC instead looks to the ethnic traditions of Asian Americans to move them spiritually. These differences result from the evangelical and mainline roots of each church; GFC aims to reach the unchurched, while PAUMC seeks to offer communion with God through many traditions, especially Asian ones. The teachings of PAUMC illustrate how the evangelical and mainline divide generates different notions of Asian American identity and community.

The Teachings of PAUMC

As a mainline liberal congregation, PAUMC teaches about social justice often and explicitly addresses issues of ethnicity and race in the context of faith, culture, and community. Evangelicals believe that the Bible offers to individuals the exclusive pathway for future salvation and provides applicable principles for living, but the mainline ministers focus more on how it teaches one to love others and to serve the community in the here and now. In effect, mainline and evangelical views on biblical interpretation, salvation, evangelism, and mission differ so that their expectations of their members vary correspondingly. Although both groups work with congregations roughly similar in generation, class, and educational attainment, they challenge them to do very different things. Because the mainline ministers do not interpret the entire Bible literally, they attempt to uncover the truths of the scriptural narratives given their social context.[11]

The teachings at PAUMC either educate members about current issues facing the community or they provide theological understandings of why the church engages in particular ministries. One year, the theme for the Lenten season was "Environmental Justice" and the next year it was "Culture, Faith, and Community Health." In one youth service, when the youth of the congregation ran the worship service upon returning from a retreat, the teenagers expressed that they wanted to engage in more community service as an expression of their faith. One young woman began to weep as she shared about how overwhelmed she felt by problems in society—homelessness, oppression, pollution, political scandal, sweatshop abuse here and in other countries. She gained comfort in the fact that Jesus walked with her just as he walked with the two disciples who grieved after the Crucifixion.[12]

The youth at PAUMC demonstrated a high social awareness about issues in society and within the Asian American community. Sweatshop abuse, in which women are paid piecemeal rates below minimum wage and receive no benefits, is a particular problem facing low-income Asian immigrant women. Asian women in developing countries also work in substandard conditions as multinational corporations make enormous profits off their cheap labor. The church youth retreat effectively connected faith, identity, and justice so that these middle-class Asian American teenagers identified with the struggles faced by Asians of different national, class, and ethnic backgrounds. Not only were the youth made conscious of these issues of justice, but they also took action.[13] As Asian Americans who claim an identity as people of color facing racism and marginalization, the church seeks to develop social consciousness among their youth and other members to build solidarity with other oppressed groups. To promote such a consciousness, the pastor and leaders directly address identity and community from the pulpit on many occasions.

Identity

PAUMC teaches that one's whole being, including one's cultural, gender, ethnic, and racial background, is sacred and that each of these aspects are connected to one's spirituality. One of the church's belief statements reads, "Within each person and all of creation, God can be known through many traditions." In this statement, they affirm the value and uniqueness of each individual because the spirit of God can be found in that individual. Another belief statement proclaims, "Having worked in our history as a Japanese American church, God continues to give us a unique role in the Asian American community and society." Here the church recognizes how God acts in history by using ethnicity and race to bless people. These statements do not merely legitimate ethnic and racial boundaries; they also intentionally affirm them as God's good creation. Given this appreciation for ethnic and racial identity, the church actively promotes a reinvention of ethnicity and the articulation of panethnicity.

In a sermon entitled "Standing in the Shadows: Honor, Shame, and New Life," Pastor Bill challenged the ethnic self-hate, stereotypes, and cultural bondage that some Asian Americans may hold. In an opening skit that introduced the topic, two sisters dealt with their rebellious teenage daughters. When one daughter was scolded for not being properly feminine, she complained, "I'm not your typical Oriental Barbie doll! I hate being Asian!" The daughter ran away, but the mother was uncomfortable in seeking counseling because she thought it would bring shame to the family.

Just as the skit directly dealt with stereotypes of being Asian, Pastor Bill addressed the virtue of Asian values such as honor and face. However, he admitted that these values can be roadblocks to spiritual health: "The values of honor and shame are virtuous but they can become barriers to seeking help. The world has changed and there are more resources for us. We have a greater awareness of how different cultures get help and seek help." He then related the scripture passage about being born again to the need to change some old patterns:

> Fundamentalists say we have to be born again to get to heaven, but there are many possibilities of what it means to be born again. We may be enclosed by culture that blocks the pathways of new life. We may need a new way of looking at things. God doesn't condemn, shame, or dishonor but offers hope and peace.

Cultural practices, if inappropriate to the changed world we now live in, need to be shed in order to obtain new life and health. Similarly, PAUMC teaches that gender inequalities need to be challenged and women's leadership roles uplifted. Like those at GFC, these teachings seek to transform traditional Asian cultural values so that people can fully embrace the love of God.

However, unlike GFC, PAUMC actively promotes a positive ethnic identity among its members by incorporating cultural traditions and by explicitly identifying strong ethnic role models. On Dr. Martin Luther King's birthday weekend, Pastor Bill explained in his children's sermon that "Dr. King was a minister living in the South when Blacks and Whites lived separately by law. He believed God thought it was wrong and he was a very special servant of God. We want to thank God for him and His life." Then Pastor Bill showed a news photograph of Fred Korematsu with President Bill Clinton (see Sandalow 1998). He asked, "Do you know what he is known for? Japanese Americans were taken away and he said he didn't think it was right and he was sent to jail. He was like Dr. Martin Luther King speaking truth that something is wrong and he fought to help others without hurting anybody." By highlighting a hero in the Japanese American community, Pastor Bill consciously provided a secular role model for the children. Dr. King is a role model, but the Japanese and Asian American community has its own leaders that fought for civil rights as well. Pastor Bill further added, "We also have people with us who speak for the truth and do the right thing." He pointed out parents in the audience who were attorneys or activists who did work in the Asian American community. By valorizing the efforts of these individuals, Pastor Bill created living ethnic symbols that the youth were to learn from and emulate.

Besides promoting a strong ethnic self-image, PAUMC teaches its members to join in solidarity with other people of color. Sermons decry the use of race in creating inequalities and call on the church to challenge racist injustices. In a sermon called "Covenanting with God," Pastor Bill shared the story of a woman near an oil refinery who got cancer. The people in the community recognized that industry pollution correlated to higher rates of cancer in that area. They also found that race is the most significant factor in determining where such facilities are to be situated. Pastor Bill continued to explain that such policies constitute "environmental racism" because industries' policies disproportionately affect people of color, the groups least likely to oppose corporations. He challenged the church to be in covenant with God and to turn away from the forces of evil. Instead of spiritual complicity with racist policies, the church was to repent of them and follow Jesus' call for justice.

PAUMC consciously and strategically integrates faith and identity by reinventing ethnicity through challenging unhealthy cultural practices, by teaching about ethnic role models, and by racializing its members through its critique of racist environmental policies. In contrast to evangelicals who interpret authentic identity as one's spiritual relationship with Jesus, PAUMC more readily embraces members' multiple identities. By reasserting its ethnicity and racial heritage, PAUMC provides an institutional space and social agenda to make its community more multiethnic and multicultural.

Community

Just as one's identity combines one's background and experiences, community can be forged through the connection of ethnic upbringing, racialized experiences, and spiritual calling to build God's kingdom in a specific location. PAUMC's notions of community, framed by its mainline Protestant perspectives, differ greatly from GFC's evangelical ones. PAUMC teaches that Christian community is built on both shared experiences and a common social agenda. According to those at PAUMC, God's spirit and hope bridges people separated by history, location, and background.

Being intergenerational, the congregation must work hard at building connections between age groupings. By sharing and relating stories during service, they attempt to close generation gaps and emphasize common experiences. On one Sunday different members of the church personally shared "The Experience of Youth." One senior spoke about attending Japanese-language school at the church and playing sports. A Chinese American young adult testified about attending church camp with other Asian American Methodists and said he felt "like he knew them all of his life." Pastor Bill summarized the stories by saying that "as we share stories, we're tied together by the same God. Kids in the '20s working with the kids in the '80s and '90s all have the same God. The tie that binds us over the generations is our common God. Think of yourself as part of a community of faith." Although Pastor Bill emphasized the common spiritual ties that bind generations, the speakers also shared their ethnic and racial experiences of growing up in the United States. These types of stories testify how church fellowship with other Asians—whether Chinese or Japanese—creates special bonds and forges a community of experience.

Another notion about community, a community of place, is that church should minister to nonchurch members, especially those with low incomes, in the local area. In a talk entitled "Embodying God's Love: The Community Developer's Program at PAUMC," Associate Pastor Christine taught that this program was founded to effect change in the community. Initiated by the denomination in the 1970s, the program funded church-community partnerships in low-income, racial and ethnic minority communities to confront racism and oppression. This program existed at PAUMC, she explained, to provide a way for members to relate to each other, to their community, and to God. "We need to relate to the community, listen to the community, and hear the cries of the community," she preached, "because Jesus helped the dispossessed know that they are loved despite their circumstances."

Community is not found through therapeutic intimacy within groups but is developed through an "engaged faith in practice." Pastor Christine shared the story of Buddhist monk Thich Nhat Hanh, who exemplified how faith could be put into practice to relieve suffering. The year before, Pastor Bill preached that the community development program helped establish the Organization of Asian Americans (OAA). This group challenged hiring practices in the local school district and participated in the creation of a multicultural center in the city. Actively confronting evil, racism, and oppression, the church helps establish Asian American community by articulating its social needs and political disenfranchisement. This makes PAUMC a community of practice, one that builds solidarity in its issue identification.

In these sermons, speakers base Asian American community on common experiences of growing up with other Asians, Asian role models, a shared political agenda, and a spiritual connection. PAUMC attempts to strengthen ethnic, racial, and political solidarity within a faith framework. In another talk on "The Power of Prayer," Pastor Bill taught that prayer puts life in perspective, builds connection, and establishes lines of energy among the congregation. He had the audience lift their hands, palms up, toward God in order to receive strength from "the Holy Other." He then had us direct our palms toward each other to share positive life energies. While the congregation seemed hesitant, they complied with this unusual physical exercise of prayer.

In PAUMC's understanding of both identity and community, the church has adopted multicultural identity of politics discourse that mainline denominations have slowly embraced since the civil rights movement. One's experiences in the United States as an ethnic and racial minority become the basis of one's identity and community. The church selects particular aspects of ethnicity and race to emphasize as the primary bonds of solidarity. These include affinity toward role models committed to the community, experiences shared with co-ethnics (language, school, sports), and a concern for the oppressed. These multiple identities intersect with one's faith identity, which provides another bond among the congregants. Their self-conscious understanding of Asian American panethnicity is expressed in the kinds of activities and programs offered in their congregational life together.

The Congregational Life of PAUMC

More than one hundred people came out on a Saturday evening to attend PAUMC's basketball program orientation. Most of these people were nonchurch members who wanted their children to participate. Besides basketball information, attendees received a packet of information about PAUMC. The contents reveal the public face of the congregation and how they want to be known in the wider Asian American community. Along with the church bulletin and brochure listing the programs and services, the packet included copies of articles about the organizations the church sponsors. One article described the Organization of Asian Americans' fundraiser to honor the school superintendent;

another, entitled "Congregations in Action," profiled the work of the Extending Connections program with elderly Nisei. A flyer invited youth and family to a luncheon and program on drug abuse with a Japanese American doctor from a local clinic. Involvement with community issues characterizes much of the life of the PAUMC.

PAUMC tailors its programs based on the age-, gender-, or language-specific needs of its members but also places a special emphasis on "cultural awareness" and "social justice," as specified in the vision statements for their programs.[14] What integrates these disparate programs are values seeking to integrate ethnic heritage, Pan-Asian community, and multiculturalism with spirituality.

The Spring Bazaar and the Ethnic "Chicken of God"

"We barbecue over seven thousand pieces of chicken," a PAUMC member proudly informed me after one Sunday service. "You'll probably cut chicken. Everybody ends up working." PAUMC held its annual spring bazaar in May and the focus was on its teriyaki chicken, which competed with other Japanese American churches for the claim of "Best Teriyaki Chicken." Originally begun in 1959 as a traditional doll festival similar to ones held in Japan, this bazaar, now one of the church's main fund-raisers and ethnic events, draws elder members and guests from the area.

Besides the draw of chicken lunches, people come for the doll display, arts and crafts sales, and carnival games. A few people in the church survey listed the bazaar as one of the main reasons why they had returned to the church after a period of absence. Relatives and friends from the Japanese Buddhist temple across the street and from throughout the Bay Area, along with church members, buy the chicken meals. Like the church's other cultural events, this bazaar is a very intergenerational affair and attracts participants of all ages.

Pastor Bill writes that the story of PAUMC's Spring Festival Bazaar traces the story of the Japanese American community in the town. When the church organized the first bazaar with a display of Japanese doll collections, they described it in their newsletter as a children's carnival, without mentioning the Japanese roots of the doll festival. This avoidance of referring to the bazaar as a cultural event stemmed from the members' ambivalence about connecting an ethnic, family custom with an American religious institution. Furthermore, during wartime internment many Japanese American families had to destroy possessions, including their doll collections, that were related to Japan. Celebrating one's Japanese cultural roots after the war could have caused backlash in this military community.

The doll festival soon disappeared from the bazaar as the sale of chicken teriyaki grew in importance. Years later, however, interest in the bazaar waned.

It required significant volunteer labor, the Nisei organizers were aging, and the primary purpose of the bazaar, fund-raising, could be accomplished with less intensive efforts.

In the 1990s, however, the Sansei generation took over coordination of the event and revived its celebration. With the influx of new families to the church, more people learned from the church elders about how to carry on this distinctly Asian American tradition. After hearing the origin of the festival, Pastor Bill provided a theological interpretation of it. He saw that as members of the community gathered together, just as Jews do for the Feast of the Passover, they shared stories of their past and the oppression they encountered on the way.

Pastor Bill suggested that the bazaar is not just a cultural event or an economic fund-raiser.

> In the gathering of the people, the Spirit of Christ will remind us that life is born of sacrifice. But in our story, the sacrificial Spirit of Christ is not the "Lamb of God," but of course, the "Chicken of God."
>
> As people gather to eat their chicken teriyaki lunches, through the eating and the fellowship, in the festivity and the storytelling, the Spirit of the community of the faithful will be remembered as a new community is born.

This bazaar is a hybrid of Japanese culture—itself a syncretic mix of Shinto, Buddhist, and Confucian influences—and American consumerism. Yet the bazaar is more than an Asian American tradition of thirty-eight years. It is now also an Asian American *Christian* tradition, used as a means to understand God's work in history and Jesus' sacrifice for humanity. By integrating a community tradition and an ethnic celebration with its Sunday service, PAUMC preserves a unique cultural identity through the explication of its symbolic meaning. Another community tradition that PAUMC has challenged and reinterpreted is its youth basketball programs.

Basketball as Pan-Asian Community

The history of the PAUMC basketball program is another example of the congregation's transition from a Japanese American institution to a Pan-Asian one. In 1999 the congregation sponsored ten teams of girls and boys ranging in age from five to eighteen years old. The mission of the program is to provide "opportunities to play basketball in a safe, well-organized environment that helps foster values of teamwork, cultural awareness and community service."[15] According to Allison Yamada, the church liaison to the basketball leagues, more than one hundred families participate in the church's teams because they want their children to socialize with other Asian Americans in a good moral environment. When asked why families join the league, she replied,

I think it's really community. You get to know the parents and you know they promote good values. Because most of the teams are church-based, they're all church people. So there are rules that don't allow taunting. It's a combination of that and keeping the cultural identity, of playing with Asian kids.

PAUMC's program began in 1992 when the congregation sponsored one team of girls playing in the East Bay Girls Athletic League, a Japanese American basketball organization. A few years later, boys' teams joined the East Bay Youth Athletic League (EBYAL), a Japanese American league that formed after World War II. However, one year in the mid–1990s, one PAUMC boys team boycotted EBYAL over what they felt were discriminatory policies. According to league rules, a team can only have three non-Japanese Americans on the team.[16] League officials argued that this policy maintained the historical purpose of the league, which was to keep the Japanese American community together. That year, the league reviewed the roster of the PAUMC team and rejected the team because it had more than three non-Japanese American players. Rather than exclude one teammate, the team voted to withdraw from the league.

To support the team, the congregation started a new league, the Asian Community Basketball Association, and drew teams from other Asian American organizations to play during the off-season of EBYAL. PAUMC teams have since returned to play in the EBYAL league, but parents still lobby to revise league policies. Allison explains:

We're church-affiliated and this is the belief of our church. We said times have changed. The league has to be open and we can't be discriminatory based on race. We'll continue to fight because we think it's wrong. We still want to instill the same values about maintaining cultural identity, but our philosophy is not to discriminate against anyone.

By wanting to maintain an Asian cultural identity while not being discriminatory, PAUMC attempts to negotiate the fine line of being proud of one's heritage and yet still being inclusive of other groups. To promote an Asian identity, teams have participated in cultural activities such as visiting the Asian Art Museum in San Francisco and sponsoring a video showing of "Rabbit in the Moon," a documentary about Japanese American internment. The basketball team coordinators particularly wanted to acknowledge its Pan-Asian church sponsorship and their inclusivity in their mission statement: "while rooted in the Asian Christian community, the Program is open to youth and families of all ethnic heritage, religion, or skill."

As Allison noted, times have changed. The Japanese American community, with high rates of out-marriage and acculturation, today contends with the question of maintaining ethnic solidarity. PAUMC currently resolves this issue by opting to develop a Pan-Asian community that is more open yet maintains cultural distinctiveness. The politics of identity, evidently, comes into question even in the world of kids' play. The church also engages in power struggles over Asian Americans' place in broader society as its social justice committee involves itself in city politics.

Asian American Community Development in a Multicultural World

One rainy winter night I entered the council chambers of the town's city hall. I joined Pastor Bill and a small group of PAUMC members to hear an agenda item regarding housing and community development needs. Participating with the coalition, Building Bridges, they wanted funding for a new multicultural community center. While we waited for the item, the pastor and other activists discussed the politics of each council member, their histories with different interest groups, and their upcoming campaign strategies. They were, in political terms, "counting their votes" to assess who and how they might need to lobby. Eventually Pastor Bill got to testify. He argued that with the growing number of immigrants to the area, the city needed "multicultural development to build relationships among disparate communities. It's central to community health." When he finished, he was greeted with much applause. A year and a half later, after much more organizing, lobbying, and planning, the multicultural center had its grand opening.

To the outside community, PAUMC is a congregation with a strong social activist agenda. As the sponsor of the denominational Community Developer's program, it has spawned several organizations and initiatives. In its efforts to promote racial justice, the church has helped to create the OAA, the Coalition for Racial Equality (CORE), and the town's multicultural center within a period of six years.[17]

Pastor Bill's own commitment to racial justice spawned the church sponsorship of these organizations and programs. As he has organized within the community, Asian Americans with similar progressive stands have joined the congregation. These include directors of local Asian nonprofit organizations, community activists, and public interest attorneys. Of all the ministries of PAUMC, the theology and practice of the Community Developer's programs exemplify the racialized consciousness that this Pan-Asian congregation seeks to develop.

As stated in the history of the congregation, Pastor Bill brought with him his own political consciousness and social activism when he was hired. After graduating from University of California at Berkeley, where he said he gained "an Asian American political identity," he worked with nonprofit community agencies in Asian immigrant communities prior to entering seminary. After being called to the pastorate at PAUMC, he founded the Sansei Legacy Project and then became involved with local officials regarding incidents of racial epithets aimed at kids in the youth group. Later, another member informed him about an Asian American school administrator who was being transferred from a school that had a large population of Asian American students. Pastor Bill recounted the situation:

> We tried to have some meeting with a group of parents. We were able to get the guy retained at the school but he got blackballed in the district. Out of that, we decided to form an organization for Asians because it was very clear there was no voice for advocacy for Asians. If it had been a Black issue, they wouldn't resolve it like that. So out of that series of events, we decided to form the Organization of Asian Americans (OAA).

To fund the new organization, Pastor Bill obtained a grant from the Methodist denomination to hire staff. To be "in mission" with the denomination and the community, the church was to engage in the empowerment of disenfranchised communities. Pastor Bill offered his theological rationale to engage with the local Asian American community:

> If we believe in justice, then we need to translate and concretize the community in terms of empowerment for people, and not just for people who are church members, but people in the community.
> What we get out of it is that we're doing God's work. And our interest should be nothing more than that. Part of defining what it means to be in mission in your community is working for social justice change. It's ushering in the realm of God in your community in a very concrete, tangible way.

OAA has since become an Asian American advocate in the hiring practices of the government and local school district, in police-community relations, and in youth leadership development. The organization is intentionally political rather than cultural and social. Pastor Bill justifies this focus by arguing that "in terms of institutional racism and the longstanding exclusion of Asians in the decision-making process, we can't afford to spend time trying to build social community and identity." In helping to found this secular organization dedicated to promoting Asian American political interests, PAUMC is at the forefront of establishing a Pan-Asian community in reaction to racism.

Following the establishment of OAA, Pastor Bill became active in forming another new group, the Coalition for Racial Equality, with representatives from the NAACP and OAA. This coalition has organized the town's multicultural center. Pastor Bill relates this community activism to the work of the church:

> As a church sponsors this multiracial coalition—we're the fiscal agent for it—we're giving support here so that people know that the church is a welcoming place. I don't think God is that concerned, per se, about

building up the membership of churches. God is concerned about the realm of God and doing what we can to usher that in. I believe our mission is to bring about—in this world—to bring about a sense of the presence of God and God's domain.

New initiatives of the Community Developer's program include advocating affordable housing, confronting community health and substance abuse issues, and creating a youth leadership training development institute.

Conclusion

Mainline theology on cultural accommodation and social justice provides the framework for the reinvention of ethnicity and the formation of racial panethnicity at PAUMC. By being religiously tolerant, the church can integrate Asian values and practices into its Christian liturgy and beliefs. Communion is combined with a memorial for ancestors so that Asian American community is built with both the saints and ethnic forebears. In concerning itself with ushering in the kingdom of God "in this world," the congregation seeks to effect social change around issues of racial justice. The church founded organizations both to advocate on behalf of Asian American concerns and to promote multicultural unity. Thus, they view Asian Americans as a political grouping that requires an equal voice in an increasingly multicultural society.

By providing institutional space to develop multiple identities around ethnic heritage, racialized community, and religious multiculturalism, PAUMC fosters Pan-Asian mobilization. Yet the institution's ethnic history also limits its panethnic development. Although some South Asian and Filipinos attend the congregation, its cultural influences remain more East Asian and Confucian oriented. Children, including Chinese Americans, learn to greet elders in Japanese before reading the scripture. Class and language barriers also preclude new immigrants from gaining access to this church.

An intriguing issue for PAUMC and mainline congregations in general is how to promote a distinctive faith that can be integrated with other aspects of the members' lives. PAUMC members pray less, give less money, and read the Bible much less than GFC members.[18] They also vary much more in their range of beliefs and share their faith to others less than those at GFC.[19] Although PAUMC has worked well in integrating the people's faith with their ethnic heritage and racial identity, it does less well in programs of spiritual formation. As mainline churches continue to dwindle in number, one wonders if congregations like PAUMC will have much of a public voice or even a significant voice in members' private lives.

Another trend at PAUMC that reflects statewide changes is the increasing number of interracial couples. About one in five couples at PAUMC were interracial, while less than 2 percent of GFC were interracial.[20] With a population of 2.1 million in the 2000 census, mixed-race Asian Americans currently outnumber all other Asian subgroups except Chinese Americans. As California becomes more multiethnic and as Asian Americans not only culturally assimilate but also structurally assimilate through intermarriage, will Asian American ministers continue to see the need for Pan-Asian churches?

8

Conclusion

Asian American Christians in a Multiethnic Society

Before visiting Dayspring Church, I checked out their Web site. The home page had a bold white-on-black graphic announcing "M7–New Series at DS 09.07.03." In the background, lines of Greek words ran across the page. Assuming that most visitors to the site wouldn't know Greek or what "M7" was, the Web masters enticed visitors with intrigue; the church seemed to be airing a television spy show.

Dayspring met at a Silicon Valley office park that would have rented to computer start-ups if the economy were better. Instead of housing cookie-cutter suites, the 21,000-square-foot building was left mostly open and bare, with large ventilation ducts running along the ceiling in full view. Upon entrance, one did not enter a brightly lit corporate office or a stained-glass church but a dim, cavernous warehouse with a postindustrial feel. The professional stage lighting spotlighted only the front platform, so congregants sat in the dark.

In front of a large black curtain, the worship team performed a fifteen-minute set of three songs. The lead singer wore a microphone headset and roamed the center of the stage as he played guitar. Two females sang backup while five musicians, including a violinist, accompanied them. The congregation sang along to lyrics projected on two screens flanking the stage, but I couldn't hear them or myself because of the four large speakers blasting the musicians' singing and instrumentals.

This morning's worship time of singing was cut short to view a multimedia extravaganza, "SCUBA–Super Cool Undersea Bible Adventure," about the children's summer program. Synchronized to upbeat songs, color photographs of the happy campers scrolled across a panorama of the ocean floor. Intermittently, but on beat, lyrics to the songs would flash on the screen: "Jump! Scream! Shout!" Immediately following, children from SCUBA sang two songs, including one rap, during which two little boys did some freestyle hip-hop moves.

Pastor Rod came on stage next, dressed in a dark crew shirt and light khaki pants. He explained that the mysterious M7 series was about the seven magnificent attributes of God. This week's talk was on Christ's humility, and sermon notes were provided. People filled in blanks to remember key points, such as the main principle of humility.

Following another closing worship set of songs, we walked out through the church's fair publicizing its small groups. Each geographic small group had a booth with photographs and descriptions of their group's activities. Some handed out candy; others gave away chocolate chip cookies. I stopped at the booth of the group meeting near my home and asked why they attended a church so far away. One young man, Peter, replied, "I like the vision of a multicultural church–there's a biblical mandate for it, but Sunday mornings are the most segregated hour in America."

Although 95 percent of Dayspring Church members are Asian American, its mission aims to "connect multiethnic and diverse people relationally with Jesus Christ and to one another."[1] Just as starting Pan-Asian churches was a major trend in the 1990s, more Asian American ministers have begun planting multiethnic congregations at the start of the twenty-first century. When I conducted my first survey of San Francisco Bay Area churches in 1998, only two congregations led by Asian American ministers saw themselves as multiethnic. Four years later, at least four Asian American ministers have started multiethnic congregations in the area, and more are considering broadening their church identity.

In his welcome letter on the church Web site, Pastor Rod writes about his vision for the church:

> Our desire is to be a vibrant, healthy church that partners with God in transforming the lives of multiethnic people. Our desire is to serve you. All of us long for genuine community, where people know your name, miss you when you are gone, and listen to you when things aren't going so well. At Dayspring, we believe you'll find that sort of community.

In its Web site, its church handouts, and its statement of values, the church repeatedly declares that it wants to be "multiethnic" and a "genuine community."

While Dayspring Church and this sample of multiethnic churches may not be fully representative of this trend, the appearance of Asian American–led, multiethnic churches across the United States raises some intriguing questions.[2]

Why have Asian American ministers developed this new vision for churches? Are these new churches a sign of the declining significance of race and the inevitable assimilation of Asian Americans? How will ethnic-specific and Pan-Asian congregations relate to our increasingly multiethnic and multiracial society?

To answer these questions, we need to first examine why and how these Asian American ministers developed their visions for multiethnicity. Of the eight ministers at multiethnic churches in this study, seven are evangelical and one is mainline Protestant.[3] Their motivations and visions for new church plants often come in reaction to their former work at ethnic-specific churches and how these churches fail to meet the needs of younger generations of Asian Americans.

Reacting against Ethnic Churches and a New Generation of Asian Americans

In starting their multiethnic congregations, Asian American ministers cite four main reasons for establishing churches with this identity. First, having started from ethnic church contexts, all these ministers feel that ethnic-specific immigrant congregations limit the church's ability to serve English-speaking members who have grown up in the United States. Second, these English-speaking members are increasingly multicultural in their social networks and sensibility. They interact with many groups of people and feel uncomfortable belonging to ethnic-specific institutions. Third, these ministers adopt a version of multiculturalism that values inclusivity and the positive affirmation of diverse ethnic groups. Apprehensions of being insular, traditional, or even racist motivate ministers to reach outside of their ethnic groups. These concerns relate to the fourth factor affecting these particular ministers, which is their theological orientation. Each of these ministers express that their churches' core values—hospitality, community engagement, and social justice—differ from those of congregations that are primarily oriented toward church growth. Together, these four factors indicate another generational shift in outlook and lifestyle, just as the emergence of Pan-Asian congregations represent generational change.

Growing Out of Ethnic Churches

These ministers specifically seek to avoid particular cultural and organizational problems facing the ethnic-specific congregation. Because this type of church caters to one cultural or ethnic group, ministers feel that it restricts potential membership and limits a church's numerical growth. While the ethnic church serves its purpose in attracting people with linguistic or cultural ties, it is not as welcoming to those of different ethnic backgrounds. Ethnic cues, such as the types of food served at meals or the jokes used in sermons, establish insiders and outsiders to the church. This minister complains that the mission of his former church, to evangelize Chinese, prevented his English-speaking members from evangelizing the local community:

> We wanted to pass out tracts to the neighborhood, inviting people to our church. But we got some flak for that because we weren't reaching Chinese people. And they figured since the population in this area is 7 percent Chinese, we're throwing flyers at 93 percent of the people that they weren't intending to come to church. And I believe there's a wider scope, in terms of looking at the Great Commission—not just simply the Chinese folks in the area.

Another problem noted by ministers is that the older immigrant population controls resources, staff, and space. As a result, the English-speaking members feel disenfranchised within their own church. In contrast, this minister says that establishing a multiethnic church helped his members gain a vision of the church as their own:

> Most of the battle for multiethnicity is a change in the people's mentality. The initial focus is "this is your church." That's what the second generation's hang-up is most of the time. They always feel that it's their parents' church. So they can't change it, they have no influence over it, they can't make it a church that reflects their culture or who they are.

He echoes the sentiments of other pastors that suburban, English-speaking members no longer have friends who are solely Chinese or Chinese Americans.

Not only does the immigrant generation fear giving up control, but they also tend to be more traditional in their thinking, explain these ministers. Seeking to preserve ethnic ways and cultural traditions could hinder the congregation's discipleship in certain ways. For example, a congregation's desire to maintain ethnic solidarity may hamper efforts against prejudice and racism. This minister notes:

> A lot of times, especially historically ethnic churches, it's very easy to come at this with a whole, static hermeneutic. And they essentially think, "Okay, we started off Chinese or Japanese or Nigerian, whatever. We're going to be true to our roots." There's no reaching out and being uncomfortable going beyond what comes naturally. I think with a redemptive hermeneutic, you're more willing to struggle with being so comfortable. And you reach into that future and try to bring it back to the present. The closer we get to heaven, the more we should start to resemble the heavenly reality because of the redemptive power of the gospel.

Because leaders of immigrant congregations have begun to realize that their individual churches do not meet the needs of the second generation, they have blessed these ministers in starting multiethnic churches.

Generational shifts are even more pronounced among those who came of age in the 1990s. Not only the mainline Protestants but also evangelicals of this Generation X, postmodern cohort appreciate performative symbols, care for the poor, and seek diversity more than previous generations (Roof 1999; Webber 2002). Younger Asian Americans belonging to this cohort have been similarly influenced growing up in neighborhoods even more diverse than previous generations.

Demographic and Generational Shifts

Robert Webber (2002) characterizes evangelicals who organized and led the generation of the 1980s and 1990s as "pragmatic." Concerned with church growth and meeting felt needs, these evangelicals' methods of establishing megachurches have begun to be institutionalized on a global scale. Asian American evangelicals have adopted this organizational model to build churches around the therapeutic, felt needs of Pan-Asian constituencies. However, further generational and demographic shifts have created new challenges for Asian American ministers. Some of the needs presumed to connect Asian Americans are no longer felt, and their personal networks have also changed.

Ministers note that for some Asian Americans who grow up in suburbs within the San Francisco Bay Area, ethnicity and race are not significant concerns. Class privilege often provides Asian Americans with educational and social opportunities not afforded to previous generations. As California has become more multicultural in ideology and in population, ministers note that younger Asian Americans feel less marginalized as minorities: "The younger ones don't have that problem [an ethnic identity crisis], partly because they grew up after the Civil Rights Act. They see themselves as having a place in society, especially if they grew up in California. They don't see the effects of racism at all." Another agrees that the next generation will have a different conception of what it means to be Asian American, especially as Asian Americans integrate more at their schools and workplaces:

> This is unique in California. Here in California, the Asians are leaders on campus. Not only academically, but also socially. I have found prom queens and kings from my youth group in my public school. You don't find that elsewhere. It helps with the identity issue. They don't have the same problems the Asians who are made to feel more of a minority.

The multicultural perspective of this generation stems from the increasingly diversified friendship networks that emerge from their school and workplace settings. The increasing number of portrayals of Asians in mainstream media, sports, and entertainment also provides positive role models and linkages to Asia.[4] As Asian Americans interact and develop friendships across ethnicity and race, they need congregations that reflect this diversity. This minister says that he hopes to encourage his members to evangelize all of their friends, not just a subset of them:

> We have to move in the direction of [multiethnicity] because of the make-up of the church. They no longer live in isolation or associate only with Chinese people. It's strange to say you can only invite your Chinese friends. At work, they work with people from India in the software business. They have friends that are Korean and Vietnamese. If you want them to have an impact, the church needs to reflect where they are.

Ironically, groups within his members' social circles that he mentions are solely Asian ethnic groups, which may reflect the engineering workforce in Silicon Valley. Nonetheless, changes in social networks correspond to changes in values regarding multiculturalism.

Multicultural Values and "Younger Evangelicalism"

Multiculturalism and diversity discourse, especially in the San Francisco Bay Area, promote identity politics as different groups seek recognition and power. In addition, multiculturalism has another consequence. Not only do the younger generation have symbolic racial identities, but they also have developed a multicultural perspective that resists the imposition of inauthentic categories. As a result, they may take pride in their heritages and backgrounds but resist stereotypes and generalizations (Flory and Miller 2000). Furthermore, Generation X members do not want to be limited in their association with others so that the idea of multiethnic congregations appeals to them.[5] Asian American ministers starting multiethnic churches seek to tap into this sentiment and reach out especially to this younger generation.

Multicultural Values

When defining multiethnicity, pastors discuss inclusivity, affirmation, and authentic community as three related values that they hope will permeate their church culture. While not necessarily new theological ideas, the language and ideas employed by ministers represents the influence of multiculturalism. They then appropriate use of this discourse for their own agendas of church growth, social justice, or church unity.

The one mainline minister who pastors a multiethnic congregation expresses a desire to be open to all groups, even if it means going against his denomination's official stance on gay ordination. In contrast to elitist institutions that have traditionally locked out women and people of color, this church seeks to welcome all groups.

> We're inclusive and intergenerational. Inclusive is one of those buzz words right now and we really struggle with what that's going to be for

us. We're inclusive of our young people and we do things that incorporate our children to our oldest. We're also progressive when it comes to
sexuality, as far as ordination of gay and lesbian folks. That goes against
our denominational policy. We're also, if you walk in here, a multiethnic
congregation. If you are Asian, you'll feel perfectly at home. If you're
white, you'll feel perfectly at home. We reflect the community now,
which is what we're striving to do.

Inclusivity is a "buzz word," but how it is put into practice is complicated. For
example, this mainline church seeks to draw together people with different ethnic, political, and religious values. Determining which values to be preached
from the pulpit or to be taught to the children becomes a contested issue. Sub-
sequently, those who might disagree can easily leave and find other churches.

Evangelicals also affirm inclusivity but have a different understanding of it.
Coming from a different organizational field, they interpret this value in terms
of evangelism rather than in terms of political inclusion. For this minister,
inclusivity is a means by which members should welcome new people to join
the church: "In our multiethnic vision, the dominant word is inclusion. I don't
think of race, but I think of a group as outward-oriented, versus inward-
oriented. We want anybody to come to our church and worship God." Evangelicals
continue to hold to a more strict set of beliefs, but they want to include newcomers into the church by building relationships with them and forging community.
They thus accommodate multiculturalist discourse to their own purposes.

Another value borrowed from the multiculturalist discourse is affirmation
of one's identity. For the most part, ministers of multiethnic congregations recognize the ethnic and racial distinctions of their members and lift up these distinctions as valuable. For example, this minister noted that these ethnic and
racial differences are to be celebrated:[6]

Some people said race shouldn't be an issue. I said that's not the right
way to approach it. We're not going to be a church that's non-racial. We
want to be a church that celebrates all the races.

Let's say if someone asked, "How important is it that you're Chinese?"
I would say, "Well, God made me this way, and I celebrate that as well." I
think everybody should celebrate the culture that they were born in and
not to discount it.

However, valuing both inclusivity and affirmation creates a tension for ministers. Some did not want to use ethnic terms or references for fear of excluding
non-Asians, but they also wanted to recognize differences as well.

To resolve this tension, ministers preach another value of postmodern
multiculturalism, that of authentic community. Because of the fragmentation
and insecurity brought on by higher divorce rates within families, economic

recession, and the events of 9/11, the younger generation especially prizes this ideal. Authentic community, as understood by this cohort, should both acknowledge and transcend ethnicity and race while offering a sense of belonging based on shared vision. That vision of multicultural community is what attracts people like Peter to Dayspring Church. This pastor analyzes the issues facing his members:

> Some of the folks—maybe it's a Gen X thing—whether they were latch-key kids or children of divorce, really have some cravings for community but don't have the tools to effectively live in community. This may be true of every generation, but it is more pronounced here. And this definitely has implications for multiethnic ministry, because people have hunger for multiethnicity, but they don't have the proper tools for multiethnicity, either.

He explains that younger Asian Americans' utilitarian views of relationships and their individualism contend with their desire for community.

To address these group unity issues, the ministers need to continually assert the idea of "authentic" community. Authentic community can both include all people while also affirming all people's differences. Furthermore, the shared *vision* of authentic community provides an alternative source of group solidarity. Without having ethnic loyalties or panethnic ties to rely upon, ministers build attachments around common beliefs and aspirations.

As with the case of Pan-Asian congregations, organizational logics shape mainline and evangelical multiethnic churches differently. Mainline Protestants, who stay more in tune with liberal ideologies, value inclusivity and affirmation as tolerance and respect for all people, no matter what their age, sexual orientation, or belief. Evangelicals also adopt this language, but inclusion means a warm welcome into the church with hopes for transformation. Affirmation involves the recognition that one is the child of God. Within the evangelical organizational field, two new religious concerns further foster the movement toward multiethnicity.

Younger Evangelicals

Besides being shaped by today's multiculturalism, younger evangelicals who come of age in the 1990s prize local community engagement and social justice more than evangelicals of the 1970s and 1980s (Webber 2002). These concerns, traditionally espoused more by mainline Protestants, encourage the establishment of multiethnic congregations. They lead Asian American Christian professionals outside of their lifestyle affinities and toward others with different felt needs.

Asian American evangelicals who utilized "new paradigm" church growth methods attracted members through social networks. Ethnic and Pan-Asian churches increased in number by meeting members' cultural needs or their social needs. They gave little regard to the church's local neighborhood because they expected to serve ethnic or panethnic communities, not geographic communities. The ministers of multiethnic congregations, however, have more of a vision to reach out to and reflect the local neighborhood. This pastor explains:

> To have people who look like the neighborhood is important to us. This change wouldn't have happened if we had stayed in the Chinese church. The Psalms teaches that God is God of all nations. The Old Testament teaches that God has a heart for all peoples. The Great Commission is to all nations and Acts demonstrates the expansion of the church to all ethnicities.
>
> We see that we can be part of the community. We participated in the 4th of July city parade and talked to 500 to 700 people in order to be a blessing to the community. We are in this situation and we are in this culture. Our motivation is to not limit the gospel.

He insists that his church should interact with its neighbors and engage the local city government. This new evangelical model of church growth, that of uniting with other churches to pray and improve the spiritual climate of the city, aims to bring about large-scale revival (see Dawson 2001 and Wagner 1997).

The second difference in evangelical thinking is these ministers' concern for social justice. To further racial reconciliation and to reflect God's vision for church unity, they believe their churches should be multiethnic. Like the previous pastor, this minister claims that pursuing social justice is a biblical command:

> From the very beginning, we had the intention of being multiethnic with a justice and racial reconciliation ministry. We did inductive Bible studies, but a lot of times, I would just preach about justice. There's a high view of Scripture in many Korean churches, so we did Bible studies and helped them to see that justice was not just a liberal thing coming from a Harvard divinity student, but was really rooted in Scripture.

By appealing to biblical mandates for justice, as well as to Korean Americans' "high view of Scriptures" and their emphasis on applying the Bible to their lives, he overcomes the group's immigrant predisposition to remain inwardly focused. Another pastor argues that the multiethnic congregation better reflects God's community of peace and justice found in Revelations:

> Definitely, we feel called to be a people that demonstrate Christ's compassion for reconciled relationships—that's the heart and soul of it— through building Sedaqah communities.[7] Community is when two or three of our people are gathered in His name and they are able to bring these values—hope, humility, and hospitality.

This emphasis on social justice demonstrates the rise of evangelical diversity in social concern, political orientation, and intellectual tradition (Webber 2002).

Together, these new evangelical theological orientations lead congregations down the path of multiethnicity. The source and promotion of these new values come from within the organizational field of Asian American evangelicals. As national campus ministries and noted church leaders took more active stances around local community engagement and social justice, they made such ministries legitimate aspects of the church's mission and responsibilities. Just as the Asian American evangelical organizational field had institutionalized Pan-Asian churches as a viable model by the 1990s, it recently has begun to recognize the importance of ministries oriented toward unity in prayer and justice.

Four of the eight ministers of Asian American–led, multiethnic congregations have strong ties with Intervarsity Christian Fellowship. In 1987 Intervarsity Urbana Missions Conference encouraged students to become involved with urban ministries that included working with the poor. While that conference had only European American speakers, the 1990 Urbana conference diversified its worship team and platform speakers. Intervarsity has since made "ethnic reconciliation and justice" one of its core values and works to "promote personal and systemic justice." These conferences significantly shaped the ministers of these congregations. One minister recalls the following:

> My involvement with Intervarsity has been very, very seminal in my shift into what I'm doing now. I'm sitting with world-class thinkers about racial reconciliation, dealing with the poor. And I'm thinking in the back of my mind, man, I can't make any argument biblically against these messages. And it was a real disconnect for me.

Over time, this pastor established a multi-Asian, multiethnic congregation that is considered one of the cutting-edge congregations among Asian American churches.

The success and dynamism at this church and other southern California churches have in turn influenced the other ministers planting multiethnic congregations.[8] The pastor of Dayspring came from one of these churches, and many of his members also attended it. The perceived success of these congregations encourages others to emulate their model, just as the initial growth of Pan-Asian congregations spurred a similar trend toward panethnicity.

However, the new multiethnic churches have not been truly successful in becoming multiracial in membership. If a multiracial congregation is defined as a church where no one racial group is 80 percent or more of the membership, only two of the eight multiethnic congregations studied here may be considered truly multiethnic or multiracial.[9] Although each of these churches has a strong mix of Chinese, Taiwanese, Korean, and Japanese, along with some other Asian groups represented, none has more than 30 percent of another racial group represented. Why have Asian American–led multiethnic congregations become not more multiracial but Pan-Asian in composition? Is the Pan-Asian majority at these congregations simply a transitional state, as most pastors suggest?

Racial Dynamics within Multiethnic Churches

In an Associated Press article, "For Asian-American Churches, Integration Proves Complicated," Michael Luo writes that cultural differences, such as the food brought to church picnics or family expectations about the role of one's mother-in-law, are barriers for non-Asians in Asian American–led churches (Luo 2002). Clearly, cultural differences in expectations and communication affect church unity, but race also plays a role. In the article, Professor Michael Emerson asks, "Will Asians be able to move past race?" These Asian American ministers want to move past race, but non-Asians have yet to attend their churches in significant numbers. I argue that racial dynamics, in terms of power relations and symbolic identities, significantly structure a church's growth and racial composition. In examining these dynamics within multiethnic churches, we must turn Emerson's question on its head and ask, "Will non-Asians be able to move past race and accept Asian American leadership?"

The Niche Overlap Effect and the Niche Edge Effect

In *United by Faith: The Multiracial Congregation as Answer to the Problem of Race*, DeYoung et al. (2003) observe that only 7.5 percent of religious institutions and 5.5 percent of Christian congregations are multiracial. Of these, half are undergoing transition from one racial group to another so that a stable, multiracial congregation is quite rare in the United States. Beyond cultural differences and prejudice, organizational factors keep American Christians divided by race. Michael Emerson and Christian Smith (2000) write that, internally, similar congregations offer identity and belonging at lower relational and emotional costs than diverse, multiethnic ones might. Furthermore, people have a "status quo bias" in that they prefer the type of congregations to which they are accustomed, even if they might value diversity highly. Consequently, not just Asian American–led multiethnic churches but any multiethnic congregation would face difficulty because the costs of attending one are higher than its benefits.

Smith and Emerson raise one other explanation for the infrequency of multiethnic churches that is particularly salient to Asian American–led congregations. The "niche overlap effect" and "niche edge effect" suggest that organizations carve out niches within the overall church landscape. Once one racial group appears dominant within a congregation, this core group will form a critical mass that shapes the perceived identity of the church. This critical mass of people attracts friends who are usually racially similar. Those who are atypical to a social group will then tend to drop out of an organization because they have fewer social similarities and ties within it. For non-Asians in Asian American–dominated congregations, their racial difference puts them on the edge of the group. With few relational ties to the core of the group and more ties outside, they are likely to leave.

Asian American ministers of multiethnic congregations observe these two effects. Because they started from ethnic-specific congregations, these pastors started their new churches with core groups that had an Asian American majority. Even though they consciously attempted to diversify this core group, members that later joined and stayed inevitably were Asian Americans. This pastor describes the process:

> There was an intention for multiethnicity at the very beginning. But a lot of my contacts were much more with Asian Intervarsity folks and that was the group that we started getting in large number, initially. We got some from multiethnic fellowships, but the number of Asians started to become overwhelming. This was similar to what happened at Columbia University Intervarsity, where the Asian folks started coming out in larger numbers.
>
> So by the end of year one, we were 70–80 percent Asian, even though in the beginning, we were half and half. There was a momentum toward pan-Asian and that was something that we didn't have to work at, at all.

Although Asian Americans do have non-Asian friends and would invite them to church, those who joined the church were Asian Americans. These visitors could more easily develop a greater number of intraorganizational ties than non-Asians, as well as feel at home in the church as the majority.

Whites at this church were thus pushed to the niche edge of the organization; they were in the unaccustomed status of being a minority.[10] While Asian Americans are familiar with predominantly white settings, whites are less likely to feel comfortable on the periphery of a group's relational networks, even if they have a leadership role. The pastor of the church further explains:

> Non-Asians in majority Asian contexts—whites, actually—are not used to being in the minority. They have some of the difficulty of "Do I belong here? Should I stay here?" They're not used to being in the minority and that dynamic is very different and unfamiliar to folks. I'm always appreciative of the white Americans, who for them being a minority is such a different thing, that they would be willing to stick that out.

Race has a symbolic effect. This minister describes the symbolic significance of having whites visibly active within the church: "We had a Caucasian guy doing announcements. One white student said he stayed because of him. He said, 'I can be here because if there's a place for this guy, there's a place for me.'" Although this person stayed, this church and Dayspring appear Pan-

Asian, so non-Asians and especially whites feel that they are on the edge of the group. This minority status in terms of perceived numbers, which has nothing to do with the amount of power that non-Asians might possess within the organization or the leadership roles that they hold, clearly affects who stays and who leaves.

As a minority, whites in Asian American–led, multiethnic churches also find that they are easily stereotyped. "Out-group homogeneity bias" is the perception that niche edge members are alike, especially because the majority have less interaction with these minority members. When this multiethnic congregation attended a joint Easter service for Asian American churches, white members complained even though the church had participated in joint services with African American churches. Their pastor expresses the white minority's viewpoint:

> They said, "We don't want to be there again this year. We feel uncomfortable at their Asian thing. We feel like we're being categorized as Asians." There's some stereotypes, about especially the white males, that they're trying to date Asians. All sorts of stereotypes were coming out.

Alienated as a minority and stereotyped as out-group members, whites in these Asian American–led multiethnic congregations pay high emotional and relational costs to remain in these churches.

Conclusion

Dayspring Church has the right ingredients to establish a multiethnic church for Generation Xers. Its facility is spacious and appropriately stark to make it edgy. The music is professional, loud, and passionate so that worship feels authentic and sincere. The lights, sound system, and media meet the technical standards of this group without overwhelming the mystery and spiritual atmosphere created by the candles in the dimly lit hall. The pastor speaks in relevant ways but with no references to his Asian background. Indeed, the worship style, the church architecture, and the sermon are each tailored for a mainstream American audience. Even the booths advertising small groups remind one of a shopping mall food court. The church is thoroughly American. The target audience is clearly multiethnic. Yet the members are predominantly Asian Americans.

The emergence of Pan-Asian congregations is a story of generational change, a story by religious entrepreneurs, and, most of all, a story about the construction and significance of race in the United States. Even when Asian American ministers establish multiethnic churches such as Dayspring Church, their congregations attract primarily Asian Americans. Analyzing the symbolic nature of race helps explain how Asian American churches have been established and the diverse church subcultures that result. The power of these symbolic racial identities draw people together, as well as keep people apart.

The large majority of Christian churches that host Asian congregations in the United States are ethnically and linguistically specific. They build solidarity and community not only around faith and tradition but also around cultural and transnational ties that remain strong among the immigrant generation. The early Chinese and Japanese American congregations, such as Chinese Grace Church, helped the first generation adjust to the United States and later promoted nationalist causes with missionary zeal. Eventually, they became family-centered congregations that transmitted cultural values to the youth. The numerous parallels between Japanese American church history and Chinese American church history stem from the racial attitudes held by white missionaries who helped found these congregations and the racism that Chinese and Japanese immigrants encountered.

Ethnic-specific churches today present organizational problems that ministers must resolve. With a shrinking target population, Japanese American churches must broaden their identity in order to survive. Chinese American churches, confronted with demographic and generational shifts, must figure out how to retain their younger members.[11] As religious entrepreneurs, Chinese and Japanese American ministers have faithfully established Pan-Asian churches to address these problems. Since the 1970s, the educational system, the market, and the government have racialized Asians in the United States to develop identities as Asian Americans.[12] The prevailing multicultural ideology in California reinforces this racial identity to be legitimated and affirmed. By claiming this new symbolic racial identity, ministers can organize their churches around different solidarities and new visions of community as they avoid generational conflicts.

Ministers construct race by defining who Asian Americans are. This process of racial formation involves the cultural articulation of racial identity and the institutional organization of the social practices of a racial group. Michael Omi and Howard Winant (1994, 56) write that "racial projects connect what race means in a particular discursive practice and the ways in which both social structures and everyday experiences are racially organized, based upon that meaning." In particular, ministers use the theologies and organizational logics from their professional networks to generate understandings about Asian Americans. Common, representative experiences, such as parents being strict about school performance or being treated as a foreigner, symbolize the Asian American group identity and establish boundaries about who belongs. Evangelical and mainline Protestants have different symbolic boundaries to define Asian Americans and so they generate different types of churches.

Evangelicals understand Asian Americans as a network of people with similar family socialization patterns and lifestyle affinities. With this group identity, Grace Faith Church targets and seeks to meet the needs of Asian Americans as a spiritual market group. They offer vibrant contemporary worship, applicable sermons, and workshops that bring "wholeness and vitality" to Asian Americans, especially in response to their psychological makeup and family upbringing. The church is attractive because members share distilled ethnic values, racial identity, and lifestyle affinities. Although GFC inculcates very American evangelical values, its Asian American identity is symbolically important; the effective leaders represent authentic, strong Christians who are Asian American as well.

Mainline Protestants, on the other hand, view Asian Americans as a disenfranchised people of color who need to reclaim their ethnic heritage. At Park United Methodist Church, members embrace this identity as part of their church's mission. They fight for Asian American political causes and introduce new forms of worship by reinventing ethnic traditions. While its use of hybridized rituals and its strong social justice stance attracts a smaller number of Asian American Christians, PAUMC is unabashed about how it is seen by others. It is an activist, Asian American church that is proud of its roots and members' heritages.

These churches thus create racial identities for their members and congregations that are symbolic. These experiences and symbols are powerful in that they resonate with Asian Americans and draw them together. On university campuses and professional workplaces, Asian Americans develop friendships and social networks. For those who attend college Christian fellowships, these networks are even more tightly knit. Pan-Asian churches and new multiethnic congregations draw from these networks that are racialized, educated, and similar in beliefs and values. Even though it wants to be multiethnic, Dayspring Church developed a core group of Asian Americans. As this core group invites friends from their racialized social networks, the church continues to grow in a Pan-Asian direction. Their pastor observes this phenomenon: "There is a niche in the market for that because you have all these Asian Americans who are very Americanized, who feel very uncomfortable in a first-generation church. We tend to attract people like that."

As this pastor noted, Pan-Asian churches develop through the racialized networks of Asian Americans despite the fact that their members are acculturated and integrated within their workplaces. And even though Asian American evangelical congregations have worship styles, teachings, and small groups heavily influenced by American evangelicalism, their members prefer to worship with fellow Asian Americans. The Asian American mainline congregations seek to integrate ethnic traditions much more into their church practices, but these rituals are still new and intermittently employed. Asian American racial identity is thus more symbolic than substantively based on any Asian American culture or concrete material interests. Moreover, Asian American panethnicity is still in its infant stages of institutionalization so that its taken-for-granted reality and a rich symbolic system remain to be developed.[13] Nevertheless, the subjective attachment to the group is strong and viable enough to build churches.

The symbolic racial identity of Asian Americans not only shapes church subcultures and members' social networks; it also shapes how non-Asians respond to these congregations. If a church has an Asian American minister and a majority of Asian Americans, then outsiders label it as an Asian American church. This identity becomes imposed based largely on how the group appears, no matter what the theology, vision, or acculturation of the congregation. Non-Asian visitors to Asian American–led multiethnic churches have to get "past race" in order to feel comfortable and gain a sense of belonging.

Asian American ministers cannot simply start a church as whites can establish a local church. Instead, if they want to reach out to their neighborhood, they must start a *multiethnic* congregation because their racial presence in the pulpit obviously makes the church different from the European American norm. Racial identity may eventually not matter to Christians as our society becomes more multiethnic, but race currently remains one of the organizing principles for congregations. The pastor of Dayspring describes how race now affects his church's growth:

> We want people to know that they don't have to be Asian to be Christian. We're proactive in who we hire and the language that we use. Not using illustrations that are Asian so that only Asian people get it. So we have to use illustrations that are universal, and that'll attract non-Asians.
>
> I don't want to be locked into and settling for homogeneous ministry. I want to keep pushing multiethnic ministry that's rooted in the gospel and let God bring the people. I see it happening overseas.

Whereas Asian American mainline Protestants complain that Christianity is too much of a "white man's religion," this minister ironically notes that "you don't have to be Asian to be Christian" in his church. To prove this point, he avoids racial and ethnic illustrations to attract non-Asians. He may hire non-Asian staff to represent the multiethnic vision of the church. Race not only influences his sermons and staff, but how he does ministry and builds church solidarity. As the face of Christianity changes both domestically and globally, the church today must deal with the same issue as the early church did in the book of Acts— how to affirm distinct group identities while maintaining church unity.[14]

Asian American Panethnicity and Identity

How can Asian American Christians affirm an authentic and distinct Asian American identity? Previous theories about ethnic and panethnic mobilization argue that congregations would adopt a Pan-Asian identity because cultural similarities, political benefits, or material interests tie people together. However, Asian Americans who have been educated in the United States and who work in professional positions have increasingly acculturated into the lifestyles of their class background. Asian American evangelical congregations assert that cultural distinctives in upbringing bond Asian Americans. Yet these churches respond more to the professional class of this group than to their distinctive cultural needs. They have tailored their church for urban professionals more characterized by their stressful careers and their busy lifestyles than by any ethnic traditions. Asian American mainline congregations assert that the political disenfranchisement and marginalization of minorities bring Asian Americans together. However, Asian Americans have faced difficulty in identifying specific community causes, whether civil rights issues or economic justice concerns, around which to organize and unite. To build an authentic identity, Asian American Christians must not only draw from the cultural or material interests of their members but also their *ideal* interests, such as their desires for meaning and their religious hopes (Weber 1958).

One "ideal interest" of Asian American ministers is to provide Asian American Christians with a calling and a sense of how God uses them as a distinct people. Unfortunately, pressures to become like white Americans, to interact with them, and to attend church with them, continue to make Asian Americans feel guilty if they remain in Pan-Asian congregations. One Pan-Asian, mainline church development started because its members felt excluded and isolated within white congregations. Yet its pastor mentions the mixed feelings his members possess:

> The thing is—and this is what I think is really funny—even our group was afraid to invite their Caucasian friends because they were afraid their friends would feel excluded or isolated in the church. But that's why they started our [Asian American] church in the first place! A lot of white churches don't feel bad being white. Why do we feel bad being Asian? White churches look around and no one says, "How come we don't have more Latinos or African Americans here?" So I try to get them to quit feeling guilty about stuff like that.

Instead of comparing Asian Americans to white ethnic Americans as the standard, I understand the group Asian Americans as a new, hybridized whole (Lowe 1996). By placing Asian Americans at the center of analysis, questions about cultural preservation, assimilation, accommodation, and marginalization become moot. All these processes occur simultaneously. What is more significant and interesting in this story is the self-definition, narrative understandings, and expression of this group identity.

The institutionalization of Pan-Asian churches offers space for the positive acceptance of an Asian American identity and the affirmation of a distinct calling. By having the freedom and resources to explore their identity, ministers and their congregations can generate new subcultures that truly express their faith and hopes. Asian American symbolic identity, although rooted in the structural marginalized experience of Asians in American society, is not necessarily an identity of victimization or alienation. Instead, ministers repeatedly claim that God gifts Asian Americans with unique heritages and experiences. Even though he leads a multiethnic congregation, this pastor notes that ignoring his ethnic roots or racial background would be inauthentic:

> I asked how the jazz group Hiroshima started with traditional Asian scales and instruments, and blended it with American jazz instruments, and you have this definite Asian American sound. And they have a multiethnic audience. He said, "The first thing that had to happen was that we had to be down with who we were first. If we showed up with our taiko drum and felt very apologetic about not being the typical American drum, no one would want to jam with us."
>
> I feel that as any group moves more down the road toward multi-Asian, multiethnic, you can't ignore exploring the roots, and the meaning, and even the redeeming of your cultural identity. Because that's what you need to bring to the table. That's what you need to bring to the jam session.

In the process of binding people together with both panethnic and faith-based ties, Asian American congregations provide creative space to pursue their calling. As they meet together, members can explore their common backgrounds and interpret their experiences. Hopefully, they can creatively memorialize and celebrate their faith journey so that "they are down with who they are" and who God made them. In evangelizing other Asian Americans, in promoting justice for Asian Americans, and in offering culturally relevant worship and ministry, Pan-Asian churches do have a distinct call and identity.

Asian American Panethnicity and Community

The calling to be a distinct people of God not only provides an affirming and redemptive identity but also binds people together. As Asian American Christians partner in the task of the gospel, they find fellowship in their shared fate and liberation in their common hopes. Although Asian American mainline and evangelical ministers remain in separate institutional networks, they have much to teach each other about the creation of community in an urban, postindustrial environment. Mainline ministers recognize the importance of reactive solidarity and the church as a sanctuary. Evangelicals see the need for face-to-face community that offers healing and intimacy. Both must fight against the individualism and fragmentation caused by our postmodern, capitalist society and base community around more stable, transcendent values.

The comfort level that Asian Americans experience in their churches is one of safety. This feeling of connectedness is partly a reactive solidarity in which members escape from the alienation or marginalization experienced on the outside. Mainline ministers often point out the need for a safe space where people can belong and feel free from racism and being considered different. For those who suffer from the impact of racist policies or distorted media images, PAUMC provides opportunities to name, confront, and challenge inequalities and injustice. A minister from another mainline congregation summarizes this need to come together:

> A whole set of racial needs have to do with understanding who you are over against American racism, America's picture of who you are. Each person has a need to counter the American view that race determines worth. That's a set of racial needs that everybody has.

Along with reacting to racism, the church that proactively seeks justice is drawn together by shared fate.

The Asian American church is not only a sanctuary for the community but also a healing place. As Asian American evangelicals explore their common upbringing and marginalization, they have developed approaches and ministries to bring wholeness to members. For those scarred from difficult family situations, GFC offers understanding and hope for restoration. An evangelical minister notes how community can bring about wholeness:

> The work ethic is very strong in Asian culture. But it also adds to the lack of relationship between parent and child. They're very well off materially but the kids are emotionally starved. When you talk about community and communication, the clash of culture, that's an alienation issue. We are alienated from God. We are also alienated from ourselves and alienated from one another.
>
> I would teach the necessity of reconciliation to overcome alienation. And I would teach love, the expression of love, and the sacrificial nature of love. If we structure a church as a community that reflects those values, that's preventative and has a healing nature.

Through this reconciliation process, the church builds community through shared hopes of transformation.

The danger for the Asian American Christian community is to become too inward and self-satisfied. As people who generally have attained a high level of affluence and enjoy career mobility, the lifestyle orientation and group patterns of those in Asian American churches promotes self-sufficiency and a sense of worldly entitlement.[15] While the church may call out for compassion and social justice, Asian American church members who are professionals too easily develop privatized lives that can shut out the cries of the poor. They can compartmentalize their lives so that they simultaneously pursue capital accumulation through the workplace and therapeutic righteousness in their spiritual lives without noting the contradictions between their two worlds. Beyond wholeness from personal oppression, the Asian American community must repent of its own complicity in the increasing polarization between the rich and the poor. Given that the socioeconomic status of many Asian American churches is professional and upwardly mobile, they must develop more just relationships with others. This process of group repentance might also bring about revival, effect structural change, and restore community.

Finally, the Asian American church also can be the home for a creative, liberating community as it looks eschatologically into the future. In forging new worship styles and liturgies, ministry programs, and small groups, Asian American church members can look to their past and present to imagine a new, beloved community. In their heritages and traditions, in their talents and experiences, Asian Americans are rich with resources to theologize, critique, and express new ways of relating in this world. For example, the anthology *Realizing the America of Our Hearts: Theological Voices of Asian Americans,* edited by Fumitaka Matsuoka and Eleazar Fernandez (2003), offers numerous, creative essays that elaborate on concepts such as *han* (frustrated hope), the *tao* (the way), and *tam tai* (three elements of reality) to provide hermeneutic lenses that are both Asian and American. These insights not only build Asian American communities but also can contribute to the broader church's understanding of God and the sacred.[16]

Asian Americans in Multiethnic America

If Asian American communities invest in the explorations of their heritage, interpret their experiences through scriptures with both the eyes of the privileged and the marginalized, and share their resources and talents in the promotion of justice, then they do have something to offer that is distinct and authentic. Rather than organizing around a difference based solely on identity, they can develop a different cultural viewpoint that is to be shared with others. But will racism and racialization prove to be insurmountable so that Americans remain divided by faith? Asian American ministers explain that true multiculturalism involves sharing gifts and burdens, as well as racial reconciliation and empowerment.

As Asian Americans lead Pan-Asian and multiethnic congregations, they want to avoid tokenizing other ethnic groups and instead actively include those on the "niche edges." As minorities in broader society, Asian Americans are sensitive to patronizing multiculturalism. One minister describes her desire for true partnership:

> [The denomination] always does this stupid stuff about, "Oh, let's make the Chinese pastor pray in Chinese!" and we'll all get a sense of our oneness.

But you know, it wasn't real and I feel all this stuff happens on the surface and there's not real partnership. It's the same people who lead and the same people who run the economics and the same people who are up front.

Instead of patronizing others, Asian American ministers of multiethnic congregations recognize they must share their power to shape their corporate culture. They are therefore conscious of identifying the people on the margins as members of their own extended family:

> If you're trying to move into multiethnicity, those who are in power to shape and name the corporate identity and corporate culture have to have an awakening to the presence of people that we're marginalizing. I try to bring them and their culture into the mix. So that they can see that they're more than tolerated. They're welcomed and invited to make this evolving culture reflect some of who they are.
>
> I'd be reading the *LA Times* and reading this article on WW II Filipino war veterans who are trying to take action against the U.S. government because they never gave them the veterans benefits. Before I would never read the story. Now I think, there are Filipinos in my own extended family, Filipino people in my church. I need to feel this pain, I need to understand this issue.

Just as racial identity may marginalize people, embracing the racial identities of church members can build a congregation's unity and strengthen its worship of God.

Racial reconciliation, then, involves the bearing of minority group burdens, the development and sharing of group gifts, and the use of power to serve others. The pastors recognize that this type of multiculturalism that includes Asian Americans requires divine grace:

> The idea out there is that there is no racism outside of black/white relations. But what does reconciliation look like when it's not black and white?
>
> It's a pain, it's a hassle to do multiethnicity. You have the power dynamics, you have racism issues, and you have the spiritual dynamic. We're going up against the strongest demonic force in America—slavery. Our battle isn't against flesh and blood. It's a challenge, but the church can do something that the world can't.

These ministers acknowledge that without God's grace, both personal sins, damaged group relations, and structural racism cannot be overcome.

"The church can do something the world can't." It has brought together Chinese and Japanese American Christians, along with other Asian groups despite their traditional enmity and their American acculturation. As they come together in sacred spaces, they can develop new eyes to see and new ears to hear. Asian American panethnicity is still emerging so that its subculture is as of yet inchoate. But new generations of Asian American churches offer the opportunity to establish affirming and redemptive identities. It provides the space for grace-filled modes of worship, authentic cultural expression, and liberated community. And as Asian American churches develop just patterns of lifestyle and action, they can offer the racial reconciliation our society desperately needs. These can be Asian American offerings of faith to America's table of multiculturalism.

APPENDIX A: RESEARCH METHODOLOGY

I initially conducted forty-four interviews with ministers of Chinese, Japanese, and Pan-Asian American congregations in the San Francisco Bay Area in 1996 and 1997. The Chinese American ministers were randomly selected from a list of 158 Chinese congregations prepared by Dr. James Chuck in his *Exploratory Study of the Growth of Chinese Protestant Congregations* (1996). I interviewed twenty ministers of the 86 Chinese American congregations that had English-speaking services. The 1995 Northern California Japanese American Religious Federation listing identified eighteen Japanese American Christian churches in the Bay Area. I interviewed nine of these ministers. Through these interviews, I believe I received a fairly representative sample of Chinese and Japanese American churches.

Midway through these initial interviews, I noticed a trend toward Asian American panethnicity. Not only were ministers establishing new Pan-Asian churches, but also some identified their historically Chinese or Japanese congregations as Asian American. I then sought out and interviewed ministers of Pan-Asian congregations, including those started by Korean American, Filipino American, and European American ministers. Twenty-two of the initial forty-four interviews were with pastors of Pan-Asian churches; two of the Asian American ministers had Pan-Asian congregations with a multiethnic focus.

My interview sessions with the ministers usually lasted ninety minutes to two hours. Besides asking about their congregation's history, demographics, and ministries, I would ask about the pastor's sense of calling and his or her views on ethnicity, race, and theology. I would also question them about the issues facing their members regarding politics, community concerns, gender and family, and work.

Interviews with the ministers revealed a trend toward panethnicity, as well as differences between fundamentalists, evangelicals, and mainline liberal thinking. From these interviews, I created ideal types, or composite portraits, of ethnic congregations, evangelical Pan-Asian congregations, mainline Pan-Asian congregations, and multiethnic congregations. The descriptions of these congregations came from site observations and interviews. No one church corresponded fully to the characteristics of the types, but they are useful for comparison purposes and for illustrating the consequences of church discourses and organizational logics.

To investigate new Asian American congregations and the religious construction of race, I chose two churches. The evangelical one, Grace Faith Church, was the largest Pan-Asian church in the Bay Area at the time. I attended services, small groups, conferences, and ministry activities at this church from 1996 through 1997. In collaboration with the church board of directors, I conducted two church censuses and shared these findings with them. The mainline congregation, Park Avenue United Methodist Church, was the most active Pan-Asian congregation in terms of political and community issues. I attended this congregation from 1998 through 1999 and observed services, community meetings, and festivals. Again, I conducted a church census to gather data on church demographics and faith practices. I also facilitated the church's long-term planning process, which culminated in the church's vision statement and five-year plan. The long-term relationships that I have with members of the two congregations, the participatory action research, and the commitment I have to Asian American churches aided in providing an insider perspective.

Since 2000, when I completed my dissertation, more Asian American–led, multiethnic congregations have been planted. I had two multiethnic congregations in my original sample, but I wanted to add the perspective of those promoting multiethnicity for the conclusion. Through snowball sampling, I interviewed four ministers of this type of church in the Bay Area and two other ministers who are recognized leaders of this movement. I have visited five of these congregations for their worship services, including Dayspring Church's Sunday worship and a small group meeting.

My current home church involvement reflects my theological beliefs and political orientation. I attend New Hope Covenant Church, an evangelical, multiethnic congregation that ministers to a low-income neighborhood. My own background certainly colors this research, but I hope that I have given Asian American ministers and their congregations voice within this book.

APPENDIX B: DESCRIPTIONS OF CONGREGATIONS

TABLE 1

Ethnicity of Ministers

Ethnicity of Minister	Type of Congregation				Number of Ministers
	Chinese American	Japanese American	Asian American	Multiethnic	
Chinese American	13		13	4	30
Japanese American	1	4	3		8
European American	1	1	3		5
Korean American			2	3	5
Filipino American			1	1	2
Total	15	5	22	8	50

TABLE 2

Theology of Ministers

Theology of Minister	Type of Congregation				Number of Ministers
	Chinese American	Japanese American	Asian American	Multiethnic	
Fundamentalist	2				2
Evangelical	7	2	18	7	34
Mainline	6	3	4	1	14
Total	15	5	22	8	50

Note: Theologies of ministers may differ from that of their congregations, especially when ministers are short-term hires.

TABLE 3

Ages of Congregations

| | Type of Congregation | | | | | |
| | Chinese | Japanese | Originally Ethnic-Specific, Now Asian | Asian | Multi- | |
Ages of Congregations	American	American	American	American	ethnic	Total
Before 1950	7	5	8	0		20
1951–1970	1					1
1971–1980	4		1	0		5
1981–1990	1		5	2	1	9
1990–2000	2			6	3	11
2000–present					4	4
Total	15	5	14	8	8	50

TABLE 4

Size of Congregations

| | Type of Congregation | | | | |
| Size of | Chinese | Japanese | Asian | Multi- | |
Congregations	American	American	American	ethnic	Total
< 100	7	3	10	3	26
100–199	3	1	4	2	9
> 200	5	1	8	3	15
Total	15	5	22	8	50

TABLE 5

Denominational Affiliation

	Type of Congregation				
Denomination	Chinese American	Japanese American	Asian American	Multi-ethnic	Total Number
Independent	5		7	2	14
Presbyterian USA	1		4	1	6
Southern Baptist	2		3		5
American Baptist	1	1	2	1	5
Methodist	1	2	1		4
Evangelical Covenant				3	3
Cumberland Presbyterian			1	1	2
Episcopal	2				2
Holiness		1	1		2
Interdenominational			2		2
United Church of Christ	1	1			2
Alliance	1				1
Catholic	1				1
Free Methodist			1		1
Total	15	5	22	8	50

TABLE 6

Location of Congregations

County	Chinese American	Japanese American	Asian American	Multi-ethnic	Total Number
San Francisco	6	2	3	2	13
San Mateo	1		4		5
Contra Costa	1		4		5
Alameda	5	2	8	3	18
Santa Clara	2	1	3	1	7
Total	15	5	22	6	48

Note: Two ministers interviewed had congregations outside of the Bay Area.

NOTES

PREFACE

1. The YaoMingMania.com Web site self-describes itself as "100% dedicated to Yao Ming's life in the NBA." In its first five months of its existence, 532 members joined and posted more than 3,100 articles. One forum, "Yao's Impact on the Asian Community," addresses Yao's impact on Asian culture and business. *PC Magazine* rated it as one of the "Top 5 Sports Nuts Sites."

2. This topic generated eighty-two responses within two months of being posted.

3. Recent anthologies that have begun to provide a better portrait of Asian American religions include Carnes and Yang (2004), Iwamura and Spickard (2003), and Min and Kim (2002). For a sociological review of the role of religion in Asian American communities, see Chen and Jeung (2000).

4. See also I. Chang (2003), Nakao (2003), and Warren (2003).

5. I worked for Mayor Art Agnos in San Francisco and council member John Russo in Oakland and have engaged in community organizing with Cambodian Americans and Latinos for the past decade.

6. For example, my neighborhood church has only about fifty members but nine different Asian ethnic groups represented. In 2000, the church helped two hundred tenants, mostly Cambodian and Latino, win a major housing settlement.

7. Like other Asians in the United States, Yao Ming has suffered from anti-Asian racial taunts. Opposing star center Shaquille O'Neal employed a fake Chinese accent to say, "Tell Yao Ming, 'Ching-chong-yang-wah-ah-soh.'" Yao Ming ignored the taunt and appealed for greater cross-cultural understanding. See Erwin (2003) and Roberts (2003).

CHAPTER 1.   INTRODUCTION

1. *Banzai* is a patriotic battle cry. Story cited in Hayashi (1995).

2. In Chuck's (2003) collection of stories by sixty-four Chinese Americans who attended First Chinese Baptist Church in San Francisco, half made references to World War II and its effect on their lives.

3. See Tu (2002), Kim (2001), Tran (1999), and Tran and Cha (1998).

4. I define the term *Asian American* as any American of Asian descent. In the 2000 U.S. Census, persons answering the race question could check off as Asian Indian, Chinese, Filipino, Japanese, Korean, Vietnamese, Native Hawaiian, Guamanian, Chamorro, or Samoan. In addition, persons can identify as "Other Asian." Asian American panethnic congregations are those that ministers self-define as Asian American.

5. Even today, Chinese and Japanese Americans have conflicting views of the Japanese invasion of China in the 1930s. Interestingly, in 1999 Japanese American California state legislator Mike Honda wrote legislation calling Japan to apologize for wartime atrocities. See Lochner (2003), Lieser and Lin (2001), Wong (1999), and Nakao (1998).

6. Dr. William Speer founded the Presbyterian Church in Chinatown in 1852, and Kanichi Miyama established Pine United Methodist Church in 1879. Both churches, originally located in Chinatown, continue to meet in San Francisco. In fact, the first panethnic congregation of Chinese and Japanese converts met within the Methodist Chinese mission in San Francisco Chinatown from 1877 to 1885. Immigrant converts met for a monthly English-language worship service until the mission work was divided in 1885. At the time of division, the mission had worked with upwards of three thousand Chinese and two to three hundred Japanese. See Pang (1995, 10–16), Suzuki (1991, 113–134), and Woo (1983).

7. Estimates of the number of Korean American churches in the United States range from 3,500 to 4,000 congregations (see J. H. Kim 2002).

8. According to the American Religious Identification Survey 2001, 21.1 percent of Asian Americans identified as Catholic. Agnostics or those claiming " no religion" was the second largest group at 20.2 percent, making Asian Americans the most secular of all racial groups. However, the nature of Asian popular religiosity makes their identification with particular religious traditions problematic. Protestants (9.6 percent), Buddhists (9.1 percent), Christians (5.8 percent), and Muslims (5.2 percent) were the other large groupings.

9. I use the term *Christian churches* to include Catholic and Protestant congregations but exclude sects such as the Church of Latter Day Saints and Jehovah's Witnesses. Statistics on weekly participation are derived from estimates from my interviews and Chuck (1996).

10. In fact, 55.6 percent of the second generation Nisei and 35.2 percent of the third generation Sansei belong to a Japanese American church or temple while only 3.5 percent and 3.7 percent respectively belong to a non-Japanese or Asian American church (Fugita and O'Brien 1991).

11. From a 1993–94 study of 1,043 Asian Americans in Los Angeles County, Lien (2001) reports that 25 percent of Chinese Americans attend church, as compared to 16 percent who participate in the PTA and 14 percent who are involved with business/professional organizations. Recreational clubs and sports (21 percent) ranked first among groups that Japanese Americans participate in, followed by church (19 percent), business/professional (18 percent), and ethnic/cultural organizations (18 percent).

12. Jung Ha Kim (2002, 205) writes that "the fact that over 70 percent of one million Korean Americans are faithfully attending their own 3,500 churches every Sunday deserves recognition."

13. Even Asian Americans joke about the number of Asian American student fellowships. In the film, *Better Luck Tomorrow*, white students taunted a group of Asian Americans crashing a party by laughing, "The Bible study is next door." See also Chang (2000).

14. The reemergence of ethnicity and of conflicts between ethnic groups remains both a theoretical and ideological concern for social scientists and policy makers. See Keyes (1981), Kivisto (1989), Omi and Winant (1994), and Yancey, Ericksen, and Juliani (1976).

15. I utilize concepts from Hechter (1987) and Olzak (1992) for these working definitions of group and ethnic solidarity.

16. In her study of Italian immigrants in Buffalo, New York, Virginia Yans-McLaughlin writes that this one ethnic group established over one hundred clubs and organizations, mostly along existing kin and friendship ties, in the 1920s. Coming from sixteen different Italian provinces, this local community was so internally divided that leaders had to organize for ten years before they could establish a united Confederation of Italian Societies. John Bodnar provides another example of the regional, social basis of religious organizations. He cites that between 1874 and 1914, Providence, Rhode Island, was the home of twenty-four separate Orthodox Jewish congregations based on homeland localities. Jon Gjerde also argues that Norwegian immigrants separated into different church communities based on place of origin even if they shared the same pastor. See Bodnar (1985), Gjerde (1985), and Yans-McLaughlin (1977).

17. Having interviewed 524 contemporary whites, Richard Alba concludes that ethnic identities tend to be reflected in some experiences that are seen as ethnic but that "the kinds and qualities of these experiences are highly variable." As ethnicity becomes more of an individual choice, Alba does not believe that religious organizations will be able to maintain ethnicity. He finds that the "broad ethnic effects of ethnic membership organizations appear small" and that "combinations of ethnic and religious identities were not very common." Symbolic ethnicity does not seem to provide a strong basis for the development or even maintenance of ethnic organizations (see Alba 1990, 296, 304).

18. In the 1970s, Asian Indians won the right to be included in the Asian and Pacific American category for the 1980 census. They wanted minority classification and the right to participate in federally funded programs. From 1950 to 1970, Asian Indians had to mark "Other" (see Espiritu 1992).

19. Testimony of Mr. William Tamayo at the Assembly Committee on Elections and Reapportionment, Sacramento, CA, hearing, 23 April 1991.

20. Min suggests that Vietnamese have cultural similarities to other East Asian groups because of their Confucian roots but does not discuss where other Southeast Asians fit in his East Asian/South Asian panethnic groupings.

21. Lien et al. (2003) surveyed 1,218 adults of Chinese, Filipino, Japanese, Korean, South Asian, and Vietnamese descents in the metropolitan areas of Los Angeles, New York, Honolulu, San Francisco, and Chicago.

22. Portes and Rumbaut note that high school students who identified as "Asian American" rose from 0.3 percent in 1992 to 4.5 percent in 1996 (Portes and Rumbaut 2001).

23. Ricourt and Danta (2003) find an opposite gendered effect in their study of Latino panethnicity. They suggest that Latinas identify more panethnically because they are more concerned than the men about their children's opportunities in the United States. Further, they view panethnic organizing as critical to improving these opportunities. On the other hand, Latinos are more likely to hold transnational identities rooted in their places of origins. Asian women, perhaps, remain more tied to their ethnic culture than Asian men and are less likely to identify as Pan-Asian.

24. In contrast, critical factors affecting Hispanic panethnic identification include Spanish language, geographic concentration, class, and gender. See Kao and Joyner (2001), Ricourt and Danta (2002), and Rosenfeld (2001, 263–276).

25. Omi and Winant (1994) borrow from Antonio Gramsci's (1971) concept of "organic intellectuals" and theorize that leaders of racial movements carry out the task of "racial rearticulation."

26. For example, Martin Luther King Jr. rallied African Americans around the ideas of the

"promised land" and "beloved community," Christian symbols understood as black liberation and interracial fellowship. Religion provides the primary symbolic source for group solidarity (Durkheim 1915).

27. For ethnographies on how popular religious practices highlight certain group experiences, see Brown (1991), Constable (1994), and Orsi (1985).

28. Mia Tuan suggests that Asian Americans who congregate in nonethnic activities, such as volleyball, do so to maintain a meaningful, distinct identity. She writes, "What is different is the intent involved in coming together. Those who join ethnic clubs and organizations are consciously choosing to do so because they place value on associating with others like themselves based on the perception of common upbringing and even experiences with marginalization" (Tuan 1998, 166).

   Furthermore, Lillian Rubin suggests that symbolic ethnicity does have consequences on the daily lives of racial minorities: "Symbols, after all, become symbolic precisely because they have meaning. In this case, the symbol has meaning at two levels: one is the personal and psychological, the other is social and political" (Rubin 1994, 179).

29. Organizational logics are imperatives that shape and constrain the development and culture of an institution, as well as the definition of a people. Both material practices, such as worship styles or evangelism techniques, and symbolic systems, such as theologies, constitute these logics (see Friedland and Alford 1991, 232–263).

30. The evangelical "symbolic universe," also known as the "cultural toolkit," includes the symbols, concepts, and resources evangelicals use to understand the world. See Emerson and Smith (2000), Swidler (1986, 273–286), and Wood (2002).

31. The widely accepted definition of American contemporary evangelicalism is that it possesses three tenets: (1) the literal interpretation of scripture, (2) a born-again experience, and (3) the commitment to converting others. See Smith (1998).

32. I grouped ministers as belonging to the mainline through their self-identification, their denomination or tradition (United Methodist, Presbyterian USA, Episcopal, American Baptist, or Catholic), and a theological orientation that differs from evangelicals.

CHAPTER 2.   CHINESE AND JAPANESE CHURCHES IN THE UNITED STATES

1. Pseudonyms of churches and ministers are employed throughout this book to protect their anonymity and confidentiality. Chinese Grace Church is one of the oldest Chinese American congregations in San Francisco's East Bay.

2. I create ideal types of ethnic, Pan-Asian, and multiethnic congregations by selecting and accentuating certain elements of these churches. Similarly, I compare ideal types of evangelical and mainline churches, but no one congregation fully corresponds to the ideal types. Appendix A reviews the methodology by which I identified the congregations in this study. Appendix B includes tables of the congregational identities, ministers' theologies, congregational ages, congregational sizes, and congregations' denominations.

3. Transnational theory posits that migrants maintain multiple relations across borders (Basch, Schiller, and Blanc 1994; Hu-Dehart 1999). Historian Madeline Hsu notes that another religious impetus for Chinese to maintain transnational connections was the desire to be buried with ancestors (see Hsu 2000).

4. Fumitaka Matsuoka argues: "To become Christian, to a certain extent, was to become American. To be American was to become Christian. This was true particularly in the

early days of the Asian immigration to the U.S. . . . . Asian Americans then viewed the churches as a major route and catalyst towards assimilation" (Matsuoka 1995, 16).

5. Hayashi (1995) theorizes that the social and political reforms made by the Meiji government in the 1860s and 1870s dismantled the feudal structure in which the samurai class held power. In search for stability and a new ethic toward which they could place their neo-Confucian loyalties, many samurai converted to Christianity.

6. Ira Condit, Methodist missionary to the Chinese in San Francisco, wrote: "[The] study of English in the Sunday School, as well as contact with Christian people and with our civilization, has brought still more into a new world, and made them into new men. It has even improved their personal appearance, and has put a new light into their countenances. When a Chinaman once learns English, he can never be the same man that he was before" (Condit 1900, 107).

7. This rate of conversion of Chinese in the United States roughly equals the percentage of Christians in China during this time.

8. Jee Gam preached that Christianity was not a white man's religion but the means for universal and national redemption. He wrote, "And by faith I venture to say right here that China will, before long, become a Christian country, and rank high when compared with all her sister nations" (Gam 1880, 311).

9. Anti-Japanese legislation at the time included 1907 Gentleman's Agreement, which limited Japanese labor immigration; the 1913 California Alien Land Act, which forbade Issei from purchasing land; and the 1924 Immigration Act, which barred all Asians from entering.

10. Timothy Smith argues that instead of looking backward toward the old country or toward homeland politics, religious leaders primarily looked forward into the future to define group boundaries. They redefine peoplehood by including more people from various regional and linguistic backgrounds and excluding those who do not belong religiously (Smith 1978, 1115–1186).

11. Judy Yung (1995), in examining the sociohistorical forces that explain social change for Chinese American women, argues that Chinese nationalism and Christianity had the greatest impact on Chinese immigrant women.

12. Paul Spickard (1996, 82) also suggests that Nisei were attracted to Christian churches more than to Buddhist temples because the former "was identified with American culture." By the 1930s, 15 to 20 percent of the Issei identified as Christians and about 90 percent of these Christians had converted after coming to the United States.

13. Interestingly, Chinese ministers also failed to eliminate social ills confronting Chinatown, such as gambling (see Cayton and Lively 1955).

14. Buddhist temples also adopted Americanized congregational forms, complete with hymnals, pews, and Sunday schools. See Horinouchi (1973) and Kashima (1977).

15. Assimilation theorist Betty Lee Sung, in evaluating the fate of ethnic churches for Chinese Americans during the 1950s and 1960s on the mainland, saw an ethnic institution in decline. Second-generation Chinese American Christians sought to attend church for religious reasons, not social ones. She suggested the generational changes exemplified a cultural shift toward acculturation and structural assimilation (see Sung 1967).

16. Fugita and O'Brien (1991) found that 69 percent of Japanese Americans belonged to at least one ethnic association. In contrast, only 2 percent of native-born whites belong to ethnic organizations (see Alba 1990).

17. Lien et al. (2003) found that their respondents were more likely to identify as ethnic Americans if they held U.S. citizenship status and were older. Interestingly, those who had greater social integration with close white friends also chose to claim this identity for reasons similar to those described here.

18. Confucian ethics value *xiao*, or filial piety, as a central way of relating within the family. *Ren*, or human compassion, is to be developed in all relationships and may be self-cultivated through education (see Tu 1994).

19. Fenggang Yang (1999) persuasively asserts that Chinese Christians maintain "adhesive identities" by selectively adhering American, Chinese, and Christian identities into one whole. Christians preserve Confucian cultural characteristics as a moral system but reject Buddhist beliefs as pagan. Churches reinforce and reconstruct Confucian values in the American context by providing an authoritative source to legitimate filial piety, education, and hard work.

20. Fugita and O'Brien (1991) write that *iemoto* encourages superior-subordinate relationships, harmony, and mutual interdependence that is adaptive in the United States.

21. Asian American scholars are fond of attacking the model minority thesis by noting that the class and educational backgrounds of new Asian immigrants, along with the exploitation of family labor, explains the perceived success of Asians in the United States. Asian American families live in regions with higher costs of living and higher salaries and have more members contributing to household income so that their incomes are on par with whites. However, Asian Americans tend to make less than whites given their educational achievement and many Asian Americans remain under the poverty level. Frank Wu (2002) cites more than fifty articles discrediting the model minority thesis in the chapter "The Model Minority: Asian American Success as Race Relations Failure."

22. Nazli Kibria (2002, 162) explains that distilled ethnicity also provides a symbolic ethnic function of establishing identity without specific behavioral commitments: "Distilled ethnicity, then, suggests a passed down ethnicity that meshes easily with established notions of a mainstream middle-class American lifestyle and sensibility."

23. Other ethnic churches meet this cultural function. See Almirol (1985), Hurh and Chung (1990), and Warner and Wittner (1998).

24. The Roman Catholic church appointed Monsignor Ignatius Wang, the first Asian American bishop of an archdiocese in the nation. A *San Francisco Chronicle* news article states, "Wang is the inspired choice of ruling San Francisco Archbishop William Levada—and it's political as well as spiritual." See Plate (2002) and Rubenstein (2002).

CHAPTER 3.   THE EMERGENCE AND INSTITUTIONALIZATION
OF ASIAN AMERICAN CHURCHES

1. As described in the introduction, Pan-Asian churches make up about 10 percent of the predominantly Chinese and Japanese churches in the San Francisco Bay Area.

2. Within the church, forms and structures are difficult to change since "religion has been the historically most widespread and effective instrumentality of legitimation" Berger (1967, 32). For example, Nancy Ammerman's (1987) ethnographic study of fundamentalists describes a church's practices that legitimate their own understandings of themselves in opposition to the outside world. Through their rituals, the

church is able to maintain a world that seems contrary to modern and postmodern sensibilities.

3. Unfortunately, there has been a dearth of new understandings of congregations as organizations, possibly because theologians tend to see secular studies of organized religion as profaning the sacred spirit of religion (see Demerath et al. 1998 and Stout and Cormode 1998, 62–78). Margaret Harris (1998, 307) laments, "scholars seeking an understanding of how congregations are organized do not have a readily identifiable body of literature to draw upon.

4. Although immigration policies have become stricter, researchers still predict the Asian American population to reach twenty million in the year 2020 (see Ong and Hee 1993).

5. During the 1995–1996 school year, more than 180 community and school representatives met for over a year to develop the district's value statement. It says simply, "We believe our schools and community must acknowledge and respect diversity" (Santa Clara Unified School District Web site, http://www.scu.k12.ca.us/purpose/purpose3.html).

6. Office of Student Research Web site, at http://osr.berkeley.edu.

7. Asian/Pacific American organizations make up 23 percent of the student organizations registered with the U.C. Berkeley Student Activities and Services office (http://www.uga.berkeley.edu/sas/stdgrplst.htm).

8. Of U.C. Berkeley's 735 officially recognized student organizations, 213 are cultural or ethnic related (see Chao 1998b).

9. In 1980, 76 Asian Americans held federal, state, or local offices in California. By 1998, 129 held office, an increase of 70 percent. Other changes in Asian American political clout include more officials elected to higher offices, greater ethnic representation of Asian American officials, and the establishment of more equitable representation of API officials in areas with high Asian American concentrations. However, the gap between Asian Americans running and those winning remained the same (see Lien 2001b).

10. See Wildermuth (1998) and McLeod and Guira (1998). On the other hand, Paul Ong and David Lee (2002, 65) write, "Little is known about whether ethnic-oriented voting among Asian immigrants extends to pan-Asian oriented voting. Pan-Asian solidarity at this time is more of a possibility than a reality for Asian immigrant voters." Similarly, Wu and Youngberg note the generational, class, religious, and transnational differences that pose obstacles to Pan-Asian political solidarity. See Wu and Youngberg (2002).

11. For a discussion of this issue, see Taylor (1994).

12. The proportion of Asian Americans who state that they have no religious affiliation, about one in five, is just above the general proportion of those who affiliate with no religion in the U.S. West (Kosmin and Lachman 1993).

13. The broader religious world of evangelicals and mainline churches are known as "institutional or organizational fields" in sociological literature. They are "groups or organizations producing similar products or services include as well their critical exchange partners, sources of funding, regulatory groups, professional or trade associations, and other sources of normative and cognitive influence" (Scott 1998, 173).

14. American Christians fall into two basic groups with mainline, liberal, and progressive Christians within one institutional field and conservatives, evangelicals, charismatics,

and fundamentalists within another. This two-party thesis is helpful in understanding the divergent expressions of Asian American panethnic congregations. See Hunter (1991), Marty (1981, 1998), Roof (1993), Warner (1988), and Wuthnow (1988).

15. The Joint Strategy and Action Committee of the Presbyterian USA adopted a resolution calling for more Asian American representation in the denomination in 1972. Similarly, the National Conference on the Concerns of Asian Americans and Pacific Islanders in the United Church of Christ endorsed Asian American leadership development. By 1977, the following denominations had officially recognized national caucuses, offices, or staff persons to deal with Asian American ministries: American Baptist (Asian American Baptist Caucus), Presbyterian USA (Asian Presbyterian Caucus), United Methodist (National Federation of Asian American United Methodists), United Church of Christ (Pacific American and Asian American Ministries of the UCC), Episcopal Church (Episcopal Asian American Strategies Task Force), Reformed Churches of America (Asian Office), Disciples of Christ (North American Pacific Asian Disciples), and the Evangelical Lutheran Church of America (Asian Ministries).

16. This center was later named the Pacific Asian Center for Theologies and Strategies (PACTS) to encourage the collaborative and intersecting work of Pacific Islander and Asian theologians. The center also developed specific strategies that would be more applicable for ministering to these groups than mainstream materials.

17. Normative pressures to become organizationally similar stem primarily from professionalization and standards set by the organizational field. See DiMaggio and Powell (1991).

18. *Mimetic isomorphism* refers to the tendency of organizations to mimic other organizations perceived to be successful. Even if the innovations do not prove to be effective in increasing church growth, they are still adopted to demonstrate that the ministers are trying to effect some kind of reform and to meet the demands of what potential members expect (DiMaggio and Powell 1983).

19. Intervarsity Christian Fellowship, through its publishing house, missions conferences, staff training, and urban missions, has made "racial reconciliation" one of its top priorities. The number of IVCF Asian American campus ministers has doubled from 1997 to 2003, and they now make up 10 percent of IVCF's staff nationwide. The last two Intervarsity Urbana Missions Conferences featured Asian American speakers.

20. Evergreen, when it cast its mission as an Asian American church, grew to 750 in ten years. Newsong grew to 3,500 members after its planting.

21. San Francisco County, for example, had 152,620 Chinese in the 2000 census, up from 82,480 in 1980. The Japanese American population declined from 12,046 in 1980 to 11,410 in 2000.

22. In California, only 30.2 percent of Chinese Americans but 67.5 percent of Japanese Americans are native-born (Lee 1998).

23. According to Lee (1998, 15), "Native-born Asians, especially Japanese, are largely integrated into the white majority community. Immigration continues to replenish the Asian immigrant community, however, and ensures the existence of Asian ethnic neighborhoods."

24. In an interesting ethnography of Japanese American beauty pageants and basketball leagues, Rebecca King (2002) hypothesizes another path for Japanese American institutions. Besides remaining ethnic specific or panethnic, they may become "transracial." As this group out-marries in high rates, Japanese Americanness is no longer

signified by a specific racial, physical appearance. Instead, with many *hapa* mixed race members, this ethnic group now has community debates over its symbolic boundaries and representations (King 2002).

25. Kao and Joyner (2001) found that Asian Americans held more panethnic friendships than Latinos did, even though more Latino groups spoke the same languages. Interestingly, Vietnamese Americans were the most panethnic of all ethnic groups, and parental educational level had no effect on panethnic sentiments.

26. There are 25.6 percent of Japanese Americans who marry outside of their ethnicity and 12.1 percent of Chinese Americans who marry outside of their ethnicity (Lee and Fernandez 1998).

27. The Japanese American church also faced conflicts between the Issei and Nisei generations over language used in service, control of church programs, and nationalist politics in the 1930s. Brian Hayashi (1995, 111) cites one Nisei woman who complains, "The young people don't care for the minister and he doesn't take much interest in them."

28. The cultural conflicts over roles and values faced by Asian Americans, especially the 1.5 and second generations, are common themes in their literature, films, and psychology texts. Asian American Christian publications that address cultural conflicts include Hertig 2002 and Lin 1995.

29. According to Nancy Ammerman (1991, 51), power within congregations involves the ability to "make decisions about how they will use the resources they have."

30. Michael Hannan and John Freeman (1977) identify internal and external constraints toward organizational adaptation applicable to traditionally ethnic specific congregations. These congregations are not likely to change because of their sunk costs, their limited information about innovations and demographic shifts, the vested interests of leaders, and the historic purposes of the church.

31. Michael Emerson and Christian Smith (2000) argue that the religious marketplace in the United States limits the extent that religious authorities can improve racial inequality. Ministers tend to embody the social location and concerns of their members because if they were too prophetic or challenging, their members would simply leave. Using the same argument, I suggest that Chinese and Japanese American ministers can only make changes toward Pan-Asian congregations that their members agree upon and approve.

CHAPTER 4. EVANGELICAL CONSTRUCTIONS
OF ASIAN AMERICAN PANETHNICITY

1. Fundamentalists subscribe to a literal interpretation of the biblical text, whereas evangelicals in this study vary in how they interpret different Bible passages. Fundamentalists differ in that they are more disengaged with society and separatist. Only two ministers in this study were fundamentalist, and they argued that ethnic-specific congregations are better tailored to evangelize to those who are co-ethnics.

2. Evangelicals understand that objective truth and ethical principles come from the Bible, an external source of authority. Postmodernity has challenged this understanding of truth so that Wade Clark Roof writes, "No religious issue separates boomers more than the question of religious authority. Is the locus of authority within the self or outside the self?" (1993, 119).

3. Michael Emerson and Christian Smith (2000) argue that evangelicals' individualistic and pietistic theology neglects structural systems and thereby reinforces racial inequalities in society.

4. Contextualization, according to evangelicals, involves making the Christian gospel relevant to a culture through use of its songs, language, and arts (see Warren 1995). Churches targeting Gen Xers, for example, emphasize more mystical elements in their worship because this group does not value scientific, objective truths and beliefs as much as older groups (see Flory and Miller 2000; Webber 2002).

5. As early as 1983, Hunter (1983) observed that over 12 percent of evangelical Christian books deal with psychology and emotional health. Mark Shibley (1996, 9), in his ethnographies of the Vineyard Christian Fellowship and Calvary Chapel, cites that "the religious culture in these congregations, mirroring the direction of change in the wider culture, is more individualistic and therapeutic than social and moralistic."

6. The Promise Keepers, an evangelical men's movement in the 1990s, targeted Asian Americans. One article promoting the organization stated that Asian Americans are "culturally trained with strong family values" and share a discomfort with too much "public vulnerability." This focus on family and therapeutic openness reflect the evangelical concern for such dynamics (see Yamamoto 1997).

7. Although recent evidence indicates that increasing educational and income levels of its members have tempered evangelical strictness, evangelicals continue to remain strong in their concern for the truth and the preaching of the truth (Hunter 1987; Shibley 1996; Smith 1998; Webber 2002).

8. Rick Warren (1995, 177) suggests "explosive growth occurs when the type of people in the community match the type of people that are already in the church, and they both match the type of person the pastor is."

9. Bill Hybels, whose church has grown from 100 to 15,000 since 1972, has written *Becoming a Contagious Christian* (1994) and *Rediscovering Church: The Story and Vision of Willow Creek Community Church* (1997). One of his strategies is that services should be designed especially for the seeker in which "everything from the music to the printed program is designed specifically for unchurched people. We minimize the cringe factor by maintaining excellence."

10. Rick Warren, whose church is recognized as the fastest-growing Baptist church in the history of the United States, has written *The Purpose-Driven Church* (1995) and *The Purpose-Driven Life* (2002).

11. Donald McGavran and C. Peter Wagner wrote *Understanding Church Growth* (Grand Rapids, MI: William B. Eerdmans Publishing, 1980).

12. One minister explains that this evangelism strategy for Asian Americans contrasts with how ethnic churches might draw new members. Whereas ethnic churches can rely on cultural bonds to draw in newcomers, Pan-Asians require bonds of friendship to make people feel connected: "If you're a Chinese who immigrates here and if you're looking for community, church is a good place to go. It's a place where you can find a lot of Chinese who get along with each other. That's a big draw. Evangelism has been easy—you just open the door and people come in."

13. Pastors refer to what they call "the Silent Exodus," a pattern described in the evangelical magazine *Christianity Today*, in which the second generation of Asian Americans leave the immigrant church because of its constrictions.

14. Ricourt and Dante also recognize that a common class background explains the for-

mation of Latino panethnicity. They argue, "The fact that Crona's Latinos are mainly working-class inhabitants of a working-class neighborhood further reinforces Latino panethnic interaction and identification" (2002, 2)

15. These affinity groups are much like what Bellah et al. (1985) coin "lifestyle enclaves." Linked most closely to leisure and consumption, a lifestyle enclave "brings together those who are socially, economically, or culturally similar and one of its chief aims is the enjoyment of being with those who 'share one's lifestyle.'" Perhaps the most distinguishing aspect of lifestyle enclaves is that they deal only with the individual's private life, their life of personal faith, networks of friends, and lifestyle affinities.

CHAPTER 5.   MAINLINE CHRISTIAN CONSTRUCTIONS OF ASIAN AMERICAN PANETHNICITY

1. Mia Tuan (1998) discusses these two Asian American stereotypes.

2. Dean Kelley (1972) includes the following denominations as the mainline: United Methodist, Episcopal, Presbyterian USA, Lutheran, and United Church of Christ.

3. Roof and McKinney group the Episcopal Church, the Presbyterian Church USA, and United Church of Christ (UCC) as liberal Protestants. Moderate Protestants include the United Methodists, Disciples of Christ, Northern Baptists, Lutherans, Reformed Churches (see Roof and McKinney 1987).

4. Smith (1998) suggests that the mainline or liberals consist of the United Methodists, Presbyterian Church USA, Episcopalians, UCC, Lutherans, Reformed Churches, and National Baptist (USA).

5. Similarly, Balmer and Winner (2002, 5) write that "evangelicals might talk about Jesus as their 'personal Lord and Savior,' but liberals generally eschew such language in favor of social concerns: civil rights, peace and justice, inclusive language, and acceptance of homosexuals, among other issues. Whereas evangelicals emphasize evangelism, bringing others into the fold, liberals talk about 'bearing witness' against evil in the world."

6. Of the mainline ministers in my sample, only four of the fourteen claimed an Asian American panethnic identity for their congregations. However, the other ministers also discussed the differences between ethnic and racial groupings, so I incorporated their interviews to construct mainline discourses on race.

7. Hoge et al. (1994, 115) conclude the following about the tenets of lay liberalism: "To sum up, lay liberals reject the view that Christianity is the only true religion. They differed in their views of what religious truth might be, but they agree that morality is an essential part of religion."

8. Similarly, Christian Smith (1998) in his survey of 2,591 churchgoing Protestants found that 91 percent of Fundamentalists and Evangelicals believed that "converting others is very important." In contrast, only 76 percent of mainline and liberal Christians assented to this statement.

9. Ann Swidler's (1986) conception of culture as a toolkit of resources and strategies that people employ is useful in this discussion of cultural transmission.

10. Asian American mainline theology takes as its starting point the grounded experiences of Asian Americans. This process may involve "the uncovering of painful stories," such as relating the pain of the Japanese American internment experience to one's relationship with God (see Ng 1996 and Yoshii 1996).

The oppression and exploitation of Asian American women is another issue that mainline ministers and theologians discussed (see Kim 1997 and Nakashima Brock 1996).

11. Roozen, McKinney, and Carroll (1985, 15) define religious presence as "simply the ways in which religion or the religious is manifest or present in a society." They typologize four types of church religious presence or mission: activist, citizen, sanctuary, and evangelist. I suggest that Asian American mainline churches are ethnic sanctuaries that also have activist/citizen orientations regarding racial issues.

12. A "theology of struggle" is Matsuoka's phrase to depict Asian American Christians' community-building efforts in the face of racism.

CHAPTER 6.   ASIAN AMERICAN PANETHNICITY AT GRACE FAITH CHURCH

1. Evergreen Baptist Church and Cerritos United Methodist Church are two congregations in Los Angeles that were formerly Japanese American and are now Asian American.

2. Evangelicals term groups with common cultural and linguistic practices as "people groups." Understanding the values and beliefs of people groups facilitates evangelistic or missionary efforts with them.

3. JEMS, the Japanese Evangelical Missions Society, is a nondenominational missions organization focusing on evangelizing Japanese, Japanese Americans, and Asian Americans. AACF stands for Asian American Christian Fellowship.

4. Church growth experts recognize that churches that have reached maximum seating capacity are unlikely to grow larger. Churches therefore seek larger facilities that allow room for growth.

5. The church's published history highlights the numerous evangelical workshops and conferences that shaped the church. These events for the congregation included a Prayer Partners Seminar (1991), a Willow Creek Community Church training (1994), a Saddleback Community Church training (1997), and the Bay Area Billy Graham Crusade (1997). Other conferences that the church sponsored but were not included in the official recent history are "Get Real: A Seminar on Relational Healing with God, Self and Others" (1997), the Asian American Men's Conference (1997, 1998) and "Living Free in Christ: A Workshop on Resolving Personal and Spiritual Conflicts" (1998).

6. In an ethnography of another Pan-Asian congregation, I explain how other corporate and Americanized processes, such as open communication and participatory decision making, as well as building common vision, become the basis of church solidarity (Jeung 2004).

7. In her essay on second-generation Korean American church services, Karen Chai (1998) described a similar worship style and form.

8. Miller (1997, 86) describes the worship format at the new paradigm churches: "The singing, or worship, portion of the service provides an extended period for the individual to commune with God, with the music triggering entry into a level of consciousness in which everyday defensiveness is abandoned."

9. In 2003, the American Baptist Seminary of the West sponsored the first conference on "Asian American Worship." They received more than twenty-seven entries for their songwriting contest. Registrants attended workshops such as "From MY Nation, Tribe, People, and Language? The Search for Asian American Worship," "What Do Asian Americans Thirst for in Worship?" and "Asian American Styles of Worship."

10. Generation X churches, on the other hand, have begun to utilize more dance, art, and ritual within their worship (Flory and Miller 2000).

11. Dr. Russell Yee, who lectures on worship at Fuller Northern California and at the seminaries belonging to the Graduate Theological Union, offered other reasons why Asian Americans lack a distinctive worship style. He suggested that because Asian American immigration has been largely voluntary, Asian Americans are generally ready to accept dominant American culture and retain only cultural practices that are advantageous to the new homeland. Also, because most Asian American evangelicals are economically privileged, they have relatively few felt needs to express their faith as oppositional or oppressed cultural groups might. Personal e-mail correspondence, October 9, 2003.

12. Sermon series are topical and included expositions from a book of the Bible, lessons on spiritual disciplines (Learning to Pray, Stewardship, Doctrine of Scripture, Sharing Your Faith), teaching on worship and community (Worship His Majesty, Life in the Spirit, Authenticity), and doctrines of the Bible (Living a Grace-Filled Life, How Faith Grows).

13. These five areas are evangelism, exalting (worship programming), enfolding (welcome and hospitality), edification (training and home groups), and empowering (networking people into ministry). An elaborate flow chart may be found in the church annual reports and illustrates the ministry structure of GFC consisting of forty-four official functional roles.

14. Milton Gordon coined the term *ethclass* to describe the relationship between ethnicity and social class background. Those of the same ethnicity tend to work in the same neighborhoods, attend the same schools, and enter similar occupations as others (Gordon 1964).

15. The top occupations of GFC members were health/medicine (13.5 percent of members), accounting/finance (10.4 percent), computers (9.0 percent), and engineering (8.6 percent). About 60 percent of the members reported working more than forty hours a week.

16. On one Sunday, the inserts included a form for sermon notes, a weekly registration form, parking information, a quilting gathering announcement, an invitation to the seventh anniversary dinner, a "Couples Connection" flyer, and a news report from the Christian History Institute's "Glimpses of the Church across the Ages."

17. Surveyed individuals rated personal development as their highest planned priority. The mean score on a scale from 1 (much less involved) to 5 (much more involved) for this activity was 4.0. The mean scores for community service, evangelism, and church attendance were 3.5, 3.4, and 3.4 respectively.

18. Sixty-two percent of GFC members report praying daily and 55 percent read the Bible daily or at least two to three times a week.

19. At its peak in 1996, GFC had eighteen active home groups throughout the Bay Area.

20. Prayer requests at one home group included seeking God's direction regarding a job change, peace over the planning of an upcoming wedding ceremony, and help in one's personal devotional life (Bible reading). One specific group that focused on healing prayer spent time praying against spiritual warfare that affected one's relationships.

21. Pastor Dan explained that the congregation members were generally apolitical: "Politics are probably not talked about at all in our church. I have not heard much discussion

around the political arena or anyone's agenda as far as that. And we don't make mention of that in our sermons or teachings. But as far as political party affiliation, discussions are nonexistent. It's just something that people are not really highly interested in for one thing."

CHAPTER 7.   ASIAN AMERICAN PANETHNICITY AT PARK
AVENUE UNITED METHODIST CHURCH

1. Similarly, other congregations are able to maintain activist efforts only if the minister also pays attention to the pastoral needs of the people (Roozen et al. 1984).

2. The church's sponsorship of youth basketball has grown from one girls' basketball team in 1992 to ten teams for both boys and girls in 1998. The seniors program, started in 1990, now meets weekly with more than forty participants. The congregation also houses a fellowship group for Japanese-speaking members, a women's fellowship, and two youth groups.

3. Conducted in July 1999, the church census of members and regular attendees obtained sixty-eight returned surveys.

4. Park Avenue United Methodist Church Vision Statement, adopted October 1999.

5. Comments from a Long-Term Planning Team meeting, June 1999.

6. Although the United Methodist Church has published an Asian American songbook, neither PAUMC nor other mainline churches have included many songs written by Asians or Asian Americans (see Asian American Hymn Book Project 1983). In 1992, David Ng and the Christ, Culture, and Community Project Team gathered members of nine Asian American congregations to share stories about the lives of their churches. He noted, "Cultural affirmation in the congregations should lead to cultural expressions of faith through prayer, worship and liturgies. But no Asian North American congregation that reported could claim any sense of accomplishment in this area of church life" (Ng 1996, xxiii).

7. Communion is observed once a month. Passing the Peace involves greeting other worshippers and blessing them by saying, "Peace of Christ be with you."

8. Celebrations of festivals and memorials are the primary symbolic occasions that reinforce the congregation's Asian American group identity. Though the mainline churches usually followed the Christian calendar and employed denominational liturgies, church services at Chinese and Japanese American congregations would often recognize Asian holidays and particularly held ceremonies to remember ancestors, a Confucian ethic. As stated previously, these ministers did not consider Asian festivals and rituals as pagan, especially since Asian Americans did not celebrate them as ancestor worship.

9. Other mainline congregations attempt to introduce some form of Asian elements to other aspects of their church setting as well. For example, a pastor describes that his church sought to reflect its members' Asian background by including artistic expressions of ethnicity in the church bulletin covers.

10. Mainline ministers at other congregations also alter the form of Christian rituals to refresh the meaning behind the practice and to make them resonate more closely with Asian Americans. One Asian American congregation served Chinese moon cakes and tea for communion. Round moon cakes *(yuebing),* filled with red bean paste or some other filling, symbolize unity and family. Eaten especially during the Mid-Autumn Festival by Chinese, the roundness of the cakes and the moon represents a

family reuniting. When combined with the Christian communion of the saints, this ritual is a poignant act for members who grew up eating moon cakes. For those who did not know about the moon cakes, the ritual is both a reminder of Christian unity and a lesson about Chinese heritage.

11. Scriptural interpretation for mainline ministers involves uncovering the meanings of the stories for the biblical people at that time and space and relating these stories to Asian Americans in their particular context. With their historicized readings of the scripture, these ministers do not absolutize biblical injunctives as necessary commandments that their members have to follow.

12. She referenced the story in Luke 24, in which the risen Jesus joined two disciples on the road to Emmaus.

13. After attending a youth organizing conference, the youth rallied against the sale of a community building in San Francisco Japantown. They argued that the title to the building was improperly transferred during wartime internment. The youth often express a commitment to community service by wanting to do projects such as neighborhood clean-up efforts or serving food to the homeless.

14. Park Avenue United Methodist Church Vision Statement, presented 17 October 1999. Programs for different age groups include youth basketball, Taiko drum lessons, youth Sunday school and programs, and "Extending Connections" activities for seniors. Women may meet in a women's fellowship group as well as participate in the United Methodist's Women, a denominationally structured organization. The Japanese-speaking members have their own group called Nichigo-bu. The Community Developer Program works on issues affecting the local community and has initiated several projects that will be described.

15. Park Avenue United Methodist Church Vision Statement, presented 17 October 1999.

16. To qualify as Japanese American, a player must be 1/8 Japanese.

17. In addition, the church supports the Sansei Legacy Project, a Japanese American ethnic organization, Renewed HOPE Housing Advocates, an affordable housing group, and Community Health Project, a collaborative with Asian Mental Health Services.

18. Forty-three percent of PAUMC versus 62 percent of GFC members pray daily. Twenty-six percent of PAUMC and 77 percent of GFC members read the Bible more than once a week. These differences between Asian American evangelicals and mainline Protestants correlate with Christian Smith's findings about the two groups in general (1998).

19. For example, 63 percent of PAUMC members agree that "their faith includes religious beliefs and practices other than Christian ones."

20. GFC had more Asian inter-ethnic couples than interracial ones. One reason for this pattern is that evangelicals stress Christian marriages and people tend to marry fellow church members. Given that the social networks of Asian American Christian evangelicals usually are other Asian American Christians, they also intermarry more.

CHAPTER 8.   CONCLUSION: ASIAN AMERICAN CHRISTIANS
IN A MULTIETHNIC SOCIETY

1. Dayspring Church Vision Statement as written on its Web site, 8 October 2003.

2. Across the country, in Seattle, Los Angeles, and Chicago, Asian American ministers have begun churches that are intentionally multiethnic. See Kang (2002), Ko (2002), and Thorngate (2001).

3. Six of the multiethnic congregations are in the San Francisco Bay Area. I interviewed two other Asian American ministers of multiethnic congregations from outside the area because they are recognized leaders of this movement.

4. For example, the number of Asians playing professional sports in the United States has dramatically increased. As described in the preface of this book, the emergence of Yao Ming as an international sports star has brought much pride to Asian Americans. In *Time* magazine's 8 September 2003 issue about the "next" superstar athletes, half of them were Asian.

5. In fact, Christian Smith and Michael Emerson (2000) found that 58 percent of white strong evangelicals and 87 percent of African American strong evangelicals believed that integrating the church would help address racism and welcomed diversity within their churches.

6. On the other hand, two of the eight ministers of multiethnic congregations downplayed cultural and ethnic affirmation and instead highlighted the unique identity that Christians have as the children of God. Although not fundamentalists, these ministers came from more theologically driven backgrounds and argued that their members should be defined by scriptures, and not by the world's categories. They did recognize ethnic differences among members in their church, but they would not identify their congregations as multiethnic.

7. *Sedaqah* is a Hebrew term meaning "righteous community."

8. Newsong Church, an Asian American-led, multiethnic church of over 3,000, planted another multiethnic church in 2003 and has racial reconciliation and social justice as core values.

9. This definition of a multiracial congregation comes from Paul DeYoung et al.'s book, *United by Faith*. Ministers of Chinese churches with different dialect congregations would argue that they are already multiethnic, since they have Mandarin, Cantonese, and English-speaking members.

10. Blacks and Latinos also attend this church in much smaller numbers. However, they expressed less difficulty about being minorities within the congregation.

11. Korean American congregations face a similar dilemma as the 1.5 and second generation use English, develop different worship tastes, and face new issues as professionals.

12. The emergence and institutionalization of these congregations have occurred in a particular space and moment in time. These congregations have sprung up following the Civil Rights Act of 1964 and the Immigration Act of 1965, the establishment of Ethnic Studies in the 1970s, and the coming of age of the third and fourth generation of Chinese and Japanese Americans during the 1980s. In 2003 California voted against a proposition that would ban the state from collecting racial data. Instead, voters acknowledged the continuing significance of race and ethnicity in determining health, education, and civil rights outcomes.

13. Certain institutional practices of Asian American churches may or may not last depending on the development of Asian American culture and communities. Walter Powell describes this stage of organizational development as "incomplete institutionalization," in which "practices that appear to have institutional support will have unequal staying power" (1991: 199)

14. Philip Jenkins (2002) argues that the most revolutionary movement in our world today is global religious change. He extrapolates that by 2025, only 38 percent of Christians will be non-Hispanic Whites.

15. Certainly, not all Asian American Christians fit the "model minority" stereotype as some Asian American churches have low-income and working class families struggling to survive.

16. Other new scholars of Asian American religion, such as Rachel Bundang (2002), Jane Iwamura (1996), Wonhee Joh (2003), and David Kim (2003) offer the theological possibilities of examining the intersection of Asian/Asian American roots and religious hopes.

BIBLIOGRAPHY

Abramson, H. 1975. "The Religioethnic Factor and the American Experience." Ethnicity 2 (2).

Alba, Richard. 1985. *Italian Americans: Into the Twilight of Ethnicity*. Englewood Cliffs, NJ: Prentice-Hall.

———. 1990. *Ethnic Identity: The Transformation of White America*. New Haven: Yale University Press.

———, and Victor Nee. 1997. "Rethinking Assimilation Theory for a New Era of Immigration." *International Migration Review* 31 (4): 826–874.

Albanese, Catherine. 1992. *American Religions and Religion*. Belmont, CA: Wadsworth Publishing Co.

Almirol, Edwin. 1985. *Ethnic Identity and Social Negotiation: A Study of the Filipino Community in California*. New York: AMS Press.

Alumkal, Anthony. 2002. "The Scandal of the 'Model Minority' Mind? The Bible and Second Generation Asian American Evangelicals." In *Semeia: The Bible in Asian America*, edited by Tat-siong Benny Liew, 90–91, 237–250. Atlanta, GA: Society of Biblical Literature.

Ammerman, Nancy. 1987. *Bible Believers: Fundamentalists in the Modern World*. New Brunswick, NJ: Rutgers University Press.

———. 1998. *Congregation and Community*. New Brunswick, NJ: Rutgers University Press.

Anderson, Benedict. 1991. *Imagined Communities*. New York: Verso.

Aponte, Edwin. 1998. "Hispanic/Latino Protestantism in Philadelphia." In *Re-forming the Center*, edited by Douglas Jacobsen and William Vance Trollinger Jr., 381–403. Grand Rapids, MI: William B. Eerdmans Publishing Co.

Asian American Hymn Book Project. 1983. *Hymns from the Four Winds : A Collection of Asian American Hymns*. Edited by I-to Loh. Nashville: Abingdon.

Balmer, Randall. 1989. *Mine Eyes Have Seen the Glory*. New York: Oxford University Press.

———. 1996. *Grant Us Courage: Travels along the Mainline of American Protestantism*. New York: Oxford University Press.

Balmer, Randall, and Lauren Winner. 2002. *Protestantism in America*. New York: Columbia University Press.

Barth, Frederick. 1969. *Ethnic Groups and Boundaries*. Boston: Little, Brown.

Barton, Josef. 1975. *Peasants and Strangers: Italians, Rumanians, and Slovaks in an American City*. Cambridge, MA: Harvard University Press.

Basch, Linda, Nina Glick Schiller, and Cristina Szanton Blanc. 1994. *Nations Unbound, Transnational Projects, Postcolonial Predicaments, and Deterritorialized Nation-States*. Langhorne, PA: Gordon and Breach.

Becker, Penny Edgell. 1999. *Congregations in Conflict: Cultural Models of Local Religious Life*. Cambridge: Cambridge University Press.

Becker, Penny Edgell, and Nancy Eieland. 1997. *Contemporary American Religion: An Ethnographic Reader.* Walnut Creek, CA: AltaMira Press.

Bellah, Robert. 1998. "Is There a Common American Culture?" *Journal of the American Academy of Religion* 66 (3): 613–625.

Bellah, Robert, Richard Madsen, William Sullivan, Ann Swidler, and Steve Tipton. 1985. *Habits of the Heart: Individualism and Commitment in American Life.* Berkeley: University of California Press.

Berger, Peter. 1967. *The Sacred Canopy: Elements of a Sociological Theory of Religion.* Garden City, NY: Anchor Books.

Bird, Frederick. 1968. *A Study of Chinese Churches in the San Francisco Bay Area.* N.p., Bureau of Community Research.

Bodnar, John. 1985. *The Transplanted: A History of Immigrants in Urban America.* Bloomington: Indiana University Press.

Bonacich, Edna. 1973. "A Theory of Middleman Minorities." *American Sociological Review* 37: 583–594.

Brint, Stephen, and Jerome Karabel. 1991. "Institutional Origins and Transformation." In *The New Institutionalism in Organizational Analysis,* edited by Walter Powell and Paul DiMaggio. Chicago: University of Chicago Press.

Brown, Karen McCarthy. 1991. *Mama Lola.* Berkeley: University of California Press.

Buenaventura, Steffi San. 2002. "Filipino Religion at Home and Abroad: Historical Roots and Immigrant Transformations." In *Religions in Asian America: Building Faith Communities,* edited by Pyong Gap Min and Jung Ha Kim, 1–14. Walnut Creek, CA: AltaMira Press.

Busto, Rudy. 1999. "The Gospel According the Model Minority? Hazarding an Interpretation of Asian American Evangelical Students." In *New Spiritual Homes: Religion and Asian Americans,* edited by David Yoo, 169–187. Honolulu: University of Hawaii Press.

———. 2003. "DisOrienting Subjects: Reclaiming Pacific Islander/Asian American Religions." In *Revealing the Sacred in Asian and Pacific America,* edited by Jane Naomi Iwamura and Paul Spickard, 9–28. New York: Routledge Press.

Calderon, Jose. 1992. "'Hispanic' and 'Latino': The Viability of Categories for Panethnic Studies." *Latin American Perspectives* 19 (4): 37–44.

Carnes, Tony, and Fenggang Yang, eds. 2004. *Asian American Religions: The Making and Unmaking of Borders and Boundaries.* New York: NYU Press.

Casteneda, Laura. 1998. "Tapping into Ethnic Markets." *San Francisco Chronicle,* 8 June.

Cayton, Horace, and Anne Lively. 1955. *The Chinese in the United States and the Chinese Christian Churches.* New York: National Council of Churches.

Cha, Peter. 2001. "Ethnic Identity Formation and Participation in Immigrant Churches: Second-Generation Korean American Experiences." In *Korean Americans and Their Religions,* edited by Ho-Youn Kwon, Kwang Chung Kim, and R. Stephen Warner, 141–156. University Park: Penn State University Press.

Chai, Karen. 1998. "Competing for the Second Generation: English-Language Ministry at a Korean Protestant Church." In *Gatherings in Diaspora: Religious Communities and the New Immigration,* edited by R. Stephen Warner and Judith Wittner. Philadelphia: Temple University Press.

Chan, Byron. 2003. "A Journey with the Lord." In *Chinatown: Stories of Faith,* edited by James Chuck, 117–118. San Francisco: First Chinese Baptist Church, San Francisco.

Chan, Kenyon, and Shirley Hune. 1995. "Racialization and Panethnicity: From Asians in America to Asian Americans." In *Toward a Common Destiny: Improving Race and Ethnic Relations in America,* edited by Willis Hawley and Anthony Jackson, 205–236. San Francisco: Jossey-Bass Publishers.

Chan, Sucheng. 1991. *Asian Americans: An Interpretive History*. Philadelphia: Temple University Press.

Chang, Carrie. 2000. "Amen. Pass the Kimchee." *Monolid* 1: 1.

Chang, Gordon, ed. 2001. *Asian Americans and Politics: Perspectives, Experiences, Prospects*. Stanford, CA: Stanford University Press.

Chang, Iris. 2003. "Fear of SARS, Fear of Strangers." *New York Times*, 21 May.

Chang, Jonah. 1991. "Movement of Self-Empowerment: History of the National Federation of Asian American United Methodists." In *Churches Aflame: Asian Americans and United Methodism*, edited by Artemio Guillermo, 135–154. Nashville, TN: Abingdon Press.

Chao, Julie. 1998a. "San Francisco's Sleeping Giant: The City's Significant Asian Population Is Joining the Electoral Process." *San Francisco Examiner*, 3 May.

———. 1998b. "Teaching the Asian American Experience: More College Students Are Reclaiming a Heritage Many Did Not Know They Had." *San Francisco Examiner*, 3 May.

Chen, Carolyn, and Russell Jeung. 2000. "Creating and Sustaining Our Communities: Asian American Religious Institutions." In *Asian American Studies: Identity, Images, and Issues—Past and Present*, edited by Esther M. Ghymn. Boston: Peter Lang.

Chong, Jia-Rui, and Carla Hall. 2003. "San Gabriel Valley Abuzz with Rumors about SARS." *Los Angeles Times*, 12 April.

Chong, Kelly. 1998. "What It Means to Be Christian: The Role of Religion in the Construction of Ethnic Identity and Boundary among Second-Generation Korean Americans." *Sociology of Religion: A Quarterly Review* 59 (3): 259–286.

Chuck, James. 1996. *An Exploratory Study of the Growth of Protestant Chinese Churches in San Francisco, 1950–1992*. Berkeley, CA: Bay Area Chinese Churches Research Project.

Collier, Victoria. 1996. "Ethnic Malls Zero in on Niches." Oakland Tribune, 7 July.

Condit, Ira. *The Chinaman as We See Him and Fifty Years of Work for Him*. Chicago: Revelle, 1900.

Constable, Nicole. 1994. *Christian Souls and Chinese Spirits: A Hakka Community in Hong Kong*. Berkeley: University of California Press.

Conzen, Kathleen Neils. 1976. *Immigrant Milwaukee: 1836–1860*. Cambridge, MA: Harvard University Press.

Conzen, Kathleen Neils, David Gerber, Ewa Morawska, George Pozzetta, and Rudolph Vecoli. 1992. "The Invention of Ethnicity: A Perspective from the U.S.A." *Journal of American Ethnic History* 12 (1): 3–42.

Conzen, Kathleen Neils, Harry Stout, E. Brooks Holifield, and Michael Zuckerman. 1996. "The Place of Religion in Urban and Community Studies." *Religion and American Culture* 6 (2): 107–130.

Cornell, Stephen. 1988. *The Return of the Native: American Indian Political Resurgence*. New York: Oxford University Press.

———. 1988. *Structure, Content, and Logic of Ethnic Group Formation*. Cambridge, MA: Center for Research on Politics and Social Organization.

Cornell, Stephen, and Douglas Hartmann. 1998. *Ethnicity and Race*. Thousand Oaks, CA: Sage.

Cousins, Don, Bill Hybels, and Bruce Bugby. 1996. *Network: The Right People . . . In the Right Places . . . For the Right Reasons*. Grand Rapids, MI: Zondervan Publishing House.

"Cupertino Business Group Formed: New Council Will Try to Expand Involvement of Asian American Community." 1998. *San Jose Mercury*, 30 July.

Dariotis, Wei Ming. 2002. "The Emerging Hapa Community." *Asian Week*, 1 November.

Davis, James, and Robert Wilson. 1966. *The Church in the Radically Changing Community.* Nashville, TN: Abingdon.

Dawson, John. 2001. *Taking Our Cities for God: How to Break Spiritual Strongholds.* Lake Mary, FL: Charisma House.

Demerath, N. J., Peter Hall, Terry Schmitt, and Rhys Williams, ed. 1998. *Sacred Companies: Organizational Aspects of Religion and Religious Aspects of Organizations.* New York: Oxford University Press.

DeYoung, Curtiss, Michael Emerson, George Yancey, and Karen Chai Kim. 2003. *United by Faith: The Multiracial Congregation as Answer to the Problem of Race.* New York: Oxford University Press.

Diaz-Stevens, Ana Maria, and Anthony Stevens-Arroyo. 1998. *Recognizing the Latino Resurgence in U.S. Religion.* Boulder, CO: Westview Press.

DiMaggio, Paul, and Walter Powell. 1983. "The Iron Cage Revisited: Institutional Isomorphism and Collective Rationality in Organizational Fields." *American Sociological Review* 48: 147–160.

———. 1991. *The New Institutionalism in Organizational Analysis.* Chicago: University of Chicago Press.

Dolan, Jay. 1985. *The American Catholic Experience.* Garden City, NY: Doubleday and Co.

Douglass, H. Paul. 1927. *The Church in the Changing City.* New York: Doran.

Durkheim, Emile. 1915. *The Elementary Forms of Religious Life.* New York: Free Press.

Duster, Troy. 1991. *The Diversity Project: Final Report.* Berkeley, CA: Institute for Social Change.

Emerson, Michael, and Christian Smith. 2000. *Divided by Faith: Evangelical Religion and the Problem of Race in America.* New York: Oxford University Press.

Epstein, Edward. 1997. "Chinese Americans Flex Political Muscle in San Francisco: Central Freeway Issue Unites Voters." *San Francisco Chronicle,* 30 August.

Epstein, Edward, and Ramon McLeod. 1997. "New San Francisco Voter Bloc Shows Clout." *San Francisco Chronicle,* 6 November.

Erwin, Diana Griego. 2003. "Shaq's 'Apology' for Racist Barb at NBA foe Yao Doesn't Measure Up." *Sacramento Bee,* 14 January.

Espiritu, Yen Le. 1992. *Asian American Panethnicity.* Philadelphia: Temple University Press.

———. 1997. *Asian American Women and Men: Labor, Laws, and Love.* Thousand Oaks, CA: Sage Publications.

Espiritu, Yen Le, and Paul Ong. 1994. "Class Constraints on Racial Solidarity among Asian Americans." In *The New Asian Immigration in Los Angeles and Global Restructuring,* edited by E. Bonacich, P. Ong, and L. Cheng. Philadelphia: Temple University Press.

Filiatreau, John. 2001. "Asian Americans Celebrate Unity, Diversity." *Presbyterian News Service,* 1 June.

Fischer, Claude. 1982. *To Dwell among Friends: Personal Networks in Town and City.* Chicago: University of Chicago Press.

Flory, Richard, and Donald Miller, ed. 2000. *Gen X Religion.* New York: Routledge Press.

Fong, Kenneth Uyeda. 1999. *Pursuing the Pearl : A Comprehensive Resource for Multi-Asian Ministry.* Valley Forge, PA: Judson Press.

Fox, Geoffrey. 1996. *Hispanic Nation: Culture, Politics, and the Constructing of Identity.* Secaucus, NJ: Birch Lane Press.

Frey, William H., and Reynolds Farley. 1996. "Latino, Asian, and Black Segregation in U.S. Metropolitan Areas: Are Multiethnic Metros Different?" *Demography* 33 (1): 35–50.

Friedland, Roger, and Robert Alford. 1991. "Bringing Society Back In: Symbols, Practices, and Institutional Contradictions." In *The New Institutionalism in Organizational Analysis,* edited by Walter Powell and Paul DiMaggio, 232–263. Chicago: University of Chicago Press.

Fugita, Stephen, and David O'Brien. 1991. *Japanese American Ethnicity: The Persistence of Community.* Seattle: University of Washington Press.

Gale, Susan, and Timothy Gale, ed. 1993. *Statistical Record of Asian Americans.* Detroit: Gale Research Institute.

Gam, Jee. 1880. "Sermon by Jee Gam." *American Missionary* 34 (10): 311.

Gans, Herbert. 1979. "Symbolic Ethnicity: The Future of Ethnic Groups and Cultures in America." *Ethnic and Racial Studies* 2 (1).

———. 1999. "The Possibility of a New Racial Hierarchy in the Twenty-first Century United States." In *The Cultural Territories of Race,* edited by Michele Lamont, 371–390. Chicago: University of Chicago Press.

Garcia, John. 1997. "Latino National Political Survey, 1989–1990." *Interuniversity Consortium for Political and Social Research Bulletin* 18 (1): 1–6.

Geertz, Clifford. 1973. *The Interpretation of Cultures.* New York: Basic Books.

Gjerde, Jon. 1985. *From Peasants to Farmers.* New York: Cambridge University Press.

Glazer, Nathan. 1997. *We Are All Multiculturalists Now.* Cambridge, MA: Harvard University Press.

Glazer, Nathan, and Daniel Moynihan. 1970. *Beyond the Melting Pot.* Cambridge, MA: MIT Press.

———.1975. Ethnicity: *Theory and Experience.* Cambridge, MA: Harvard University Press.

Glenn, Evelyn Nakano. 1986. *Issei, Nisei, War Bride: Three Generations of Japanese American Women in Domestic Service.* Philadelphia: Temple University Press.

Gordon, Milton. 1964. *Assimilation in American Life.* New York: Oxford University Press.

Gotanda, Philip. 2001. "Citizenship Nullification: The Impossibility of Asian American Politics." In *Asian Americans and Politics,* edited by Gordon Chang, 79–101. Stanford, CA: Stanford University Press.

Grace Faith Church (GFC). 1996. "Worship at GFC." *1996 Annual Report.*

———. 1997. "Membership." *1997 Annual Report.*

———. 1998a. "Vision Statement." *1998 Annual Report.*

———. 1998b. "Ministry Focus." *1998 Annual Report.*

Guilermo, Emil. 1998. "Boxer Rebellion." *Asian Week,* 22 October.

Gutmann, Amy, ed. 1994. *Multiculturalism: Examining and the Politics of Recognition.* Princeton, NJ: Princeton University Press.

Handlin, Oscar. 1951. *The Uprooted.* Boston: Little, Brown.

———. 1966. *Children of the Uprooted.* New York: George Braziller.

Hannan, Michael. 1979. "The Dynamics of Ethnic Boundaries in Modern States." In *National Development and the World System: Educational, Economic, and Political Change, 1950–1970,* edited by John Meyer and Michael Hannan, 253–275. Chicago: University of Chicago Press.

Hannan, Michael, and John Freeman. 1977. "The Population Ecology of Organizations." *American Journal of Sociology* 82: 929–964.

———. 1984. "Structural Inertia and Organizational Change." *American Sociological Review* 49: 149–165.

Hansen, M. L. 1937. *The Problem of the Third Generation Immigrant.* Atlanta: Augustana Historical Society.

Hardy-Fanta, Carol. 1993. *Latina Politics, Latino Politics.* Philadelphia: Temple University Press.

Harris, Margaret. 1998. "Religious Congregations as Non-Profit Organizations." In *Sacred*

Companies: Organizational Aspects of Religion and Religious Aspects of Organizations, edited by N. J. Demerath, Peter Hall, Terry Schmitt, and Rhys Williams, 307–317. New York: Oxford University Press.

Hayashi, Brian. 1995. *For the Sake of Our Brethren: Assimilation, Nationalism, and Protestantism among the Japanese of Los Angeles, 1895–1942.* Stanford, CA: Stanford University Press.

Hechter, Michael. 1975. *Internal Colonialism: The Celtic Fringe in British National Development, 1536–1966.* Berkeley: University of California Press.

———. 1987. *Principles of Group Solidarity.* Berkeley: University of California Press.

Herberg, Will. 1955. *Protestant, Catholic, Jew.* Garden City, NY: Anchor Press.

Hertig, Young Lee. 2002. *The Cultural Tug of War: Korean Immigrant Church and Family in Transition.* Nashville: Abingdon Press.

Ho, Pensri. 2002. "Young Asian American Professionals in Los Angeles: A Community in Transition." In *Contemporary Asian American Communities,* edited by Linda Vo and Rick Bonus, 134–146. Philadelphia: Temple University Press.

Hoge, Dean, Benton Johnson, and Donald Luidens. 1994. *Vanishing Boundaries: The Religion of Mainline Protestant Baby Boomers.* Louisville, KY: Westminster/John Knox.

Hogg, Michael. 1992. *The Social Psychology of Group Cohesiveness.* New York: NYU Press.

Hopewell, James. 1987. *Congregation: Stories and Structures.* Philadelphia: Fortress Press.

Horinouchi, Isao. 1973. "Americanized Buddhism: A Sociological Analysis of Protestantized Japanese Religion." Ph.D. diss., University of California, Davis.

Hsu, Madeline. 2000. *Dreaming of Gold, Dreaming of Home: Transnationalism and the Migration between the United States and South China, 1882–1943.* Stanford, CA: Stanford University Press.

Hu-DeHart, Evelyn, ed. 1999. *Across the Pacific: Asian Americans and Globalization.* Philadelphia: Temple University Press.

Hunter, James. 1983. *American Evangelicalism.* New Brunswick, NJ: Rutgers University Press.

———. 1987. *Evangelicalism: The Coming Generation.* Chicago: University of Chicago Press.

———. 1991. *Culture Wars: The Struggle to Define America.* New York: Basic.

Hurh, Won Moo, and Kim Kwang Chung. 1990. "Religious Participation of Korean Immigrants in the Unites States." *Journal for the Scientific Study of Religion* 29 (1): 19–34.

Hybels, Bill, and Mark Mittelberg. 1994. *Becoming a Contagious Christian.* Grand Rapids, MI: Zondervan Publishing House.

Hybels, Lynne, and Bill Hybels. 1995. *Rediscovering Church: The Story and Vision of Willow Creek Community Church.* Grand Rapids, MI: Zondervan Publishing House.

Iannaccone, Laurence. 1994. "Why Strict Churches Are Strong." *American Journal of Sociology* 99: 1180–1211.

Isaacs, Harold. 1975. *Idols of the Tribe.* New York: Harper and Row.

Iwamura, Jane Naomi. 2003. "Envisioning Asian and Pacific American Religions." In *Revealing the Sacred in Asian and Pacific America,* edited by Jane Naomi Iwamura and Paul Spickard, 1–8. New York: Routledge Press.

Iwamura, Jane Naomi, and Paul Spickard, eds. 2003. *Revealing the Sacred in Asian and Pacific America.* New York: Routledge Press.

Jacobsen, Douglas, and William Vance Trollinger Jr., eds. 1998. *Re-Forming the Center: American Protestantism, 1900 to the Present.* Grand Rapids, MI: William B. Eerdmans Publishing Co.

Jenkins, Philip. 2002. *The Next Christendom: The Coming of Global Christianity.* New York: Oxford University Press.

Jeung, Russell. 2002a. "Asian American Pan-Ethnic Formation and Congregational Culture."

In *Religions in Asian America: Building Faith Communities,* edited by Pyong Gap Min and Jung Ha Kim, 215–243. Walnut Creek, CA: AltaMira Press.

———. 2002b. "Evangelical and Mainline Teachings on Asian American Identity." In *Semeia: The Bible in Asian America,* edited by Tat-siong Benny Liew, 90–91, 211–236. Atlanta: Society of Biblical Literature.

———. 2002c. "Southeast Asians in the House: Multiple Layers of Identity." In *Contemporary Asian American Communities,* edited by Linda Vo and Rick Bonus, 60–74. Philadelphia: Temple University Press.

———. 2003. "New Asian American Churches and Symbolic Racial Identity." In *Revealing the Sacred in Asian and Pacific America,* edited by Jane Naomi Iwamura and Paul Spickard, 225–240. New York: Routledge Press.

———. 2004. "Creating an Asian American Christian Subculture: Grace Community Covenant Church." In *Asian American Religions: The Making and Unmaking of Borders and Boundaries,* ed. Tony Carnes and Fenggang Yang. New York: New York University Press.

Johnson, Chip. 2000. "Christian T-shirt Crusade Group Makes U.C. Student a Campus Icon." *San Francisco Chronicle,* 22 April.

Jones-Correa, Michael, and David Leal. 1996. "Becoming "Hispanic": Secondary Panethnic Identification among Latin American-Origin Populations in the United States." *Hispanic Journal of Behavioral Sciences* 18 (2): 214–254.

Kanda, Shigeo. 1978. "Recovering Cultural Symbols: A Case for Buddhism in the Japanese American Communities." *Journal of the American Academy of Religion* (December): 445–475.

Kang, K. Connie. 2001. "Building on the Gospel of Inclusion: The Rev. Ken Fong Guides His Historically Japanese American Congregation into a Multiethnic Look." *Los Angeles Times,* 8 December.

Kao, Grace, and Kara Joyner. 2001. "Do Hispanics and Asian Adolescents Practice Panethnicity in Friendship Choices?" Paper presented at the American Sociological Association Meeting. Anaheim, CA.

Kashima, Tetsuden. 1977. *Buddhism in America: The Social Organization of an Ethnic Institution.* Westport, CT: Greenwood Press.

Kelley, Dean. 1972. *Why Conservative Churches Are Growing: A Study in the Sociology of Religion.* San Francisco: Harper and Row.

Keyes, Charles. 1981. "The Dialectics of Ethnic Change." In *Ethnic Change,* edited by Charles Keyes. Seattle: University of Washington Press.

Khanh, Truong Phuoc. 2002. "Leadership of Big, English-Speaking Churches Seems Out of Reach, Many Asian American Pastors Say." *San Jose Mercury News,* November 2.

Kibria, Nazli. 1996. "Not Asian, Black or White? Reflections on South Asian American Racial Identity." *Amerasia Journal* 22 (2): 77–88.

———. 2002. *Becoming Asian American: Second-Generation Chinese and Korean American Identities.* Baltimore, MD: Johns Hopkins University Press.

Kim, David. 1993. "Becoming: Korean Americans, Faith, and Identity." Master's thesis, Harvard University.

———. 2003. "Enchanting Diasporas, Asian Americans, and the Passionate Attachment of Race." In *Revealing the Sacred in Asian and Pacific America,* edited by Jane Naomi Iwamura and Paul Spickard, 327–340. New York: Routledge Press.

Kim, Eunjoo Mary. 2002. "Hermeneutics and Asian American Preaching." In *Semeia: The Bible in Asian America,* edited by Tat-siong Benny Liew, 90–91, 269–290. Atlanta: Society of Biblical Literature.

Kim, Jung Ha. 1997. *Bridge-Makers and Cross-Bearers: Korean American Women and the Church*. Lanham, MD: Scholars Press.

———. 2002. "Cartography of Korean American Protestant Faith Communities in the United States." In *Religions in Asian America: Building Faith Communities*, edited by Pyong Gap Min and Jung Ha Kim, 185–214. Walnut Creek, CA: AltaMira Press.

Kim, Ryan. 2001. "Asians Pursue United State." *San Francisco Chronicle*, 2 August.

King, Rebecca. 2002. "'Eligible' to Be Japanese American: Multiraciality in Basketball Leagues and Beauty Pageants." In *Contemporary Asian American Communities*, ed. Linda Vo and Rick Bonus, 120–133. Philadelphia: Temple University Press.

Kivisto, Peter, ed. 1989. *The Ethnic Dilemma: The Salience of Ethnicity for European-Origin Groups*. Philadelphia: Balch Institute Press.

Ko, Michael. 2002. "Church Makes Community, Not Religion, Focus of Center." *Seattle Times*, 2 November.

Kosmin, Barry, Egon Mayer, and Ariela Keysar. 2001. *American Religious Identification Survey 2001*. New York: Graduate Center of the City University of New York.

Kosmin, Barry, and Seymour Lachman. 1993. *One Nation under God: Religion in Contemporary American Society*. New York: Harmony Books.

Kuramoto, Mary. 1986. *Dendo: One Hundred Years of Japanese Christians in Hawaii and the Nuuanu Congregational Church*. Honolulu: Nuuanu Congregational Church.

Kurashige, Lon. 2002. *Japanese American Celebration and Conflict: A History of Ethnic Identity and Festival, 1934–1990*. Berkeley: University of California Press.

Kurien, Prema. 1998. "Becoming American by Becoming Hindu." In *Gatherings in Diaspora: Religious Communities and the New Immigration*, edited by R. Stephen and Judith Wittner Warner. Philadelphia: Temple University Press.

———. 2002. "'We Are Better Hindus Here': Religion and Ethnicity among Indian Americans." In *Religions in Asian America: Building Faith Communities*, edited by Pyong Gap Min and Jung Ha Kim, 71–98. Walnut Creek, CA: AltaMira Press.

Kwon, Soo Ah. 2003. "Asian and Pacific Islander Youth Activism: Examining Pan-Ethnic Consciousness and Inter-Ethnic Relationships." Paper presented at the Association of Asian American Studies Meeting, San Francisco.

Lai, James. 2003. "Asian Pacific Americans and the Pan-Ethnic Question." In *Asian American Politics: Law, Participation, and Policy*, edited by Don Nakanishi and James Lai, 247–260. Lanham, MD: Rowman and Littlefield Publishers.

Landberg, Mark, and Reynolds Farley. 1985. "Residential Segregation of Asian Americans in 1980." *Sociology and Social Research* 70 (1): 71–75.

Law, Eric. 1993. *The Wolf Shall Dwell with the Lamb*. St. Louis: Chalice Press.

Leadership Education for Asian Pacifics (LEAP), ed. 1993. *The State of Asian Pacific America*. Los Angeles: LEAP.

Lee, Helen. 1996. "Silent Exodus: Can the East Asian Church in America Reverse the Flight of Its Next Generation?" *Christianity Today*, 12 August, 50–53.

Lee, Sharon M. 1998. "Asian Americans: Diverse and Growing." *Population Bulletin* 53 (2): 2–41.

Lee, Sharon M., and Marilyn Fernandez. 1998. "Trends in Asian American Racial/Ethnic Intermarriage: A Comparison of 1980 and 1990 Census Data." *Sociological Perspectives* 41 (2): 323–343.

Lien, Pei-te. 1997. *The Political Participation of Asian Americans: Voting Behavior in Southern California*. New York: Garland Publishing.

———. 2001a. "Comparing the Voting Participation of Chinese to Other Asian Americans in U.S. Elections." *Chinese America: History and Perspectives* 17 (January): 1–13.

——. 2001b. *The Making of Asian America through Political Participation.* Philadelphia: Temple University Press.

——. 2001c. "Voting Participation: Race, Gender, and the Comparative Status of Asian American Women." In *Asian American and Politics: Perspectives, Experiences, Prospects,* edited by Gordon Chang, 173–196. Stanford, CA: Stanford University Press.

Lien, Pei-te, M. Margaret Conway, and Janelle Wong. 2003. "The Contours and Sources of Ethnic Identity Choices among Asian Americans." *Social Science Quarterly* 84 (2): 461–481.

Lieser, Ethen, and Sam Chu Lin. 2001. "APIAs Say the 50th Anniversary of 1951 U.S.-Japan Peace Treaty Is No Reason to Celebrate." *Asian Week,* 20 September.

Liew, Tat-siong Benny. 2002. "Whose Bible? Which (Asian) America?" In *Semeia: The Bible in Asian America,* edited by Tat-siong Benny Liew, 90–91, 1–26. Atlanta: Society of Biblical Literature.

Lin, Tom. 1995. *Losing Face and Finding Grace.* Downer's Grove, IL: Intervarsity Press.

Lincoln, C. Eric, and Lawrence Mamiya. 1990. *The Black Church in the African American Experience.* Durham, NC: Duke University Press.

Lochner, Tom. 2003. "Japanese Atrocities Disclosed." *Contra Costa Times,* 20 January.

Loo, Dennis. 1974. "Why an Asian American Theology of Liberation?" *Church and Society* (January–February): 49–54.

Lopez, David, and Yen Le Espiritu. 1990. "Panethnicity in the United States: A Theoretical Framework." *Ethnic and Racial Studies* 13 (2): 198–224.

Lott, Juanita. 1998. *Asian Americans: From Racial Category to Multiple Identities.* Walnut Creek, CA: AltaMira Press.

Lowe, Lisa. 1991. "Heterogeneity, Hybridity, Multiplicity: Marking Asian American Differences." *Diaspora* 1: 24–44.

——. 1996. *Immigrant Acts: On Asian American Cultural Politics.* Durham, NC: Duke University Press.

Lubman, Sarah. 1998. "Latinos, Asians Gain Influence in Elections." *San Jose Mercury,* 27 April.

Luo, Michael. 2002. "For Asian American Churches, Integration Proves Complicated." *Associated Press,* 20 January.

Mamiya, Lawrence. 1994. "A Social History of the Bethel African Methodist Episcopal Church." In *American Congregations,* edited by James Wind and James Lewis. Chicago: University of Chicago Press.

Mark, Diane. 1989. *Seasons of Light: The History of Chinese Christian Churches in Hawaii.* Honolulu: Chinese Christian Association of Hawaii.

Marsden, George M. 1980. *Fundamentalism and American Culture: The Shaping of Twentieth-Century Evangelicalism, 1870–1925.* New York: Oxford University Press.

Martin, Glen. 1998. "State May Move to Ban Import of Turtles, Frogs—Asian Americans Say It's a Ploy to Halt Live Food Sales." *San Francisco Chronicle,* 27 January.

Marty, Martin. 1971. *Righteous Empire: The Protestant Experience in America.* New York: Dial Press.

——. 1981. *The Public Church: Mainline-Evangelical-Catholic.* New York: Crossroad.

——. 1998. "The Shape of American Protestantism: Are There Two Parties Today?" In *Re-Forming the Center,* edited by Douglas Jacobsen and William Vance Trollinger Jr., 91–108. Grand Rapids, MI: William B. Eerdmans Publishing Co.

Matsuoka, Fumitaka. 1995. *Out of Silence: Emerging Themes in Asian American Churches.* Cleveland, OH: United Church Press.

Matsuoka, Fumitaka, and Eleazar Fernandez. 2003. *Realizing the America of Our Hearts: Theological Voices of Asian Americans*. St. Louis: Chalice Press.

McGavran, Donald, and C. Peter Wagner. 1980. *Understanding Church Growth*. Grand Rapids, MI: Eerdman.

McIntosh, Peggy. 1988. "White Privilege and Male Privilege: A Personal Account of Coming to See Correspondences through Work in Women's Studies." Working paper, Wellesley, MA, Wellesley College Center for Research on Women.

McLeod, Ramon, and Maria Alicia Guira. 1998. "Crossover by Democratic Voters Helped Put Fong Over the Top." *San Francisco Chronicle*, 4 June.

Mendoza Strobel, Lenny. 1996. "'Born-Again Filipino': Filipino American Identity and Asian Panethnicity." *Amerasia Journal* 22 (2): 31–54.

Miller, Donald E. 1997. *Reinventing American Protestantism: Christianity in the New Millennium*. Berkeley: University of California Press.

Min, Pyong Gap. 1992. "The Structure and Social Functions of Korean Immigrant Churches in the U.S." *International Migration Review* 26: 1370–1394.

———. 2002. "Introduction: A Literature Review with a Focus on Major Themes." In *Religions in Asian America: Building Faith Communities*, edited by Pyong Gap Min and Jung Ha Kim, 1–36. Walnut Creek, CA: AltaMira Press.

———, ed. 2002. *Second Generation: Ethnic Identity among Asian Americans*. Walnut Creek, CA: AltaMira Press.

Min, Pyong Gap, and Jung Ha Kim, eds. 2002. *Religions in Asian America: Building Faith Communities*. Walnut Creek, CA: AltaMira Press.

Min, Pyong Gap, and Rose Kim, eds. 1999. *Struggle for Ethnic Identity: Narratives by Asian American Professionals*. Walnut Creek, CA: AltaMira Press.

Min, Pyong Gap, and Kyeyoung Park. 1999. "Second-Generation Asian Americans' Ethnic Identity." *Amerasia Journal* 25 (1): ix–xx.

Mittleberg, David, and Mary Waters. 1992. "The Process of Ethnogenesis among Haitian and Israeli Immigrants in the United States." *Ethnic and Racial Studies* 15 (3): 412–435.

Moberg, David. 1984. *The Church as a Social Institution*. Grand Rapids, MI: Baker Book House.

Moy, Russell. 2002. "Resident Aliens of the Diaspora: 1 Peter and Chinese Protestants in San Francisco." In *Semeia: The Bible in Asian America,* edited by Tat-siong Benny Liew, 90–91, 51–68. Atlanta: Society of Biblical Literature.

Mullins, Mark. 1987. "The Life Cycle of Ethnic Churches in Sociological Perspective." *Japanese Journal of Religious Studies* 14 (4): 321–334.

Nagasawa, Mako. 2000. "The Best of Both Worlds." *Regeneration Quarterly* 6 (Fall).

Nagel, Joane. 1986. "The Political Construction of Ethnicity." In *Competitive Ethnic Relations,* edited by Susan Olzak and Joane Nagel, 93–112. Orlando, FL: Academic Press.

———. 1994. "Constructing Ethnicity: Creating and Recreating Ethnic Identity." *Social Problems* 41: 152–177.

———. 1995. "American Indian Ethnic Renewal: Politics and the Resurgence of Ethnicity." *American Sociological Review* 60: 947–965.

Nakanishi, Don, and James Lai, eds. 2003. *Asian American Politics: Law, Participation, and Policy*. Lanham, MD: Rowman and Littlefield Publishers.

Nakao, Annie. 1996. "Asian Americans Vote in Big Numbers." *San Francisco Examiner*, 15 December.

———. 1998. "Bitterness Over Nanking Massacre Dies Hard." *San Francisco Examiner*, 13 September.

———. 2003. "Asians in the News: Masked and Unmasked." *San Francisco Chronicle*, 22 April.

Nakashima Brock, Rita. 1996. "Clearing the Tangled Vines." *Amerasia Journal* 22, 1 (Winter): 181–186.

Ng, David, ed. 1996. *People on the Way: Asian North Americans Discovering Christ, Culture, and Community.* Valley Forge, PA: Judson Press.

Nguyen, Daisy. 2000. "A Guiding Light in a New World." *Contra Costa Times,* 15 October.

Niebuhr, H. Richard. 1929. *The Social Sources of Denominationalism.* Cleveland, OH: World Publishing Co.

———. 1951. *Christ and Culture.* New York: Harper.

Oboler, Suzanne. 1995. *Ethnic Labels, Latino Lives.* Minneapolis: University of Minnesota Press.

Okamoto, Dina. 2003. "Toward a Theory of Panethnicity: Explaining Asian American Collective Action." *American Sociological Review* 68 (6): 811–842.

Okihiro, Gary Y. 1984. "Religion and Resistance in America's Concentration Camps." *Phylon* 45 (September): 220–233.

———. 1994. *Margins and Mainstreams: Asians in American History and Culture.* Seattle: University of Washington Press.

Olzak, Suzanne. 1992. *The Dynamics of Ethnic Competition and Conflict.* Stanford, CA: Stanford University Press.

Olzak, Suzanne, and Joane Nagel. 1986. *Competitive Ethnic Relations.* Orlando, FL: Academic Press.

Omatsu, Glenn. 1994. "The Four Prisons and the Movements of Liberation: Asian American Activism from the 1960s to the 1990s." In *The State of Asian America: Activism and Resistance in the 1990s,* ed. K. Aguilar-San Juan, 19–69. Boston: South End Press.

Omi, Michael, and Howard Winant. 1994. *Racial Formation in the United States.* New York: Routledge.

Ong, Paul, and Suzanne Hee. 1993. "The Growth of the Asian Pacific American Population: Twenty Million in 2020." In *The State of Asian Pacific America,* edited by Leadership Education for Asian Pacifics (LEAP). Los Angeles: LEAP.

Orsi, Robert. 1985. *The Madonna on 115th Street: Faith and Community in Italian Harlem, 1880–1950.* New Haven: Yale University Press.

Padilla, Felix. 1985. *Latino Consciousness: The Case of Mexican Americans and Puerto Ricans in Chicago.* Notre Dame, IN: University of Notre Dame Press.

Palinkas, Lawrence. 1981. "The Force of Words: Rhetoric and Social Change in a Chinese Christian Community." Ph.D. diss., University of California, San Diego.

Palmer, Albert. 1934. *Oriental in American Life.* New York: Friendship Press.

Pang, Wing Ning. 1995. "The Chinese American Ministry." In *Yearbook of American and Canadian Churches, 1995,* edited by Kenneth Bedell, 10–16. Nashville, TN: Abingdon Press.

Park, Andrew Sung. 1996. *Racial Conflict and Healing: An Asian American Theological Perspective.* Maryknoll, NY: Orbis Books.

Park, Robert. 1950. *Race and Culture.* New York: Free Press.

Park, Sharon. 1998. "Korean American Churches." Paper presented at the Pacific Sociological Association, San Francisco.

Phan, Peter, ed. 1991. *Ethnicity, Nationality, and Religious Experience.* Lanham, MD: University Press of America.

Phan, Peter, and Jung Young Lee, eds. 1999. *Journeys at the Margin: Toward an Autobiographical Theology in American-Asian Perspective.* Collegeville, MN: Liturgical Press.

Plate, Tom. 2002. "Welcome Bishop-to-Be Wang." *San Francisco Chronicle,* 20 December.

Portes, Alejandro, and Robert Bach. 1985. *Latin Journey: Cuban and Mexican Immigrants in the United States.* Berkeley: University of California Press.

Portes, Alejandro, and Ruben Rumbaut. 1996. *Immigrant America.* Berkeley: University of California Press.

———. 2001. *Legacies: The Story of the Immigrant Second Generation.* Berkeley: University of California Press.

Powell, Walter, and Paul J. DiMaggio, ed. 1991. *The New Institutionalism in Organizational Analysis.* Chicago: University of Chicago Press.

Qian, Zhenchao, Sampson Lee Blair, and Stacey Ruf. 2001. "Asian American Interracial and Interethnic Marriage: Difference by Education and Nativity." *International Migration Review* 35: 557–586.

Ricourt, Milagros, and Ruby Danta. 2003. *Hispanas de Queens: Latino Panethnicity in a New York City Neighborhood.* Ithaca, NY: Cornell University Press.

Roberts, Selena. 2003. "Sports of the Times: Yao Proving a Bigger Man Than O'Neal." *New York Times,* 18 January.

Rodriguez, Clara. 2000. *Changing Race: Latinos, the Census, and the History of Ethnicity in the United States.* New York: New York University Press.

Roediger, David. 1991. *The Wages of Whiteness: Race and the Making of the American Working Class.* New York: Verso.

Roof, Wade Clark. 1993. *A Generation of Seekers.* New York: Harper Collins.

———. 1999. *Spiritual Marketplace: Baby Boomers and the Remaking of American Religion.* Princeton, NJ: Princeton University Press.

Roof, Wade Clark, and William McKinney. 1987. *American Mainline Religion.* New Brunswick, NJ: Rutgers University Press.

Roozen, David, William McKinney, and Jackson Carroll. 1985. *Varieties of Religious Presence.* New York: Pilgrim.

Rosenfeld, Michael J. 2001. "The Salience of Pan-national Hispanic and Asian Identities in U.S. Marriage Markets." *Demography* 38 (2): 161–175.

Rubenstein, Steve. 2002. "Asian Bishop Is a First for SF and Nation." *San Francisco Chronicle,* 14 December.

Rubin, Lillian. 1994. *Families on the Fault Line: America's Working Class Speaks about the Family, the Economy, Race, and Ethnicity.* New York: Harper Collins.

San Buenaventura, Steffi. 2002. "Filipino Religion at Home and Abroad: Historical Roots and Immigrant Transformations." In *Religions in Asian America: Building Faith Communities,* edited by Pyong Gap Min and Jung Ha Kim, 143–184. Walnut Creek, CA: AltaMira Press.

Sandalow, Marc. 1998. "A Defiant Stand for Freedom: Japanese American Honored Years after Arrest, Internment." *San Francisco Chronicle,* 16 January.

Sano, Roy. 1985. "Transforming Suffering: Struggling with Life as an Asian American." In *Changing Contexts of Our Faith,* edited by Lefty Russell. Philadelphia: Fortress Press.

Sawyer, Mary. 1998. "Black Protestantism as Expressed in Ecumenical Activity." In *Re-Forming the Center,* edited by Douglas Jacobsen and William Vance Trollinger Jr., 284–299. Grand Rapids, MI: William B. Eerdmans Publishing Co.

Scott, W. Richard. 1998. *Organizations: Rational, Natural, and Open Systems.* Englewood Cliffs, NJ: Prentice-Hall.

Shibley, Mark. 1996. *Resurgent Evangelicalism in the United States: Mapping Cultural Change since 1970.* Columbia: University of South Carolina Press.

Shinagawa, Larry, and Gin Pang. 1996. "Asian American Panethnicity and Intermarriage." *Amerasia Journal* 22 (2): 127–152.

Shinto, William. 1975. "The Role of Religion in Asian American Communities." Paper presented at the 1975 Education for Mission Conference, Hawaii Council of Churches and Asian Center for Theology and Strategies, Honolulu.

Sikkink, David. 1998. "'I Just Say I'm Christian': Symbolic Boundaries and Identity Formation among Church-going Protestants." In *Re-Forming the Center,* edited by Douglas
Jacobsen and William Vance Trollinger Jr., 49–71. Grand Rapids, MI: William B. Eerdmans Publishing Co.

Singh, Jaideep. 2003. "The Racialization of Minoritized Religious Identity: Constructing
Sacred Sites at the Intersection of White and Christian Supremacy." In *Revealing the
Sacred in Asian and Pacific America,* edited by Jane Naomi Iwamura and Paul
Spickard, 87–106. New York: Routledge Press.

Smith, Christian. 1998. *American Evangelicalism: Embattled and Thriving.* Chicago: University of Chicago Press.

———. 2000. *Christian American: What Evangelicals Really Want.* Berkeley: University of
California Press.

Smith, Tim. 1978. "Religion and Ethnicity." *American Historical Review* 83 (5): 1115–1186.

Sollors, Werner, ed. 1989. *The Invention of Ethnicity.* New York: Oxford University Press.

Sowell, Thomas. 1981. *Ethnic America: A History.* New York: Basic Books.

Speer, William. 1853. "China and California: Their Relations, Past and Present." San Francisco, n.p.

Spickard, Paul. 1996. *Japanese Americans: The Formation and Transformations of an Ethnic Group.* New York: Twayne Publishers.

Steinberg, Stephen. 1981. *The Ethnic Myth.* Boston: Beacon Press.

Stout, Harry, and D. Scott Cormode. 1998. "Institutions and the Story of American Religion." In *Sacred Companies: Organizational Aspects of Religion and Religious Aspects
of Organizations,* edited by N. J. Demerath, Peter Hall, Terry Schmitt, and Rhys
Williams, 62–78. New York: Oxford University Press.

Strasburg, Jenny. 2002. "Abercrombie and Glitch: Asian Americans Rip Retailer for Stereotypes on T-Shirts." *San Francisco Chronicle,* 18 April.

Strobel, Lee, and Bill Hybels. 1993. *Inside the Mind of Unchurched Harry and Mary: How to
Reach Friends and Family Who Avoid God and the Church.* Grand Rapids, MI: Zondervan Publishing House.

Sugirtharajah, Rasiah S. 1999. *Asian Biblical Hermeneutics and Postcolonialism: Contesting
the Interpretations.* Sheffield, UK: Sheffield Academic Press.

Sung, Betty Lee. 1967. *Mountain of Gold: The Story of Chinese in America.* New York: Collier Books.

Suzuki, Lester E. 1979. *Ministry in the "Assembly" and Relocation Centers of World War II.*
Berkeley, CA: Yardbird Publishing Co.

———. 1991. "Persecution, Alienation, Recognition: History of Japanese Methodist
Churches." In *Churches Aflame: Asian Americans and United Methodism, edited by
Artemio Guillermo, 113–134.* Nashville, TN: Abingdon Press.

Swidler, Ann. 1986. "Culture in Action: Symbols and Strategies." *American Sociological
Review* 51: 273–286.

Takahashi, Jere. 1997. *Nisei/Sansei: Shifting Japanese American Identities and Politics.*
Philadelphia: Temple University Press.

Takaki, Ron. 1987. *From Different Shores.* New York: Oxford University Press.

Taylor, Charles. 1994. "Multiculturalism and the Politics of Recognition." In *Multiculturalism: Examining the Politics of Recognition,* edited by Amy Gutmann, 25–61. Princeton, NJ: Princeton University Press.

Taylor, Verta, and Nancy Whittier. 1992. "Collective Identity in Social Movement Communities." In *Frontiers in Social Movement Theory,* edited by Aldon Morris and Carol
Mueller, 104–129. New Haven: Yale University Press.

Thorngate, Stephen. 2001. "Multiethnic Church Plant Set for Chicago Northside." *Covenant News*, 10 July.

Tilly, Charles. 1986. *The Contentious French*. Cambridge, MA: Harvard University Press.

Tokunaga, Paul. 2003. *Invitation to Lead: Guidance for Emerging Asian American Leaders*. Downers Grove, IL: Intervarsity Press.

Tomikawa, Collin, and Sandy Schaupp. 2001. "Two Views Regarding Ethnic Specific and Multi-ethnic Fellowships." Intervarsity Christian Fellowship, at http://regions.ivcf.org/multieth/2607.

Tran, De. 1998. "Strip Malls Emerging as Ethnic Crossroads." *San Jose Mercury*, 5 April.

Tran, De, and Ariana Cha. 1998. "Congregations at the Crossroads: Asian American Christians Leaving Their Parents' Style of Worship Behind." *San Jose Mercury News*, 12 April.

Tran, Tini. 1999. "Pan-Asian Churches Emerging." *Los Angeles Times*, 8 March.

Trottier, Richard. 1981. "Charters of Panethnic Identity: Indigenous American Indians and Immigrant Asian Americans." In *Ethnic Change*, edited by Charles Keyes, 271–305. Seattle: University of Washington Press.

Tseng, Timothy. 1994. "Ministry at Arms' Length: Asian Americans in the Racial Ideology of American Mainline Protestants, 1882–1952." Ph.D. diss., Union Theological Seminary, New York.

———. 1999. "Chinese Protestant Nationalism in the United States, 1880–1927." In *New Spiritual Homes: Religion and Asian Americans*, edited by David Yoo, 19–51. Honolulu: University of Hawaii Press.

———. 2002. "Second-Generation Chinese Evangelical Use of the Bible in Identity Discourse in the North America." In *Semeia: The Bible in Asian America*, edited by Tat-siong Benny Liew, 90–91, 251–267. Atlanta: Society of Biblical Literature.

———. 2003. "Trans-Pacific Transpositions: Continuities and Discontinuities in Chinese North American Protestantism since 1965." In *Revealing the Sacred in Asian and Pacific America*, edited by Jane Naomi Iwamura and Paul Spickard, 240–272. New York: Routledge Press.

Tu, Janet. 2002. "Ethnic Churches Drawing Crowds." *Seattle Times*, 12 March.

Tu, Weiming. 1994. *The Living Tree: The Changing Meaning of Being Chinese Today*. Stanford, CA: Stanford University Press.

Tuan, Mia. 1998. *Forever Foreigners or Honorary Whites? The Asian Ethnic Experience Today*. New Brunswick, NJ: Rutgers University Press.

Ue, Kathleen. 2003. "The Precious Gift of Freedom." In *Chinatown: Stories of Faith*, edited by James Chuck, 75–76. San Francisco: First Chinese Baptist Church, San Francisco.

U.S. General Accounting Office. 1990. "Asian Americans: A Status Report." Washington, DC: Government Printing Office.

Vecoli, Rudolph. 1979. "The Resurgence of American Immigration History." *American Studies International* 27 (Winter): 46–66.

Vo, Linda. 1996. "Asian Immigrants, Asian Americans, and the Politics of Ethnic Mobilization in San Diego." *Amerasia Journal* 22 (2): 89–108.

Vongs, Pueng. 2003. "Troubled Times: Anxiety Gripping Asian American Communities." *Pacific News Service*, 23 April.

Wagner, Peter. 1997. *Breaking Strongholds in Your City: How to Use Spiritual Mapping to Make Your Prayers More Strategic, Effective, and Targeted*. Ventura, CA: Regal Books.

Warner, R. Stephen. 1988. *New Wine in Old Wineskins: Evangelicals and Liberals in a Small-Town Church*. Berkeley: University of California Press.

———. 1993. "Work in Progress Toward a New Paradigm for the Sociological Study of Religion in the United States." *American Journal of Sociology* 98 (5): 1044–1093.

———. 1994. "The Place of the Congregation in the Contemporary American Religious Configuration." In *American Congregations*, edited by James Wind and James Lewis. Chicago: University of Chicago Press.

Warner, R. Stephen, and Judith Wittner, ed. 1998. *Gatherings in Diaspora: Religious Communities and the New Immigration*. Philadelphia: Temple University Press.

Warner, W. L., and L. Srole. 1945. *The Social Systems of American Ethnic Groups*. New Haven, CT: Yale University Press.

Warren, Marcus. 2003. "SARS Spreads Racial Tension as Toronto Feels Pariah Status." *Toronto Globe*, 23 April.

Warren, Rick. 1995. *The Purpose-Driven Church*. Grand Rapids, MI: Zondervan Publishing.

Waters, Mary. 1990. *Ethnic Options*. Berkeley: University of California Press.

Webber, Robert. 2002. *The Younger Evangelicals*. Grand Rapids, MI: Baker Books.

Weber, Max. 1958. *The Protestant Ethic and the Spirit of Capitalism*. New York: Charles Scribner's Sons.

Wei, William. 1993. *The Asian American Movement*. Philadelphia: Temple University Press.

Wildermuth, John. 1998. "Boxer Bids for Asian Voters: She Fears Losing Them to GOP." *San Francisco Chronicle*, 13 August.

Williams, Raymond. 1988. *Religions of Immigrants from India and Pakistan*. New York: Cambridge University Press.

Williams, Raymond Brady. 1994. "Swaminarayan Hindu Temple of Glen Ellyn, Illinois." In *American Congregations*, edited by James Wind and James Lewis. Chicago: University of Chicago Press.

Wind, James, and James Lewis, eds. 1994. *American Congregations*. Chicago: University of Chicago Press.

Wong, John. 1998. "Why Church Membership?" *The Challenger: A Monthly Publication of Grace Faith Church* (May): n.p.

Wong, William. 1999. "Entangled Asian American Loyalties." *San Francisco Examiner*, 31 August.

Woo, Westley. 1983. "Protestant Work among the Chinese in the San Francisco Bay Area, 1850–1920." Ph.D. diss., Graduate Theological Union, Berkeley, CA.

Wood, Richard. 2002. *Faith in Action: Religion, Race, and Democratic Organizing in America*. Chicago: University of Chicago Press.

Wu, Frank. 2002. *Yellow: Race in America Beyond Black and White*. New York: Basic Books.

Wu, Frank, and Francey Lim Youngberg. 2002. "People from China Crossing the River: Asian American Political Empowerment and Foreign Influence." In *Asian Americans and Politics: Perspectives, Experiences, Prospects*, ed. Gordon Chang, 311–353. Stanford, CA: Stanford University Press.

Wuthnow, Robert. 1988. *The Restructuring of American Religion*. Princeton, NJ: Princeton University Press.

———. 1992. *Rediscovering the Sacred*. Grand Rapids, MI: Eerdmans Publishing Co.

———. 1994. *Sharing the Journey*. New York: Free Press.

Yamamoto, J. Isamu. 1997. "Silent No More." *New Man Magazine*, May.

Yancey, William, Eugene Ericksen, and Richard Juliani. 1976. "Emergent Ethnicity: A Review and Reformulation." *American Sociological Review* 41 (3): 391–403.

Yang, Fenggang. 1998a. "Chinese Conversion to Evangelical Christianity: The Importance of Social and Cultural Context." *Sociology of Religion: A Quarterly Review* 59 (3): 231–257.

———. 1998b. "Tenacious Unity in a Contentious Community: Cultural and Religious Dynamics in a Chinese Christian Church." In *Gatherings in Diaspora: Religious Communities and the New Immigration,* edited by R. Stephen Warner and Judith Wittner, 333–364. Philadelphia: Temple University Press.

——. 1999. *Chinese Christians in America: Conversion, Assimilation, and Adhesive Identities.* University Park: Penn State University Press.

——. 2002. "Religious Diversity among the Chinese in America." In *Religions in Asian America: Building Faith Communities,* edited by Pyong Gap Min and Jung Ha Kim, 71–98. Walnut Creek, CA: AltaMira Press.

Yans-McLaughlin, Virginia. 1977. *Family and Community: Italian Immigrants in Buffalo, 1880–1930.* Ithaca, NY: Cornell University Press.

Yau, Cecilia, ed. 1986. *A Winning Combination: ABC/OBC Understanding Cultural Tensions in Chinese Churches.* Petaluma, CA: Chinese Christian Mission.

Yep, Jeannette, Peter Cha, Paul Tokunaga, Greg Jao, eds. 1998. *Following Jesus without Dishonoring Your Parents: Asian American Discipleship.* Grover's Down, IL: Intervarsity Press.

Yoo, David. 2002. "A Religious History of Japanese Americans in California." In *Religions in Asian America: Building Faith Communities,* edited by Pyong Gap Min and Jung Ha Kim, 121–142. Walnut Creek, CA: AltaMira Press.

——, ed. 1999. *New Spiritual Homes: Religion and Asian Americans.* Honolulu: University of Hawaii Press.

Yoshida, Ryo. 1989. "A SocioHistorical Study of Racial/Ethnic Identity in the Inculturated Religious Expression of Japanese Christianity in San Francisco." Ph.D. diss., Graduate Theological Union, Berkeley, CA.

Yoshii, Michael. 1996. "The Buena Vista Church Bazaar: A Story within a Story." In *People on the Way: Asian North Americans Discovering Christ, Culture, and Community,* edited by David Ng, 3–62. Valley Forge, PA: Judson Press.

Yung, Judy. 1995. *Unbound Feet: A Social History of Chinese Women in San Francisco.* Berkeley: University of California Press.

Zald, Mayer, and John McCarthy. 1998. "Religious Groups as Crucibles of Social Movements." In *Sacred Companies: Organizational Aspects of Religion and Religious Aspects of Organizations,* edited by N. J. Demerath, Peter Hall, Terry Schmitt, and Rhys Williams, 24–49. New York: Oxford University Press.

Zhou, Min, Carl Bankston III, and Rebecca Kim. 2002. "Rebuilding Spiritual Lives in the New Land: Religious Practices among Southeast Asian Refugees in the United States." In *Religions in Asian America: Building Faith Communities,* edited by Pyong Gap Min and Jung Ha Kim, 37–70. Walnut Creek, CA: AltaMira Press.

INDEX

acculturation, 2, 17, 23, 88, 141; panethnic church and, 101, 123
affirmative action, 10
African Americans, 5, 76, 114
aging. *See* elderly, the
Alameda County, 44
Ambassadors for Christ, 26
America. *See* United States
Americans, 29, 32, 68; disidentification as, 3, 20, 89, 97; identification as, 7, 13, 43, 129
American Baptists, 83
American Baptist Seminary of the West, xiii, 92
American Born Chinese (ABC), 29, 54, 107
American Indians, 10, 12
Americanization, 23, 24, 63, 121
ancestor worship, 87, 89, 90, 132
ancestral homeland, 18, 24, 39, 41
Andover Theological Seminary, 18
Anglo Japanese Training School, 19
anti-Asian violence, 9, 10, 100
anti-Japanese legislation, 19, 20, 179n9
architecture/space, 58; of CGC, 16; of Dayspring Church, 146; of GFC, 103–105, of PAUMC, 125, 131
Asian American Bay Area Fellowship, 50
Asian American Caucus of the United Methodist Church, 27
Asian American Christian Fellowship, xii, 49, 106, 107
Asian American churches, xii, xiii, 2, 28, 58; number of mainline, 126; reasons for, 110, 129
Asian Americans, 1, 42, 100; as activists, xii, 4, 14; categorization of, 9, 45; diversity of, 63, 71, 101; experiences of, 10,

63, 82, 185n10; identification as, x, 6, 13, 177n22; invisibility of, 3; population changes among, 44; as politicians, 45–46; as professionals, 11, 79, 118; religious affiliations of, 3, 176nn8, 11; representation of, 68–69, 98; sports leagues for, 106; student organizations for, xii, 45, 106; as term, 11, 14, 17, 62, 63, 175n4
Asian Americans for Community Involvement, 99
Asian American Studies, 13, 106
Asian Community Mental Health Services, xi
Asian Health Services, 49, 95
Asian Indians, 3, 150, 177n18
Asian Law Caucus, 9, 10, 49
Asian Neighborhood Design, 49
Asian Pacific Americans and Religion Research Initiative, xiii, 48
Asian Pacific Islander Health Forum, 10
Asians, 38; culture of, 34, 87; physical features of, 28, 31, 88, 101
assimilation, 5–6, 23, 28, 35, 74; institutional, 2; rejection of, 74, 101; social, vii, 21; structural, 123, 145, 179n15
authenticity, 38, 75; cultural, 31; relational, 117; shame and, 54–56
authoritarianism, 36, 54, 78
autonomy, 28, 70

baby boomers, 55, 85, 107, 127
basketball, ix, xii; league, 99, 111, 129, 182–183n4; Pan-Asian community and, 140–142
Bay Area Asian American Youth Fellowship, 50

Contra Costa County, Calif., 17
converts, 18, 19, 20, 86, 97
cross-cultural ministry, 57
culture, vii, 29, 78, 85; code, 78, 80; definition of, 29, 31; differences between Asian and American, 28, 29, 30, 57, 72, 110; ethnic, 21, 29; ethnicity in church, 29–37, 50; pan-Asian, viii; transmission of, viii, 23, 33, 35, 56, 99
Cupertino, Calif., 45

demographic change: within Asian American population, 2, 43, 51–53, within churches, 22; between generations, 150
demographics: of GFC, 105, 107, 108, 187n15; of PAUMC, 129, 131
denominations: identification with 20, 24; mainline, 41, 91, 97
dialect. See language
discipleship, 110, 111
discourse, 3, 5, 10, 152; evangelical, 111, 117; mainline, 100, 126
discrimination: institutional, 68, 95, 141; racial, 14, 38, 84, 93, 100
district, 7; association, 20, 23
diversity, 47, 66–70, 93, 108
doctrine, 85
Durkheim, Emile, viii

East Bay, Calif., 47
ecumenism, 92, 95
education: attainment of, 96, 97; panethnicity and, 14; system, 22, 54; as a value, 12, 33–34, 64
efficiency, 59, 123
elderly, the: churches and, 42, 51; at GFC, 106, 107, 108; at PAUMC, 127; respect for, 89, 110
engagement with the world, 64, 69, 96, 99. See also community: involvement
English language, 17, 82, 107, 109; churches, 3, 17, 51, 72, 148; ministers, 42, 52, 57, 63, 106; songs, 115
entrepreneurs, 1, 14, 158
Episcopal church, 83, 86, 88, 90, 91, 98
"ethclass," 118
ethnic: competition and conflict, 7, 166; enclaves, 22, 52, 84, 91, 94, 95; identity

capital, 10; institutions and markets, 45; pride, viii, ix, 25, 34, 46, 89
ethnic churches, 17, 29–40, 93, 180n23; reactions to, 148–150; study of, 2–4; worship style at, 36, 41, 56, 114
ethnicity, 5, 7–8, 17, 94; definition of, 7; distilled, 12, 54, 122, 160, 180n22; invention/reinvention of, 89, 101, 126, 135, 160; shifting understandings of, 17
Ethnic Studies. See Asian American Studies
ethnocentrism, 66
Eucharist. See communion
European Americans, ix, 10, 28, 155, 157. See also white ethnics
evangelical Christianity/Christians, xii, 71, 97; Asian American churches, 28; definition of, 64, 178n31; growth of, 4; organizational field, 49–51; younger, 153–156
evangelism, 64, 86, 106, 110; of Asian Americans, 42, 73–80; of Chinese Americans, 28, 149; and friendship, 75; of Japanese Americans, 40
Evergreen Baptist Church, 51, 106, 182n20

face, 54, 117, 135
family, 40, 56, 86; associations, 20; church as, 22, 25–27, 41; dynamics, 71, 110; filial piety and, 33–35; upbringing, 72, 73; value for, 31, 89
fellowship. See small groups
felt needs, 64, 65, 66, 78
festivals, 29, 35, 89, 101; Japanese American, 7, 36, 131, 139
filial piety and responsibility, 33, 36, 180n19
Filipino Americans, xi, 3, 10, 50, 95, 108; panethnicity and, 11, 12, 13, 76, 128; veterans benefits for, 166
First Chinese Baptist Church, 26, 175n2
First Chinese Church of Christ, 22
food, 16, 22, 57, 104, 116, 126, 139
foreign-born populations vs. native-born, 14, 32, 52, 57, 102
Fuller Seminary, 49, 75
fundamentalism, xii, 35, 71, 180n2; Chinese American, 26; difference from evangelicalism, 120, 183n1; difference from mainline Protestantism, 90, 96, 135; and theology of race, 65, 66

National Conference on Chinese Christian Churches, 23
nationalism, 18–21, 41
nationality, 17, 20
National Origins Act of 1924, 3, 24
nation-state. *See* state
neighborhoods, 2, 7, 9, 93, 154, 182n23. *See also* community: geographic; ethnic: enclaves
networks, 105, 123, 148, 160; friendship, xi, 62, 76, 110, 150; professional, 4, 47, 50, 62
new paradigm churches, 92, 113, 115, 153
Newsong Church, 51, 190n8
"niche edge effect"/"niche overlap effect," 156–158, 165
Niijima, Shimeta, 18
Nisei, 7, 60, 116. *See also* generation: second
Nisei Week, 7
nonprofit organizations, 49, 142
North American Congress of Chinese Evangelicals, 26
Northern California Japanese Christian Church Federation, 24, 169

Oakland, Calif., xiii, 69
Omi, Michael, xiii, 9
oppression. *See* discrimination
organizational field, 15, 43, 62, 155, 181n13; evangelical, 59–51; mainline, 47–49
organizational logic, 15, 105, 153; evangelical, 64, 80; mainline, 84, 100
Organization of Asian Americans, 128, 143
Orientalism, 18, 19, 21, 30
orthodoxy, 85
out-group homogeneity bias, 158
out-marriage, 60, 101, 141, 144, 183n26
Overseas Born Chinese (OBC), 29
Overseas Missionary Fellowship (OMF), 39

Pacific Asian North American (PANA) Institute, xiii, 48
Pacific Citizen (newspaper), 25
Pacific Islanders, 9, 97, 125
Pacific Rim, 45
Pacific School of Religion, 48

Pan-Asian churches, 17, 42, 83, 106; numbers of, 43; worship at, 114, 115, 188n6
Pan-Asians: friendships among, 53, 64, 72, 76; marriages among, 53, 72; national organizations for, 13
panethnicity, xi, 5, 6, 135; barriers to, 101; definition of, 10; formation of, 101; theories of, 10–13. *See also* racial: formation
parachurch, 28
parent-child relations, 4, 33, 64, 71, 80, 110
paternalism, 18, 19
peace, 21, 84, 96
perfectionism, 71, 72, 73, 80, 116
personal growth, 70
politics, 14, 45, 99, 123, 142, 187–188n21; homeland, 20, 23
popular culture, 133
popular religiosity, 4, 133
postmodernism, 70, 163
power, 57–61, 166; dynamics, 44, 149
prayer, 73, 89, 104, 133, 138, 144; meetings, 35; ministry, 71
Presbyterian Board of Foreign Missions, 18
Presbyterian Church, USA, 47, 83, 85, 91
primordial ethnicity, 11, 13, 22, 25, 32, 88
professionals, 4, 71; Asian American, 63, 105, 118; lifestyle of, 85; urban, 79
Promise Keepers, 50, 122, 184n6
prophetic voice, 131; and morality, 84
Proposition 227, 44
proselytization. *See* evangelism
Protestant ethic, 35
psychology, 27, 71, 73, 81, 105, 110
public policy, 9, 88
purpose-driven churches, 78, 111

Qing Ming, 22, 89, 90

race, 5, 8–10, 17, 19; definition of, 9; as an organizing principle, 5, 161; relations, 23, 64, 68
racial: dynamics in church, 156–158; formation 10, 43, 158; identity play, 10; projects, 159; reconciliation, 49, 50, 66, 154, 166; segregation, 21, 97
racialization, x, 5, 8, 44–47, 63, 108, 126
racism, xi, 27, 91, 97, 134; against Chinese Americans, 19; environmental, 136;

ABOUT THE AUTHOR

An assistant professor of Asian American studies at San Francisco State University, Russell Jeung received his Ph.D. in sociology at the University of California, Berkeley. He lives with his wife, Joan, in Oakland, where he is active in the Asian American community and in church work.